NEIL WAGNER

ALL OUT

NEIL WAGNER

ALL OUT

with James Borrowdale

PENGUIN BOOKS

PENGUIN

UK | USA | Canada | Ireland | Australia
India | New Zealand | South Africa | China

Penguin is an imprint of the Penguin Random House group of companies, whose addresses can be found at global.penguinrandomhouse.com

First published by Penguin Random House New Zealand, 2024

Text © Neil Wagner, 2024
Photography © Neil Wagner, 2024, unless otherwise credited.
Images on pages 70, 184, 208, 257 and 282 © Photosport NZ.

The moral right of James Borrowdale to be identified as the author of this work has been asserted.

All rights reserved. Without limiting the rights under copyright reserved above, no part of this publication may be reproduced, stored in or introduced into a retrieval system, or transmitted, in any form or by any means (electronic, mechanical, photocopying, recording or otherwise), without the prior written permission of both the copyright owner and the above publisher of this book.

Design by Cat Taylor © Penguin Random House New Zealand
Front cover photograph by Victoria Birkinshaw
Back cover photograph by Photosport NZ
Printed and bound in Australia by Griffin Press, an Accredited ISO AS/NZS 14001 Environmental Management Systems Printer

A catalogue record for this book is available from the National Library of New Zealand.

ISBN 978-1-77695-116-1
ISBN 978-1-77695-906-8 (audio)
eISBN 978-1-77695-406-3

penguin.co.nz

For Lana, Olivia, Zahli and Joshua

CONTENTS

FOREWORD
BY BRENDON McCULLUM
8

PRELUDE:
A WINDOW
11

CHAPTER 1:
LATE LAMB
17

CHAPTER 2:
IN-BETWEEN
27

CHAPTER 3:
CHOOSING CRICKET
40

CHAPTER 4:
ABROAD
54

CHAPTER 5:
SCARFIE
69

CHAPTER 6:
BLACK CAP AND DARK DAYS
87

CHAPTER 7:
CHASING VICTORY
105

CHAPTER 8:
THE SHORT STUFF
123

**CHAPTER 9:
GOLDEN SUMMER
145**

**CHAPTER 10:
LEAVING TOWN
165**

**CHAPTER 11:
CHANGING TIMES
183**

**CHAPTER 12:
TOWARDS
THE TOP
195**

**CHAPTER 13:
CHAMPIONS
215**

**CHAPTER 14:
LAST HIGHS
237**

**CHAPTER 15:
FINAL SUMMER
261**

FOREWORD

The first few times I met Neil Wagner I wasn't sure what to make of him. Here's this guy from South Africa, charging in and roaring at the opposition, yet off the field he was fairly quiet. But as I got to know Neil, I could see that behind the aggressiveness and hostility with ball in hand was someone with a huge heart — someone that epitomised the team-first attitude we were trying to build in the Black Caps.

As anyone following the game of cricket anywhere in the world will already know, that big heart and his relentless drive to succeed was key to so many of New Zealand's test victories over the past decade. The long spells and his often unique plan of attack sometimes undersold his skill, but boy it was effective.

At the time, I wasn't aware of all the challenges Neil was going through off the field, the ones he shares so openly in the following pages. It's a reflection on his character that he seems to have always found a way to bounce back from disappointment. We knew he was a resilient cricketer — I'm not sure everyone realises just how hard those long spells are on a bowler's body and mind — but it goes to show those characteristics are ever-present in Neil the person, too.

Test cricket is a tough game, and tough characters have to find a way and they do. Neil Wagner is one of the toughest that I've come across. I had the pleasure of captaining him for a long period of time, and then coaching against him, and there are very few players that you'd rather have in your corner when the going gets tough.

BRENDON McCULLUM

PRELUDE:
A WINDOW

I just want to fall.

If I close my eyes, I can still experience it through the mind of the 26-year-old I was on my third tour with the Black Caps, when I felt hopelessly lost off the field and was not yet wanted on it. I was in the hallway of the team hotel, standing in the cool bite of air-con, the windows on one side looking over the swimming pool. On the other side, the hotel car park shimmered through the muggy heat of a Colombo day. It was some time in November 2012, in the days leading up to what would be Ross Taylor's final test match as captain. A couple of months earlier, I had achieved my childhood dream of playing test cricket. But the elation of that moment was forgotten in the agony of this one, the lowest of my life. One of the windows was open and all that went through my mind was what it might feel like to lean forward and fall through it, to tumble into the blackness and be done with all of this. I felt useless. I felt worthless and insecure, trying so hard to be someone I wasn't — and feeling like I was failing at that, too.

I just want to fall.

In that moment, I was almost exactly where I hoped to be when I had made the journey to freezing Dunedin from sun-drenched Pretoria just over four years before. I had finally qualified to represent New Zealand, and I already had a couple of test matches behind me. Sure, I hadn't exactly set the world on fire in those two games against the West Indies, only taking four wickets at an average of over 50, but I'd given everything I had on a couple of lifeless pitches. I'd fought hard with the bat, too, twice coming in as a nightwatchman and both times surviving through to stumps. We lost the series two–nil, but I'd shown enough to keep my place in the squad for the next two tours — India and now Sri Lanka — even if I hadn't done much but train and run drinks throughout the subcontinent.

In my years in Dunedin, playing cricket for Otago as I worked through the qualification period, I had a great bunch of mates who appreciated the heart and hard work I put into trying to win games for the team. I did it in my own way, with the bravado and aggression I had learned to play with growing up in South Africa, picking verbal battles with batsmen to get me into the fight and also to help chase my insecurities out of my mind. I felt valued in the Otago setup.

But that had taken time. I grew up speaking Afrikaans. English never came naturally. Many times I found myself walking away from conversations thinking, *Hang on, they haven't understood me here*. I'd get frustrated with myself and the limits of my English. *Why can't you see it like I see it? That's not what I mean.* But time and familiarity with the guys made these misunderstandings far less frequent. The gap between what I meant and what others thought I meant shrank.

In the Black Caps environment, sharing a changing shed with people I had played against domestically, some of whom had taken issue with the way I played the game, I had to start over. I felt totally alone, and that loneliness was devastating.

I was also young and arrogant. The South African cricket culture I came from was so cut-throat and competitive that I had always distrusted the advice of others, thinking they might have ulterior motives. I took that lesson of distrust with me to New Zealand. I desperately wanted to fit in, to show the guys that I was a normal bloke who just wanted to be mates, have a good time and play some cricket. But I didn't know how to let down the barriers of my upbringing.

Craig Cumming, my captain at Otago, had become something like an older brother, but I didn't want to call him up out of the blue from Sri Lanka and burden him with my shit. I didn't want to confide in Mike Hesson, the recently appointed Black Caps coach who I knew well from his years of coaching Otago, or Ross, either. They might send me home, or they might think I didn't have the mental strength to perform at this level. My international career would be over almost before it had begun. I'd worked so hard to get here. I wanted to prove my strength, not show my weaknesses. I was also feeling increasingly isolated from my family in South Africa, through no fault of theirs. This didn't feel like the time to try to reach out — I didn't want them to worry.

And things weren't exactly rosy in the Black Caps changing shed. Ross would soon be replaced as captain by Brendon McCullum, and the team was swirling with speculation and rumour. I was so new to the environment that I knew almost nothing of what was going on, other than how it felt to walk into a hotel bar and witness a bunch of teammates who'd been excitedly chatting go silent when you came near. I was in such a deep hole, my thinking so scattered and my depression so self-centred, that all I could think was, *Shit, were they just talking about me?* It became easier just to order room service and eat alone in front of the TV than it was to risk rejection.

All of this swirled through my mind as I contemplated that window. I should've been happy, but inside I was miserable, feeling like a failure who was letting down the people who had made so many sacrifices to help an Afrikaans boy from the working-class suburbs of Pretoria chase his dream of playing cricket at the highest level. Maybe it was all a huge mistake. Even my faith in God seemed to desert me — and anyway, what kind of God would leave His son feeling this broken?

I looked at the window again.

I just want to fall.

My head was spinning. But then I started visualising the headlines: *Test match cancelled because New Zealand squad member dies in a Sri Lankan hotel.* What about my teammates? What would it be like for them, filing into their seats on the plane for the long flight home, my horrible death gnawing at their minds? I hate to let people down. It's not always the healthiest instinct, but maybe here it saved my life, overriding that awful weight of negative emotion in my mind.

I can't do this.

I escaped back to my room — shaking, jittery — and stepped into the shower. Everything felt wrong as I stood there with the water washing over me. A hot shower wasn't what I needed so I tried a cold one. Not right either. I fidgeted with the temperature, but I couldn't get comfortable. I got out, dried myself and went to the bed, staring at the ceiling, flat on my back, trying desperately to empty my racing mind.

I'm not sure quite how much time passed before I looked over at my phone. There was a message waiting from my friend Lana. We had met years ago, in Pretoria, and had sporadically kept in touch over the years — but more so recently after, unable to sleep one night, I had seen her online and sent her a message. We got chatting — just general stuff to start with — but the conversation had quickly deepened and soon I was confiding in her how low I had been, and telling her I felt I had nobody to talk to. And she said, 'Well, you can always talk to me.' She had quickly become my biggest means of support.

And now, when I needed a friend more than ever before, here she was. As I saw her name on my screen, I realised how close I had come to losing everything that I had worked so, so hard to build. I felt warm relief flood through my body as I typed my reply.

CHAPTER 1:
LATE LAMB

I am what is known as a *laat lammetjie*.

Translated literally from Afrikaans, it means 'late lamb' and it is what we call a child born long after their siblings. I have two older brothers: David, who is nine years older than me, and Mark, who is seven years my senior. My first memories are from the sidelines of their Pretoria sports fields — cricket in the summer, rugby in the winter — and from the middle of the ferocious cricket contests that raged up and down the driveway of our home. I can't remember a time when I didn't love cricket, and even then — when I knew nothing else — I knew I wanted to be a cricketer.

Pretoria is the administrative capital of South Africa, founded when the *voortrekkers*, on the run from British rule in the south, headed north centuries ago. My mum, Doreen, traces her lineage back to those early pioneers. She was born and raised there in a military family and is what we call proper Afrikaans. My dad, Steve, grew up in Cape Town in an English-speaking family, but he fell in love with Mum and took the train to the north to be with her. As kids, we only ever really heard him using English when he'd lose his temper and express his anger in the language of his childhood.

I was born in 1986. We lived in the suburb of Pretoria North, bordered to the south by the Magaliesberg mountains, running laterally across the city, and to the east the Apies River, the city's green spine. Mum and Dad, at least for the first decade of my life, worked for the same real estate company. We usually welcomed the weekends with a *braai*, the extended family gathering on a Friday evening. Mum has always been a fantastic cook, and the spread was invariably incredible — fat coils of spicy *boerewors* sausage spitting on the grill; big plates of *bobotie*, a spicy sweet baked beef mince dish; lamb chops; heaped bowls of *pap*, the ubiquitous corn porridge served as the equivalent of mashed potato; *braaibroodjie*, grilled sandwiches tossed on the barbecue last to absorb the flavours of the meat that had gone before. For dessert, there were *pampoenkoekies*, sweet pumpkin fritters, and *koeksisters*, something like traditional twisted doughnuts, and *melktert*, a creamy sweet tart. In my memory, the aroma of the food mingles with the scent of freshly cut lawn. There was always sport on the TV — the local rugby team, the Bulls, or the Springboks, or Formula One, or a game of cricket being played somewhere. Our house on Sandappel Avenue sat on a big section, shaded by a couple of huge trees, where, with stomachs bloated, we would begin our own game of cricket almost as soon as we'd put down our cutlery.

My brothers and I played with a taped-up tennis ball that may as well have been a cricket ball, it was that hard. As the youngest, it was usually my job to bowl. The order of our birth, more than anything, probably sealed my fate as a bowler. My hero was legendary speedster Allan Donald — I would literally get goosebumps when I sat down in front of the TV to watch him — and I used to spread white Nivea face cream over my lower lip in imitation of that characteristic zinc-smeared Donald look that gave his scowl such menace. I wanted to be like him, I wanted to bowl like him. So despite bowling left-handed, I modelled my action on his, charging in for hours on end at David, an opening batter, and Mark, a fast-bowling all-rounder in the mould of Andrew Flintoff.

On one of the rare occasions that I managed to wrestle the bat from their hands, Mark wasn't very happy about it, and he absolutely steamed in at me, using every advantage in strength and height each one of his extra years had given him. His bouncer, speared into the driveway from the trajectory allowed him by his 1.9-metre height, caught me flush on my ear and I keeled over in pain, clapping my hand over what I assumed was the bloody mess my brother had just made of my ear. But when I drew my hand away, it was dry. Stung into a shade of bright pink, but otherwise unharmed. I wanted to run to Mum and Dad, I wanted to cry. 'Harden up. Stop being such a pussy,' Mark told me. So instead I tried to do as he told and kept my mouth shut. I was six or seven.

It wasn't long after that I remember pestering David to come out and play cricket with me as he lay inside in front of the TV one afternoon watching *Days of Our Lives*. Despite the bigger age gap, David was the brother I was closest to as I was growing up, and I usually had more success persuading him to come outside and be bowled at. This time, though, he was happy where he was. I squirted him with my water pistol to try and get him to move, but he wasn't amused. 'Do that again and there will be consequences.' Of course, I pulled the trigger once more. He drew himself up from the couch and lunged after me as I bolted to what I thought was the safety of one of the two big trees on the front lawn, where we used to kick a rugby ball around.

I scaled the brick wall at the front of the property and jumped onto the branches of the tree, thinking David wouldn't bother to follow — but he did, tall enough to skip the brick wall. And when he got close, still threatening unnamed consequences, and I had nowhere to go, I jumped. My foot landed on one of the tree's big, exposed roots, and I collapsed in agony. 'Stop faking,' David told me — he still wanted revenge and didn't want this to prevent it. But I was crawling on the grass, crying for Mum and Dad, tears streaming down my face.

'Stand up. I'll give you a one-second head start,' David said.

So I got up and tried to run, hobbling a few paces before my leg gave way with the pain and I collapsed again. Still he didn't believe me — until he looked down and saw my ankle, already blue and swollen to double its usual size. Mum, when I got to her, gave me a great big serve about it.

'What have you done now?' she scolded.

It was off to the hospital — my ankle broken in two places. I was eight, and that year's cricket season was over before it had begun. These were the joys of having two much bigger brothers, but in their large shadows I learned to grow up quickly.

In Pretoria, the atmosphere changed on a Friday, when the whole city seemed to anticipate the weekend of sport. It was the worst day of the week to be given detention because you would sit there in a stuffy classroom, mindlessly copying out the school rules thousands of times as everyone else geared up for the weekend.

Both my brothers, like me, played rugby and cricket — and Mark would later play rugby as a loose forward to a high level, his career only ruined by a gruesome ankle injury sustained in Pretoria club rugby. Thousands and thousands would turn out for rugby games between schools, with grandstands packed with students in their school colours — adults in their thousands, too — cheering for their team. And there was me, clowning on the athletics track that surrounded the rugby field, running up and down, kicking a rugby ball and trying to divert as much attention towards me as I could. I clearly remember thinking, as I looked out at my brothers in the middle of the field and then up at this mass of people cheering them on, that I wanted that for myself. *One day I will be out there.* I wanted this many people — more, even — cheering me on.

My brothers were coached by a primary-school teacher called Francois du Plessis. His son was named after him and so, to avoid confusion, the boy went by a nickname: Faf. The future Proteas captain and I would sometimes play cricket together on the sidelines of my brothers' games. In my very early days, the du Plessis family called me Turtle, as I was crazy about the Teenage Mutant Ninja Turtles.

Faf was a year and a half older than me. Later, when I was 10 or 11, I had private cricket lessons with Faf's dad every Tuesday evening at the du Plessis family home, where they had a cricket net set up in the garden. I remember, even then, that Faf made every sport he turned his hand to look so easy — especially cricket and rugby, where, like me, he played first five-eighth.

We all wanted to grow up and play for South Africa, whether as Proteas or Springboks, Allan Donalds or Joost van der Westhuizens. I have vague memories of the 1992 Cricket World Cup, the first

South Africa had competed in since readmission following the fall of Apartheid, but it was the rugby fever that enveloped my world during the 1995 Rugby World Cup that sticks in my mind. Every evening, the kids of Sandappel Avenue would spill barefoot onto the street to re-create the famous moments of that tournament — Chester Williams dotting down for four tries against Samoa; the semifinal against France in Durban, where torrential rain turned Kings Park into a mud bath before the 'Boks muscled a four-point win; and the final, when Joel Stransky slotted the winning drop goal with seven minutes remaining in extra time to beat the All Blacks. I viewed the New Zealanders with massive respect, but nothing could've been further from my mind then of ever becoming one, and I must've slotted that winning Stransky drop goal a thousand times, creating goalposts out of whatever suburban architecture was in range of my left foot — streetlights, clotheslines, roofs — to defeat the All Blacks time and time again.

I was young — I turned nine in 1995 — and lived in a typical Afrikaans bubble of sport and family and faith. Mum was a Sunday-school teacher at our local Dutch Reformed Church, where, like most conservative Afrikaans families, we would go every Sunday. So the political importance of that 1995 Rugby World Cup and what it meant for the birth of the Rainbow Nation, emerging from the ashes of Apartheid, was completely lost on me — even that magic moment when President Nelson Mandela and captain Francois Pienaar together held the Webb Ellis Trophy aloft in front of the screaming Johannesburg crowd. It wasn't really until I started making representative cricket teams, from under-11s onwards, that my horizons started to broaden and I began playing with and against other kids from beyond my Afrikaans circles — English-speaking whites, black and coloured kids who spoke Tswana or Sepedi.

But even as cricket widened my world, it simultaneously encouraged a kind of tunnel vision. It was so competitive and cut-throat, even at that early age, that it was better to put your blinkers on and think only about yourself and your own performances. Life is hard in South Africa — it was a dog-eat-dog kind of place to grow up — and you are raised with a certain amount of selfishness, to look after yourself and your family and to not look too far beyond that. I wasn't educated about the history of Apartheid, and it was easier for a child to turn a blind eye to what the lives of teammates must have been like away from the cricket pitch. I was taught to focus on my goals and what I wanted to achieve, because in a country with the kinds of structural problems that South Africa has, you need to rely on your own fierce will to get there.

But my childhood wasn't all cricket and naivety.

One day I'd been out playing cricket — Mum with me, scoring my game. Dad had taken my brothers to their rugby match. We arrived home, Mum and me pulling into the driveway from one direction, Dad and my brothers from the other. There was a small concrete patio at the front of the house, with a sliding glass door leading inside. As we got near, we realised it was half open.

'This is odd. Why is the door open?' Mum asked into thin air.

We'd been robbed.

I remember clothes — those that hadn't been stolen, which was most of them — lying everywhere, in the living room and strewn down the hallway. Random pieces of furniture remained — a few barstools and the cabinet on which the TV had formerly sat — but almost everything else was gone. For the previous Christmas, us three boys had each been given a stereo with two cassette players so we could make our own mix tapes, a gift that had been all the rage that year. My brothers had bigger ones and I had a small one that followed me throughout the house and the section, playing music wherever I ended up. All three were gone.

I remember looking at the space where the TV had been. My mum was crying, Dad was in a white-hot rage, and I can't repeat the words that were frothing from his mouth as he charged through the house inspecting the damage. I looked at the TV cabinet, in front of which I had spent hours watching cricket and rugby, and was just lost in the confusion of what had happened. My young mind couldn't comprehend it, it was just blank.

Later, we found out from the neighbours, who were new and who we didn't yet know well, that they thought we must've been moving. A group of men had backed a truck down the driveway and then systematically cleaned us out, packing our comfortable lives onto the cargo bed and carrying them away into the Pretoria afternoon. Our stuff was never recovered. Those men would never be found. I'd never really — perhaps because of those same blinkers my upbringing had given me — given much thought to the security situation in my country before that day, but I remember from then on hearing more and more about other families suffering similar misfortunes, or worse.

That robbery wasn't the end of the misfortune that visited us in that home. Not too long afterwards, the real estate company that both Mum and Dad worked for went bust, and they lost their jobs in an instant. Later, unable to keep up with the mortgage payments, we had to sell the house on Sandappel Avenue, the site of so many happy memories and some painful ones, too. We had to move onto the property of some close family friends, where we rented their granny flat. Mum and Dad hustled and hustled to get back on their feet, Dad finding work as a landscaper, Mum as a caterer. They had to take whatever work they could get, fighting every day as hard as they could to keep our family afloat. But, although we may not have had much to our name, our family was never short on love.

The tenacity Mum and Dad showed for the family when things were at their lowest is something I've never forgotten — and it was a lesson I put to use almost immediately. When I started high school at one of Pretoria's most prestigious and expensive educational institutions, where competition for a place in the top cricket teams was intensely fierce, we still couldn't even afford a house of our own.

CHAPTER 2:
IN-BETWEEN

Both of my brothers went to the local public school, Pretoria North High School, nestled in the northern lap of the Magaliesberg mountain range, close to the home we would lose. But by the high standards of Pretoria, it wasn't a very strong cricket school, and I was told that following in the footsteps of Mark and David wouldn't be good for my game. I was offered a cricket scholarship at St Albans College, a renowned private school on the leafy outskirts of the city, but it was an English-language school and my English wasn't very good. Mum worried that I would fall behind academically if I couldn't study in Afrikaans, and so she ruled it out.

Schoolwork had never been a strong point, and I much preferred to spend the daylight hours playing cricket, risking a hiding at school or home, rather than doing my homework. When I decorated my exercise books at the outset of the school year, I chose plain brown paper I could cover in stickers depicting my heroes — Allan Donald, Jonty Rhodes, Hansie Cronje. Often, in class, I would pass the time drawing cricket pictures — a favourite doodle was of stumps shattered by a searing yorker — with my mind at the top of my bowling mark, even as it should've been focused on the teacher at the head of the class. I remember a girl I sat next to once telling me to just get over cricket, to grow up, that I would never make it. I felt my ambition harden against her doubt. *I'll show you*, I remember thinking. *Nothing will stop me*.

But it wouldn't have happened without a lot of help. And this was one such occasion when it came my way. Northerns, the representative cricket team I'd been selected for every year since I was 10, brokered a deal for me to go to another top-class sporting school, Afrikaanse Hoër Seunskool, to which Northerns would also contribute a significant share of the fees, unaffordable for our family.

Founded in 1920, Affies, as the school is known, was the first Afrikaans-language high school in South Africa, and it sits in the shadow of another Pretoria sporting institution, Loftus Versfeld, whose structure is visible from the school grounds. Across the road was Pretoria Boys High School, another prestigious English-language school and Affies' sworn rival, where my great mate and Northerns opening bowling partner, Jonathan Bowles, went to school. Affies was most famous as a rugby school, but it was starting to turn out excellent cricketers, too. Future world-class batter and wicketkeeper AB de Villiers was a couple of years above me, in the same year as Faf and Heino Kuhn, who also went on to represent South Africa. Future Black Caps teammate Kruger van Wyk had gone through the school just before I arrived, as had future Proteas batter Jacques Rudolph. At Affies I would play with and against the best.

In some ways that made it a familiar environment for me. Playing for Northerns, cricket had often taken me onto the school grounds, and even into the boarding hostels where lunch would be served under photos of austere old boys looking down at you from the walls. In many other ways, it was a big adjustment from life at my local primary, Laerskool Danie Malan. I was now surrounded by the Pretoria elite on the southern side of the mountains at a time my family to the north couldn't even afford to supply me with my own cricket gear. Throughout my younger days, that had to come from a woman we knew as Auntie Ella who ran a local sporting goods store called Sportoria and had taken an interest in my development. Later, the company of a local businessman, Natie Botha, sponsored me through high school.

I was embarrassed about my family's circumstances and it made the adjustment to Affies difficult. Kids bullied me about the inexpensive brands of clothing I wore, and on school cricket tours, when they came later, I had to be very careful with what little money I had so I could do all the things the team expected, and to which my teammates never gave a second thought — like eating out at restaurants as a group, where I would make do with a single serving of chicken wings or a meal quietly taken care of by Stanley Buckle. I remember Faf once shielding me from the fines being dished out in a team meeting. Unlike most of my teammates, he knew the story of my family's misfortune and that my funds were running low. I'll always be grateful for that kindness.

I was shy and insecure, and even away from cricket I never wanted people to know why I couldn't go with them to the movies or out to a restaurant — so I would just say no. I missed out on a lot of friendships as a teenager because of those insecurities, and lots of my peers probably just thought I was someone who was happier to be alone. My mum could be quite protective, and we weren't allowed to go for sleepovers at mates' places, so I never invited them to stay at mine. I hated the idea of receiving sympathy, of people feeling like they needed to pay for my share or help me out. It made me fiercely independent. Even so, I had a tight crew of close friends — Stanley and Juan Buckle, Tiaan de Beer, Douglas Hewitt, Wilco Marais and Francois le Clus — who helped me negotiate the ups and downs of being a teenager.

I initially made the First XI as a 14-year-old, breaking into an incredibly strong team. Almost every member of it would go on to play first-class cricket, if not going further. Faf and AB were two of the most dominant schoolboy cricketers in the country, obviously destined for great things. In the years I joined them in the First XI, the team, under the leadership of coaches Deon Botes and Colin Dettmer, would escape the shadow of the First XV, joining the rugby boys as the top-ranked school team in the country. (My own rugby ambitions fell away when I started to worry about the effect a rugby injury, like that suffered by my brother, might have on my cricket.) Over two consecutive seasons, the First XI lost only one game.

Faf tells a story about Deon once asking the wider training group of about 30 boys to raise their hands if their goal was to play international cricket. Every single one of us did, and then Deon told us, statistically speaking, that perhaps only one would make it — and even then only if that person worked harder than anyone else there. For whatever reason, four of us in and around that team would make the international grade. It was an incredibly competitive group of young cricketers to be a part of.

In that atmosphere of intense competition, my cricket flourished. There was so much talent around that you were essentially always on trial. There were always two or three bowlers who could've stepped straight into my shoes and probably done just as well. There was another left-arm quick who was also a top swimmer with the resulting big upper body: taller, stronger and quicker than me. There was a bit of talk that perhaps he would take my spot, but that competition just drove me to want to get better and better — training every day that I wasn't playing — and the reward was improved performance on the pitch. This was the good side of the selfishness and self-centredness of a sporting culture built on ultra-competitiveness. You may not always have trusted the voices of those around you, but the environment pushed you to the limits of yourself in the pursuit of improvement.

Although, throughout my teenage years, my batting started to fall away. I'd always loved to bat, and even used to open in the days before bowling began taking precedence. My slide down the order began when an early rep coach, unhappy with a quickfire 40 scored in a way then thought inappropriate for an opening batter, banished me to the lower-middle order. When I made the Affies First XI, I batted at 10. The running joke in that team was that if you batted below number nine, you didn't even need to take your kit out of your parents' car — AB and Faf almost always scored enough runs at the top to make the rest of the batting order basically redundant. My ambitions as an all-rounder weren't helped by this lack of opportunity — too much competition for time at the crease, in this case — but it was a joy to fit into such a high-performing team in any way I could.

In addition to First XI cricket for the school, there was rep cricket for Northerns. Perhaps the first time I put myself on the national radar was the 2001 PG Bison Week, a week-long national under-15s tournament sponsored by PG Bison, a South African interior-design company. That year it was held in East London. I did really well, taking lots of wickets — and played against future Black Caps teammate Colin de Grandhomme, then representing Zimbabwe. Later, I represented Northerns at the under-17 week held that year in Pietermaritzburg, the hometown of another famous South African cricketing expat, Kevin Pietersen. I was selected from that tournament for the national under-17 squad, which went on to compete against the regional under-19 teams in the Coca-Cola Khaya Majola Week that followed immediately. I had a problem, though: I had only budgeted for the initial week and my wallet was empty. Luckily the tournament was in Cape Town that year, and my dad's parents still lived in the southern city. They were able to deliver a care package and some money to the hostel where we were staying.

The first time I played in the Coca-Cola Khaya Majola Week for Northerns, in Durban in 2003, it was a disaster. Our team was billeted at Durban High School and, as with every other team who stayed there, we got severely sick — we were vomiting, and worse, on the cricket field — and understandably didn't play well. The following year, the tournament was held in Pretoria, and in the familiar conditions I was one of the tournament's leading wicket-takers as our team squandered a promising start to finish fifth.

I was hopeful, though, changing into a pair of chinos and my Northerns blazer, that I'd be named in the South African under-19 team at the end-of-tournament function. I remember sitting at the table as the names were read out, nerves rising, until there were no names left to call and mine had remained unsaid. I was sitting next to my friend Francois le Clus — later a best man at my wedding — who'd been selected as captain, and I remember being stoked for him. I was frustrated to miss out — it would mean I would never get to play at an ICC Under-19 World Cup — but I wasn't too cut up about it, until I was told the reason for my omission a few days later, apparently because I had failed to take a five-wicket bag throughout the tournament, even though I had consistently been taking three or four wickets a game.

All the representative teams I'd been selected for since I was a young kid were subject to quotas — four or five players of colour in the 12 of the match-day squad, an effort to rectify just a tiny part of the harm that had been done to so many under Apartheid. It would sometimes mean, depending on the make-up of the side, that I was competing for one of as few as two spots for white bowlers in any given team. I was still a self-centred kid, the product of a conservative Afrikaans upbringing, entirely intent on making my future what I had always dreamed it would be, so perhaps I would've acted with even more anger had I been told that they couldn't fit me in because of the quota system, but I wasn't given the chance to know all the reasons.

What I do know is that it felt like the mostly white structures of South African cricket were so uneasy about this system that it was as if its name couldn't even be uttered. Instead of being honest with young talent, it seemed as though they had to invent strange excuses — no five-fors, seam not straight enough — for non-selection, even when a bulging wickets column should have justified it. It further fuelled my distrust of outside help, and redoubled my belief that if I wanted to make cricket happen for me I could only rely on myself, my work ethic and my own desperation to make the most of whatever talent I had. I couldn't trust the South African structure —

in part because of its dishonesty about the quota system, but not necessarily because of the system itself.

In other ways, however, I was starting to feel more assured of my place in the South African cricket setup. Throughout my time with Northerns, the club had taken pains to familiarise us with eminent cricketers of the generation that preceded us. As an 11-year-old, I first met my idol Allan Donald, when he presented us with our caps following a game in which his team, Free State, had played Northerns. I was in awe, starstruck, to be shaking the hand of the man who had inspired me. Later, I would sit mesmerised in front of our TV, watching that legendary battle Allan waged against England opener Michael Atherton at Trent Bridge in 1998, transfixed by the aggression, passion and sheer electrifying pace with which the quick tried to unsuccessfully pry out the stubborn Englishman. The spectacle of that spell — replayed on YouTube many times over the years — contained every element of fast bowling that made me want to dedicate my life to the craft. I would stay in touch with Allan throughout my career.

As I got older, stronger and faster, Northerns would arrange for us to bowl in the nets against international cricketers, both those visiting the Republic and the South Africans themselves. I remember once catching the edge of Herschelle Gibbs' bat and the opener just laughing it off as one of those things that happens in the nets — but for me it meant everything in the world. Bowling to Jacques Kallis almost made me feel like I was floating them down at the speed of an off spinner, he just had so much time. But I beat him a couple of times outside off, and hit him on the pads once for what would've been a close shout. It was absolutely surreal to be bowling to, and sometimes troubling, legends like this.

The 2003 Cricket World Cup, which took place in South Africa, gave me the opportunity to bowl at a smorgasbord of international cricketers, everyone from Sachin Tendulkar to Ricky Ponting. But the batter I remember most vividly was Matthew Hayden, the big, burly Australian opener. I got him to nick one outside off, and I remember feeling absolutely amazing, 10-feet tall and bulletproof. I was so chuffed — until the very next ball I bowled at him. He walked two steps down the wicket and flat-bat smashed it straight past my head, so close I heard the ball whirr past my ear. It was as if he was saying, 'Go fetch that, youngster.' My puffed-up chest instantly deflated, but it was invaluable for a young bowler to get a sense of what it was like to bowl to batters of that level — and to learn how much more I needed to improve.

During the World Cup, my mate Wilco Marais and I skipped school to head down to Centurion to watch New Zealand take on India, the searing pace of Shane Bond bowling to Sachin Tendulkar my enduring memory of the game. But even more valuable was time with some of the great bowlers of that era. Colin Dettmer, my coach at Affies who died at 51 in 2010, was a huge driver behind our success, and really strove to show us the realities of international cricket. He also worked with the Australians as their local liaison when they toured the country, and he arranged for the defending — and future — champions to spend some time with us. I'll never forget Brett Lee and Glenn McGrath, two legends whose belligerent on-field personas gave no indication of how kind and generous they would be face-to-face, taking the time to pass on some wisdom. Brett even picked up my kit bag as the two fast bowlers walked me across the University of Pretoria field to where my parents were

waiting in the car. I can still picture the long, lanky figure of Glenn McGrath leaning with a forearm resting on the blue roof of our little Volkswagen, chatting with Mum and Dad, who had climbed out of the car to shake the great bowlers' hands in the lovely evening light. They kept the team bus waiting in order to see me to my car.

I've sometimes thought there was maybe another reason why my batting never flourished like I thought it could, why I always seemed to lose my wicket playing one flashy shot too many, that I couldn't always put the expansive shots away and graft through the tough times. As I progressed through Affies, it became clear that the reasons I struggled academically weren't solely because I put cricket above all else.

At 16 I began to fall even further behind in quite a few subjects, and the extra tuition didn't seem to help. I was simply too slow. I saw a psychologist and underwent lots of tests and eventually the results came back: I had Attention Deficit Hyperactivity Disorder. I was told that if I didn't follow the necessary steps, I wouldn't pass high school.

I was prescribed Ritalin, but I refused to take it. At first I was embarrassed about this thing I felt was wrong with me, and I also had a suspicion that, somehow, the drug would affect my cricket — and I wasn't prepared to take that risk. I never have been. For a while, I kept Mum under the impression that I was taking the pills, but instead I was throwing them down the drain every day. It was just stubbornness and I should've listened to the doctors, but once I'd made my decision, nothing could change my mind. I thought that this was just another roadblock, something I'd have to push through to prove the world wrong.

Sometimes, in those moments after people are talking to me and I can't concentrate because my head is spinning elsewhere, I wonder whether my life would have been different had I decided to medicate. Fortunately, I think I've mostly been able to channel my personality into the right areas — but I know that everyone is different. Dr Pierre Edwards, Affies' principal and a former Springbok, was instrumental for me in making sure I had all the support I needed, pointing out that when it came to bowling, at least, the ADHD didn't seem to be an issue. That attitude didn't make school any easier, though somehow I kept scraping through, reaching my final high-school exam in my last year at Affies.

Business studies, I think. It was a hot day, at least 35 degrees, and we were crammed into the cavernous school hall, in rows of 20 or so. The white noise of the fans whirring overhead mixed with the clearing of throats, the squeak of chairs being readjusted, the scratch of pens flying over paper. The doors were open and from where I was sitting I could see a segment of the sports field where the First XI was warming up, soon to play Pretoria Boys High in our local derby. I was allowed to sub into the team as soon as I finished my exam. When the game began — we were bowling first — I heard the *ooohs* and *aaahs* of the bat being beaten, and then, as the opposition openers grew accustomed to the attack, the smack of willow against leather, the 'Yes!' and 'No!' of runs being accumulated. I didn't hear any big celebrations marking the fall of wickets.

The struggle to concentrate was intense as I laboured through the exam. Eventually, a true or false section — *waar* and *onwaar* in Afrikaans — gave me the chance to skim through, choosing answers basically at random. Then I spotted a particular essay question which, luckily, I had studied and studied and studied, and my left hand cramped as I fought with my memory to get it all down on paper. I finished the essay and there were still four or five questions left. I looked up and outside at the segment of the cricket field I could see, and it was as if the decision was already made. I folded my unfinished exam and delivered it to the teachers at the front of the hall. I was the first to leave. They looked at me as if to ask, 'What are you doing?' But off I went.

'How did it go?' asked Deon when I arrived at the field.

'Not very well. I don't think I am going to make it,' I said.

'Then why did you leave?'

'Because I wanted to be here,' I replied, and then — as if finishing my answer — ran onto the field and took four wickets, setting up the two-day game for the team.

Afterwards, in the car, as Mum and Dad fretted about the exam, I sat there smiling as we glided past Pretoria suburbs — Eloffsdal, Mayville — on the R101, heading back over the Magaliesberg mountains.

We're going to win this game tomorrow, and I played a huge role. I'm so stoked and I couldn't care less about anything else.

CHAPTER 3:
CHOOSING CRICKET

Centurion was wrapped in a wreath of barbecue smoke, bright white where it was caught by the highveld sunlight. The smell of *boerewors* cooking drifted across the ground. I could almost taste the beer washing it down. The crowd was dotted with familiar faces. I could hear my name being called when I furiously chased the ball to within earshot of the boundary, firing it back to Shaun Pollock, Makhaya Ntini or Jacques Kallis at the bowler's end or Mark Boucher at the keeper's. Pakistan were batting. Inzamam-ul-Haq was captaining the touring side. I had a South African flag on my chest. I was 20 — and so close to something I had dreamed of for as long as I could remember dreaming. I was 12th man, and on the field for the Proteas on my hometown ground of Centurion. I spent 20-odd overs on the park

— usually at deep square or fine leg, with a couple of overs closer to the action at midwicket, the whole time tense with the thought: *Hey, a catch could come my way at any moment here, switch on.*

If you had told me, walking out of that final exam at Affies and into a cricket game, that only two years later I'd be on the field during *this* cricket game at Centurion, even just as a reserve, I would scarcely have believed you. That fact did, however, flatter to deceive somewhat: it's not as if I was anywhere even remotely close to representing the South African team. I was pretty comfortable around the group, having played cricket with or against most of the guys in that squad — my Affies teammate AB de Villiers was opening the batting in that team — and Graeme Smith, the South African captain, had an incredible knack for making me feel as though I were an integral member of the side, as if running drinks and changes of gloves out to the batters in the middle was nearly as important as the runs they were scoring against Shoaib Akhtar and Mohammad Asif. But the truth is that I was nothing more than a useful local cricketer picked from obscurity to help out. As the tour moved on to Port Elizabeth, no doubt a useful cricketer local to the Eastern Cape city would fill that role, and I would return to the same domestic obscurity, locked in the dogfight of trying to get ahead in an era of South African, Transvaal and Pretoria cricket overflowing with talent.

Still, I couldn't sleep that night. I lived at home in North Pretoria and it felt strange to be twisting and turning in my teenage bed having spent the day among these men I revered. Adrenaline was still pouring through my veins and every time I closed my eyes all I saw was another memory. I almost couldn't believe I had spent a significant portion of the day fielding for the Proteas. The ambitions of the little boy on the sidelines of his brothers' games had almost been met. *I want more of this. I'd give anything to play for South Africa for real.*

I left school with one thing clear in my mind: I was going to be a cricketer.

It was 2005 and I played my first year of club cricket for Tshwane University of Technology (TUT). The Pretoria club scene was absolutely brimming with battle-hardened veterans, many with years of first-class experience, battling it out with the talented youngsters coming through. For example, in that TUT team, captain-coach Grant Morgan — also my coach at the South African National Academy, where I would spend two winters — had played 50-odd first-class games, and brothers Johann and Stephan Myburgh, more or less my contemporaries, would both go on to have significant professional careers, the former playing in New Zealand and in England, the latter representing the Netherlands.

If bowling at international superstars in the nets had given me a sense of how much I needed to improve my skills to make it at the top level, club cricket with and against tough, tough men gave me an idea of how mentally strong I'd need to be. It was another kind of step up from the schoolboy cricket where I had made my name. There'd been plenty of sledging there, too, but naturally it hit harder when it came from men a decade older. It wasn't just random, either: in search of material to try and get under your skin, clubs did their homework. Playing against the University of Pretoria club — nicknamed Tuks, an acronym derived from its Afrikaans name, Transvaal Universiteitskollege — meant being subject to a torrent of abuse from their captain, the sort of old-school player that gave Pretoria club cricket its abrasive character. I walked out to bat and the abuse began immediately. It soon got very personal. He somehow knew I had struggled academically on account of my ADHD: I was reminded again and again how supposedly stupid I was. The things you heard on a Saturday afternoon in Pretoria were many times worse than anything the Australians, for example, would dish out years later.

It didn't stop me helping TUT to the title that year, meaning we qualified for the South African National Club Championship, a prestigious competition for which even international players would return to their club side if their schedules allowed. I remember the thrill of taking four wickets as we won our first match that year against the Northwood Crusaders, a team from KwaZulu-Natal featuring the great Proteas all-rounder Shaun Pollock.

I would play in that tournament a further two times. But it would be for a new club. When Grant, my captain and coach, moved to Tuks, I followed him. A few Affies old boys also played their club cricket at Tuks — Kruger, Faf and AB — so there were some very familiar faces in the dressing room. As well as one terrifying one: that same captain. He shook my hand and welcomed me to the team as if he had no memory of the words he had used to try and unsettle a kid in his first year of senior cricket. Before long, he was throwing me the new ball and telling me what he needed from me on the pitch, then drinking with me after the match. In South Africa sledging was just part of the game. You had to find a way to ignore it or use it as fuel for your performance. Otherwise you would sink.

I managed to swim. In early 2006, following my good form in the previous season of club cricket, I was selected to make my first-class debut for the Northerns senior team. I was 19. The South African first-class system had recently been overhauled, with the 11 provincial teams that had previously competed at the top level combining to form six new franchises. The Northerns and the Easterns had joined forces to form the Titans, who would compete against the five other newly formed franchises in the four-day SuperSport Series. The best players from Northerns and Easterns were syphoned into the Titans, while the rest would continue to play for the original associations in an amateur, but still first-class, second-tier domestic competition. It was in this competition, called the South African Airways Provincial Three-Day Challenge, that I played my debut first-class game for Northerns.

It came against North West in Potchefstroom — a town, and a cricket ground, that I happened to know well. My brother Mark had gone to university in Potch, as it is known, and had played some of his rugby for the local Currie Cup team, the Leopards. As a kid, our family had often piled into the Volkswagen and made the two-hour drive to the student town to watch him play. Sometimes, I used to wander off during his games to the cricket field — deserted for the winter — next to the rugby ground, where I could mark out my run-up and charge in a few times to bowl a few phantom balls at phantom batters, visualising a time when I would play on the ground for real. Those visions were about to turn into reality.

This time, I got a ride from Pretoria with Northerns captain Pierre Joubert, a stalwart of Pretoria cricket who my brothers had played with and against years earlier. He was another of the old-school cricketers who had learned to play the game in that same hard way. If you weren't bowling well enough, he would definitely let you know about it later, as I had the displeasure of finding out a few times. It was a different era and cricket teams were structured in a conservative, almost militaristic way — they were very hierarchical — and I was the most junior member of the team. Pierre spent the entire drive, as the distance between me and my debut decreased, the arid farmland sliding by, ribbing me and trying to convince me I had packed the wrong kit. The drive did nothing to decrease my nerves.

We bowled first, and I took the new ball for the second over. The ground was like a billiards table — get it through the infield and it seemed to accelerate across the grass on its way to the boundary. At the top of my mark all that ran through my mind was *Don't go for four, don't go for four* — and of course I was immediately hit for a couple of boundaries, going wicketless in my first spell. When I came back later my rhythm clicked: that nervousness was gone and the ball was obedient as it left the touch of my fingertips as thousands had before. The pitch, usually notoriously flat, had a bit more pace in it than usual. It was swinging and carrying through nicely to the keeper, the familiar face of Kruger. My first wicket was opening batter and the innings' top-scorer Jimmy Kgamadi for 72 — caught in the cordon by another Affies old boy, Heino Kuhn — and a weight slipped off my shoulders. I took the next three in quick succession, North West declaring nine down to deny me the chance of a five-wicket haul on first-class debut. I knew this was exactly what I wanted to be doing with my life. This was where I needed to be. I was promoted as nightwatchman in both innings, and took another four wickets when North West batted again. We won. I was away, a first-class cricketer.

I made my senior one-day debut in the fixture that followed, bowling economically and snaring a wicket, nervous but excited to bowl in front of the biggest crowd — this was in the days when a domestic one-day game could still attract a lot of spectators — of my young career, feeding off the energy it gave me. I played another three first-class games for Northerns that season, ending with 14 wickets at an average under 18. We won both the first-class and list-A competitions, although I only played two list-A games and didn't make the team for the Provincial Challenge final. I hoped I'd done enough to force my way in, but with several Titans players dropping back down for the most important game of the season, I wasn't selected.

At the time, my methodology for taking wickets was pretty simple. I was essentially a new-ball swing bowler, pitching it up at a decent pace — consistently in the region of 135kph-plus back then — and looking to swing it back into the pads of the right-handed batters, or go searching for their outside edge with one that went straight. I was short for a fast bowler, but my bouncer was also an important part of my armoury, and batters had often told me that because of the lower angle and the different trajectory, it was a delivery that seemed to get onto them quicker than they expected. It was always an important weapon, though something I used sparingly.

By my second season with Northerns, I had found my feet. I was in great form, and would end the season at the top of the wicket table, with 39 wickets at 16.43. But it was already clear that the road to higher honours — even just a contract with the Titans, which would mean I could pay my own way in the world — was going to be a very difficult one.

The bowling resources that Northerns and the Titans could call on were truly world-class. Dale Steyn was establishing himself as the most feared fast bowler in the world, first choice in any team on the planet. Morne Morkel wasn't too far behind him, and Morne's older brother Albie represented South Africa many times as a fast-bowling all-rounder. Andre Nel was another test veteran ahead of me in the pecking order, as were domestic stalwarts Ethy Mbhalati, a bowler who would take over 350 first-class wickets, and Alfonso Thomas, a man who was incredibly unlucky to only have the opportunity to represent his country in a single T20I in a career that netted him nearly 550 wickets at first-class level. Then there were three international spinners the Titans could call on: Imran Tahir, Paul Harris and Roelof van der Merwe were variously available, depending on injuries and their selection for the national teams. Sometimes when Morne and Andre weren't required for international duty, even they couldn't crack the Titans team, dropping down to the Northerns to play alongside me in what amounted to a domestic B team — or demoting me to the bench.

The quota system complicated this further. Alfonso, who is coloured, and Ethy, who is black, were incredible bowlers, both much better than I was at the time. Alfonso, in particular, was one of the most skilful bowlers on the domestic scene, I thought, and was someone I had always tried to learn from — he was a similar height, perhaps a bit quicker, and he swung the ball both ways.

Their quality meant the Titans could meet their quota requirements and lose absolutely nothing in the potency of their attack. When the franchise could choose from its full roster, there were usually only two slots for white fast bowlers and as many as four or even five international-level bowlers vying for them. I had little chance of forcing my way through.

And, in attempting to do so, I was straining my action for every little bit of speed I could find. Just as in high school, I knew that coaches would always look a little bit longer at a bowler capable of pure, electrifying pace. I strove to get as close as possible to those speeds whenever I was called on to bowl to the Titans boys in the nets. Once, I remember bowling to Martin van Jaarsveld and Jacques Rudolph — both would play test cricket, Jacques almost 50 times — and Englishman Richard Pybus, the coach, was standing in conversation with Albie, casting their eyes over the bowling stocks. As I walked back to my mark I heard Albie mention my name.

'Looks good, he's got something about him, this kid. But I think he's undercutting the ball a bit here.'

I knew what he meant, and in striving for the thing that seemed valued above all else, I was losing the other weapons — primarily swing and accuracy — that had served me so well at first-class level. It only made me more nervous to hear it had been noticed, and my mind went into overdrive: *I'm doing something wrong here, I need to try and fix it.* I knew that if I dropped my pace that would go a long way towards sorting out the issues, but it didn't seem like something I could do if I was serious about making a case for my inclusion. It would've been the perfect time for a senior player or a coach to offer me some wisdom, but it never came — and I didn't ask. The independence I'd learned throughout my upbringing made it difficult for me to reach out for help. Here was another instance when, because of that, I was left to muddle through myself.

I only ever played two four-day games for the Titans. The first was in early 2007, bowling alongside Ethy and Alfonso against the Cape Cobras in Benoni when Morne, Dale and Andre were unavailable due to injury or international duty. I took a solitary wicket — JP Duminy, bowled — in the game and was sent back down to Northerns when Morne and Dale returned for the following fixture. The next year — I took 26 wickets at 21 for Northerns that season — I was called up in similar circumstances, taking another couple of wickets, but nothing to challenge the incumbents in that team, who were more than delivering for the franchise.

The Titans won the SuperSport Series the year I made my debut for them and, despite only having played the single fixture, I was invited out for a drink with the squad to celebrate the victory. I wasn't sure that I could go. I didn't have a car or even a driver licence so I would have to negotiate a ride to the bar with one of my teammates, then coordinate a ride home with my brother. But at the last minute I managed to get it lined up, and joined the team for a few drinks in a place called News Cafe, an upmarket establishment in the Menlyn suburb of Pretoria.

I remember looking across the busy restaurant. My eyes fell upon the most beautiful woman I had ever seen. I was there to celebrate the Titans' victory, but that suddenly didn't seem so important. Cricket itself had momentarily lost its lustre. I am not the kind of person who would ever normally approach a woman I didn't know in a bar, but something compelled me on this occasion and I felt myself moving across the room. I can't remember exactly what I said first — something generic, I think, like asking if she was having a good night, or if I could buy her a drink — but I certainly remember the response: a withering look as if to ask what the hell I was trying to do. I slunk away, humiliated by how resoundingly I'd been shot down. I would find out many years later that Lana, a very shy person, hadn't meant it that way at all.

But throughout the night — before my brother picked me up at midnight — I couldn't help but notice this woman dancing and laughing with mutual friends. The next morning, one of them tagged her in a photo. Lana Koekemoer. My cursor hovered over the 'Add Friend' button and on a whim I clicked. To my surprise, she accepted. And for a few years, that was the extent of our connection.

I started a sports science degree at Tuks, but it quickly proved too difficult to keep up with during the cricket season. We would be away for four or five days in a row, playing cricket almost every day, with a one-day fixture often following on the heels of a first-class game, and then I would get back to the hotel room in the evening and have to try and study. I had always struggled academically, and this was a bridge too far, especially as much of the work was supposed to be completed in groups. Without all the technology that would make it easier these days, I realised I was doing neither myself nor my classmates justice. I gave it up. Part of me enjoyed working towards a qualification and having something else with which to try and secure my future. When I dropped out, all I had left was cricket.

But I wasn't getting paid for it. Everything below the Titans level was entirely amateur. Accommodation and food was taken care of, but nothing else. I tried a few different things to get by, first working as a sales rep for Canterbury, the New Zealand clothing company. I got a few schools to sign up to do their uniforms through my employer, and a few other sports teams to use Canterbury for their kit. I made a little bit of money through that, but never much. I was doing some coaching, too. Heinrich Malan was a player-coach at Tuks who would later coach domestically in New Zealand and internationally for Ireland, and he roped me into his clinics, in which six or seven schools would combine for a week of coaching. From nine until five every day I ran the bowling programme. Later, I started one-on-one coaching also. It gave me some spending money, but again not enough to be self-sufficient. The first time I was ever paid for playing cricket itself was when I was 12th man for the South African side. I literally fell to my knees when I saw how much they had paid me. I had to make it last a long time.

Other than the winter months, when I lodged at the South African National Academy at Tuks' High Performance Centre, I was still living at home. I was the only member of the Northerns whose parents had to drop me off and pick me up from home games, often combining the chore with their drive to work, meaning I was almost always one of the first to arrive. It was embarrassing and it accentuated my growing impatience with the stage of life I found myself in — playing cricket full time but not being paid to do so. I was desperate to get out into the world and make a name for myself. As my frustrations started to mount, I began working with an agent, Marco Cesaro, who lined up a gig in the Liverpool and District Cricket Competition with a club called Ormskirk for the South African off-season of 2008. At least that would bring in some money.

Throughout the 2007/08 summer, however, playing mostly for Northerns, all the talk from the board and the coaches had led me to believe that I would be taken care of, that there would be a Titans contract for me in the not-too-distant future and that I could expect to be playing regularly before too long. So I had that to look forward to. Then, as the first-class season wound down, I was picked in the

National Academy team for the winter tour to Bangladesh. I had hoped to have a contract signed with the Titans before leaving, so I could use the tour and then my time in England to keep in top shape to challenge for a permanent spot in the XI the following season.

Those hopes were dashed the day before we flew to Bangladesh. I was called into a meeting. Coach Richard Pybus was there, as was Northerns coach Chris van Noordwyk. They sat me down and got to the point.

'We're very sorry but we're not in a position to offer you a contract.'

The bowling stocks were too full already, they said, and there just wasn't the money for another fast bowler. All they could do was offer me what was called a rookie contract, but it was only worth the equivalent of something like $700 for the entire season — basically nothing. I would have to coach junior cricket to get by. It was extremely deflating. I felt as if I'd been punched in the stomach, but part of me could understand as I looked around at the talent available. *Hey, I'll keep fighting, there's always next year*. And the Bangladesh tour with the South African Academy offered me another and immediate chance to prove myself.

The next day, the cricketers selected for the tour gathered at OR Tambo International Airport in Johannesburg. We had come from every corner of South Africa, and as we waited for our flight I heard a voice congratulate someone on their Titans contract. My head swung round. I could hardly believe it, but a fast bowler who had spent the season recovering from a stress fracture in his back, and who'd had to do a lot of rehabilitative work on a bowling action deemed so suspicious it was thought he could be no-balled for chucking, was accepting those congratulations. I felt gutted all over again, embarrassed, too. I felt like I hadn't been told the truth by the franchise I had dreamed of representing. I'd had real success at first-class level but here they were taking a speculative long-shot on a bowler with an uncertain future. *Am I actually good enough? Has my success to date just been luck? Why won't anybody be honest with me?*

As I sat on the plane, I couldn't escape the sense that I wasn't being valued for the skills I could bring. It felt like that same old story — the Titans would rather take a chance on a faster, taller bowler than go with me. I had taken 79 wickets at a touch over 18 for Northerns — a record I was proud of — but I could feel the South African dream starting to slip through my fingers. In a moment of clarity, I suddenly knew that I might have to look outside the country of my birth if I wanted to make a living playing the game I loved.

CHAPTER 4:
ABROAD

I thought I knew what a flat wicket looked like until I wandered out to the middle to examine the surface on which we were to play the opening game of our National Academy tour of Bangladesh. The pitch at Tuks, for example, would by the end of each sun-baked day resemble a tarmac road: hard, unforgiving and full of fast runs if bowlers got it wrong. Late-season wickets in Port Elizabeth and East London could be slow and low. Durban wickets, too, on occasion. But I had never played on anything that looked like the surface that awaited us at Shamsul Huda Stadium in Jashore, a mid-size city towards the country's western border with India. There wasn't a single blade of grass on what was essentially 22 yards of rolled mud, criss-crossed by a filigree of tiny cracks, between which, as the match wore on, chunks of dirt would break off and dissolve into dust. When I first looked at the wicket — jet-lagged, overwhelmed by the sensory experience of the subcontinent, still feeling the disappointment about what had happened back home — I thought, *What the hell am I supposed to do on this?*

Our coaches on that tour, Rob Walter, later to coach in New Zealand as well as the Proteas, and Grant Morgan, who I knew well from Pretoria, told us bowlers to embrace the challenge of these pitches, to use our time here to experiment and explore new ways of taking wickets. As an opening bowler who predominantly leaned on a swinging new ball to take the majority of mine, in Bangladesh, that might work for perhaps the first over. When you got the ball back to begin your second, it was as if a dog had mauled it in the interim, so hard were the ground and abrasive the pitches. And after that, there wouldn't be even a hint of movement in the air. A common criticism of my game had been that I never really had a method for taking wickets once the ball stopped swinging. In Bangladesh, I would have to find one.

At first, my approach — typically South African — was to bang it in as fast as possible to try and coax something out of the wicket, but all that resulted in was sweat-drenched fatigue in the unrelenting humidity. The Bangladesh soil just seemed to suck energy from the ball. The first couple I bowled, despite giving them everything I had, limped through to the keeper below knee-height. I very quickly realised that I was going to have to come up with something entirely different. Nothing that I had previously learned about bowling was going to help me.

It was a really strong Bangladesh Cricket Board Academy XI. Imrul Kayes opened the batting and Mushfiqur Rahim shepherded the middle order. All but a couple of the players in the team would go on to play international cricket. And it showed. In that first game, Bangladesh replied to our first-innings score of 311 with 507-8 declared, Imrul scoring 151, Mushfiqur a quickfire 50. I bowled 32 overs for no reward, and Bangladesh won by an innings when the spinners ran through us for 128 on a footmark-pocked pitch in our second innings.

By the second four-day game, down the road in Khulna, I had assimilated some of those lessons. I still remember how strange it felt to hold a newish red ball cross-seamed in my hand — on the pitches I grew up bowling on, where it was all about landing the ball on a dead-straight seam to keep it swinging for as long as possible, you would never consider it. But in Bangladesh I was searching for anything that might make the ball behave differently off the pitch. Gone were the conventional three slips and a gully: anything with a hint of width was travelling very fast to the off-side boundary, so I came around the wicket and tightened my line onto the stumps, with a couple of catching midwickets and a short cover ready for anything miscued in the air. For the first time in my life, I was made to really think hard about bowling and consider that there were other currencies with which you sometimes needed to buy your wickets. I took four dismissals across nearly 40 overs in the game and soaked up over 100 balls with bat in hand to help us escape with the narrowest of draws. Formative lessons were being learned.

For many of us in that squad, myself included, it was our first time out of Africa. We threw ourselves into it, taking every chance to walk the streets and visit the markets, embracing the experience of a different culture. Wherever we went, we'd see cricket in all its organic forms. One evening, after training, we jumped the fence and into the tight-packed neighbourhood surrounding the ground, where a tennis ball, an old bat and a few boxes sitting on top of each other had dragged kids into the dusty street to emulate their idols. We played for an hour as our bus waited nearby, the smiles as broad

on our faces as they were on those of our hosts.

There was still more serious stuff to play. We moved on to the teeming city of Chattogram, where we had a one-day tri-series against Bangladesh and a Pakistan Academy team — also very strong, featuring the likes of Azhar Ali, Mohammad Amir, Imad Wasim and Yasir Shah — to contemplate. We were thrashed in every game, as our batting order failed to combat opposition spinners on surfaces seemingly made for them. I played two of the four games, bowling fairly well in the strange conditions, taking a couple of wickets at an average in the low thirties. It was only a short tour, but I'd learned so much about the skill of bowling on the kinds of pitches that usually gave fast bowlers allergies. And about persevering in the aftermath of disappointment.

I confided in Grant and Rob how I was feeling about the Titans, and they urged me throughout Bangladesh to use the tour as a chance to make a statement. They reminded me that you never knew what might happen in professional sport, who might succumb to injury or whose form might fall from a cliff. Another member of the support staff, Barney Mohamed, worked with the Cape Cobras franchise back home, and he thought they might be happy to sign me, a chance I would have jumped at, as I had started to think that my time in Bangladesh could be my last push for a top-flight career in South Africa. Another couple of seasons without cementing my spot in the top league could mean a frustrating bit-part career before I'd be forced to look at doing something else with my life. I had Ormskirk on the horizon, but I also let Marco know that he should spread our net as far as possible when we thought about what came after that.

When I later tried to follow up with Barney he said he was sorry but the Cape Cobras weren't in a position to offer me anything. It was out of his hands. With none of the other South African franchises showing any interest, either, it gave me the brutal clarity of despair. I kept wondering whether I'd been deluding myself. *Am I actually good enough?* I had played 20 first-class games, taking 89 wickets at an average of 18.30. *Surely that wasn't just luck? Was there something unlikeable about me as a person that was preventing me from moving up the ranks?* It didn't seem fair. I left for England with much on my mind.

Not before a couple of days at home in the Pretoria sunshine, however, saying goodbye to family and friends, got me used to familiar and warm weather before the frigid shock of England's north. From Johannesburg I flew to Heathrow, somehow managing to negotiate that airport alone and make my connection to the north. I arrived safely, but my suitcase didn't, and facing the freezing Liverpool weather in the clothes I had left sun-drenched South Africa in did nothing to soften the transition. Club captain Adam Waterhouse picked me up from the airport and drove me the half hour north to Ormskirk, the small student town whose cricket team I'd be representing for the English summer. Although 'summer' had never seemed so relative a concept.

The apartment was another shock. I'm not an ungrateful person, and I was hardly spoiled by my upbringing, but this apartment was grim. As soon as I stepped foot inside, I felt the damp chill of the air and my nostrils were assaulted by the smell of mould. The TV was the size of an iPad. I didn't say anything, and hoped I kept my disappointment to myself, but my first thought was that this was going to be a pretty rough six months. Luckily, when another teammate stopped by to introduce himself, he took one look around the place and said, 'You can't live like this.' By chance, his parents owned an empty flat near the centre of town, and I was able to upgrade to a modest but warm and dry apartment. It was perfect. I borrowed some money from the club to buy a change of clothes, a toothbrush and enough food to see me through until my first pay cheque. When I made my Ormskirk debut a few days later I was still waiting for my suitcase to arrive.

It was an away fixture against a St Helens XI featuring Anthony Bullick, a Dunedin man I would reconnect with later. When we turned up, it was wet, freezing cold, with icy rain periodically soaking the ground. I knew there would be no play and I was secretly very pleased about that. But then Adam turned up in the dressing room to tell us the toss was in five minutes — get ready, we'll be looking to bowl first. I thought he was pulling my leg, winding up the new recruit. In South Africa, you would never play in conditions that bleak, on a wicket that was literally wet. But he wasn't kidding.

We subsequently lost the toss and I scored 34 batting at number six as we put on 222. Then future one-test England spinner Simon

Kerrigan and I shared nine of the 10 wickets to fall as St Helens crumbled to 54 all out in reply. Like Bangladesh — but at the same time its complete opposite — conditions were utterly unlike anything I had experienced before. And they would vary intensely throughout the season — one week a fast, true surface, the next something slow and docile. My education continued.

I had spent the previous two South African winters billeted during the week with the National Academy — home for the weekends — but this was a new level of independence, the first time I truly had to fend for myself. I already knew my way around a barbecue, but anything else more complicated than a fried egg was beyond me. There were several catastrophes in the kitchen before I asked Mum to send a few recipes she thought I could handle. A chicken pasta dish of hers became a staple — as did pies from the Morrisons supermarket across the road, plus a pub meal or two with guys from the team every week. They would often end in the small hours of the morning, fuelled by one-quid snakebites.

Ormskirk, I soon came to realise, was the perfect town for me, its red-brick centre small enough that I could walk everywhere I needed to go. I loved the student energy that Edge Hill University, set among the patchwork crop fields on the outskirts of town, gave to the area, reminding me a little of Potchefstroom, the town where my brother had studied. I'd often felt, back home in Pretoria, that I had missed out on many valuable post-match dressing-room lessons because we lived too far from where I played most of my cricket and where most of my teammates lived, and I usually had to shoot off quickly after a game to get a ride back to Pretoria North with Mum or Dad or one of my brothers. In Ormskirk, I could be the last to leave if I wanted, soaking in the storied history and culture of Lancashire cricket as I listened to the banter of my teammates, learning as I did so. Usually, after a game — we played Saturday and Sunday, sometimes a T20 on Friday evening — we'd hit the showers, chuck on a polo shirt and a pair of jeans and migrate to the bar in the Tudor-style pavilion, where the tales continued, getting louder, and perhaps taller, as pint glasses accumulated around us.

Once, after a victory in which I took a five-for, the club chairman appeared in the midst of post-match drinks to criticise my performance. The game had been close and I apparently should have done more. As an overseas professional, there was pressure on me to do well, to earn the seven or eight thousand pounds the club had invested in me for the season. My teammates told me that other clubs could be far more brutal on their overseas pros, and I would always just laugh off comments like that or — depending on how many beers I had sunk — give my opinion back. And, anyway, I enjoyed the pressure. I had left South Africa feeling unwanted by the system there. The pressure to perform for Ormskirk felt like another way of letting me know I was needed, that my efforts were appreciated. I thrived on it. And for the first time in my life I was paying my own way playing the game I loved. I was 22 and could finally call myself a professional cricketer. It meant everything in the world to me.

Marco, from his Durban base, had also been busy, investigating what options were out there for me following my season with Ormskirk. During my time in the UK, I began to think my future might be in the English county game — and maybe, one day, that would open the door to play for England. Marco arranged a trial with Lancashire — where, by chance, Faf had ended up for the season. Nothing much came of that, other than an invitation to do some net bowling before test matches at Old Trafford later in the summer. I also had a trial with Hampshire when they played Lancashire at Old Trafford that season, bowling in the nets as the team prepared for the match. There was talk that I might play a Second XI game for them at some point. Marco had even sent my footage further afield, to Dunedin, New Zealand, where we started a conversation with Otago's new coach, Mike Hesson, who was looking for a left-armer to supplement his pace-bowling stocks.

The Black Caps were touring England that year, and the second test was at Old Trafford, where I was called in as a net bowler. England netted first, and the superstars of that squad — Kevin Pietersen, Michael Vaughan, Andrew Flintoff — were friendly enough but kept pretty much to themselves. When the Black Caps replaced them in the afternoon, the atmosphere changed utterly — it was relaxed, jokey and they just seemed like a good bunch of laidback guys. Aaron Redmond was cracking everyone up, Daniel Flynn and James Marshall made an effort to have a chat, and Jacob Oram, in particular, stood out for how friendly and welcoming he was. Grant Elliott, the South African-born all-rounder, was on that tour, too, and we had a brief chat. I admired the power of Brendon McCullum up close, in awe of the batter I had watched one morning on the TV in the Ormskirk clubroom smash a brutal century in the inaugural game of the Indian Premier League. I was given a couple of tickets to the test and I took Faf along to watch the game. Ross Taylor hit 17 fours and five sixes in scoring a rapid 150 and I realised as I watched New Zealand struggle in a losing cause, dodging the rain that interrupted the game, that I had no interest in playing for England. For some reason, I just didn't feel that this was the team for me. Although nor did New Zealand really enter my thoughts at the time, either.

Ever since the 1995 Rugby World Cup, I can remember having a huge respect for New Zealand's sporting culture, mostly on the back of rugby. At Affies, touring teams would often use the school facilities to train and, once, Andrew Mehrtens, when the visiting Crusaders were done with their own training, took us through a kicking clinic. Me and a bunch of mates went to the game that followed, across the road at Loftus Versfeld, waiting outside the gates when it was over, hoping for another glimpse of our heroes. Most of the Bulls players walked straight past without even raising an eyebrow. But Mehrts remembered exactly who we were, and came to shake hands and chat with us. It was the kind of thing a sports-mad kid never forgets, and it gave me a template for what I thought New Zealanders must be like. Later, links between New Zealand and South African cricket started to strengthen — Dave Nosworthy, who I had a bit to do with when he was at the Titans, went off to coach Canterbury. Johann Myburgh went that way also. Grant Elliott had already made a name for himself in Aotearoa. I still remember wondering, at Kruger van Wyk's going-away party back in Pretoria, why the hell he was going all the way to New Zealand to play his cricket — but perhaps watching him make that move had planted a seed in my own mind.

I did manage to play a couple of games for the Sussex seconds, including a three-day game against Surrey at The Oval. I almost didn't make it, emerging from London's Euston Station to find myself instantly lost in that unforgiving city, somehow ending up on the wrong line on the Underground, and then ignored by busy Londoners as I tried to find someone to help. Eventually a lady took pity on me and directed me to the right line and station, from which I emerged to drag my suitcase and kit bag around in search of the hotel. In the chaos of London, I found myself wanting to escape back to small, manageable Ormskirk. I almost broke down in tears, deciding finally to splurge on a taxi to get me to the hotel — I didn't care how much it was going to cost.

The cabbie, when I asked him to take me, just broke into a grin: 'Mate, look behind you.'

I turned and looked straight into the foyer of the hotel I had been searching for.

I didn't produce my best performance on a flat Oval surface, leaking a lot of expensive runs for a solitary wicket. But after the game, South African Mark Davis, Sussex's coach whose first-class playing career had also begun with Northerns, caught up with me in the pavilion. I looked over the historic ground, the nervousness building, as I awaited Mark's verdict. I'd been completely honest with him about my prospects — including the fact there'd been some initial interest shown in me from Mike Hesson in New Zealand. Mark said that, yes, Sussex would look to offer me a two-year contract — but that, if he could speak honestly, there was a lot of uncertainty surrounding the rules governing South African players in the county game and that, if he were in my shoes, he would think really hard about accepting an opportunity in New Zealand should it come. It would give me a better chance, he thought, of one day playing international cricket.

I headed back to Ormskirk. A couple of days later, Hess rang me up and said, 'Look, we know there's an offer on the table from Sussex, just give us twenty-four hours to put something together before you sign anything.' Grant Elliott got in touch to help sell New Zealand. Anthony Bullick, when I informed him what was going on, told me how much I'd love Dunedin. All of a sudden, after feeling unwanted for so long, I was being courted on opposite sides of the world. But it was Mark's honesty, in opposition to his best interests, that rang in my ears when Hess called. Otago could only offer a six-month contract, Hess told me, but they would do their best to look after me through the time it would take to qualify for New Zealand, if that's what I wanted. He said he saw in me a bowler with the potential to play international cricket, provided I was prepared to work hard to improve — and that he wanted to help me do exactly that. These were words I had wanted to hear all my life and suddenly it felt as though my dream wasn't an impossible one. He was warm, honest and friendly, just as his compatriots had been in the Old Trafford nets. I wanted to accept immediately but I had to talk to my Mum and Dad first. They told me to follow my gut.

I called Hess back: 'Where do I sign?'

It began a period of frantically trying to get all my paperwork in order. Relying largely on the goodwill of English mates and access to their cars, I criss-crossed England's northwest: a hospital in Liverpool for this medical test, another in Manchester for that. Down to London again to the New Zealand High Commission. Andy McLean, then the manager for Otago Cricket, was directing me from afar through all the hoops I needed to jump in order to get to Dunedin for the first ball of the season. He was incredible, as was everyone else who I was in touch with at Otago, from Hess to the late Ross Dykes, then the chief executive. They all gave me the impression they couldn't wait to have me, and the simple fact of being wanted meant I could hardly wait to jump on the plane to get down there.

There was the remainder of the season to play with Ormskirk, and a few ends to be tied up in South Africa, but it really felt — even before I had stepped foot in New Zealand — that I had made a definitive break with my homeland. I knew that I would never be able to return with my tail between my legs, asking for another shot at the Titans or elsewhere. This was it. This was my chance to play cricket at the highest level possible. I yearned to get my life properly under way, to escape the period of stagnation that my life and my cricket seemed to have fallen into since high school had finished. I wanted to support myself — and one day, I hoped, a family — with cricket. I didn't think about the potential of playing on the international stage in terms of a desire to represent New Zealand *per se* — it was, at that point, a country I had never been to — but instead as the pinnacle of cricket, to which I hoped one day to climb.

That meant saying goodbye to the boyhood dream of playing for South Africa. But my time in England had done nothing to dilute the frustration and anger I felt about how I'd been treated by the game there, and it wasn't until fairly late in the piece that I even called the Titans to touch base. They weren't too happy about my decision. Or at least that's the impression I got from the media coverage about my move, which dwelt on how I was apparently chasing money — which is why, naturally, I chose a six-month contract with the famously lucrative Otago Cricket Association over county opportunities — and how if I had kept the Titans in the loop about my New Zealand plans I would've been looked after better. I didn't like the tone of the coverage. Why should it take me leaving for my home franchise to want to take care of me?

Then there was the other angle the media took. I was 22 and had never done a minute of media training in my life. My English was far from fluent. I had just made the biggest decision of my life so far, and my emotions were all over the place. Then interview after interview — only one of which was conducted in Afrikaans — returned again and again to the quota system. Are you leaving because of the quota system? Is the quota system to blame? How has the quota system contributed to your departure? The journalists kept coming back to the question, asking it in different ways until I hardly knew what I was saying and they had evidently got what they were after. What I had wanted to express was that, yes, the quota system exists in South Africa and of course it is a complicating factor of representative cricket in the country, but in truth it was the impenetrable block of talent — black, white, coloured — ahead of me at the Titans that really made me look elsewhere to try and build a livelihood from cricket. When I saw the headline — something like 'Neil Wagner Blames the Quota System' — I couldn't believe how much my words had been taken out of context.

It put me in an awkward position with friends of mine, like Alfonso and Ethy, insinuating that the only reason I thought they were ever picked ahead of me was because of their colour. My brother, I remember, told me to just forget about it — you're leaving, it's not your problem anymore. But it left a bitter taste in my mouth — as well as giving me another hint that I was making the right move — as I wrapped up my season with Ormskirk and headed home. The team would win the league, closing out the final few games without me. I needed the extra few days to wrap up my South African life, getting ready to head down the road to OR Tambo International Airport in Jo'burg and jet off to my new life, whatever that would turn out to be.

It was a night flight. I remember, sitting in the plane as it lingered on the tarmac, having said goodbye to my family at the departure gate, feeling overcome by the gravity of the choice I had made. I felt like I'd reached a fork in the road of my life, knowing that my decision to see where this path would take me meant closing the door on others I would never even know. I had my earphones in, my iPod on shuffle. U2's 'Where the Streets Have No Name' came on. The song's theme of struggle, of being assaulted by the elements, and of the respite we might find from it in the place with the anonymous streets, was incredibly apt. Dunedin, a little gothic Scottish city on the other side of the world, was still — for the next 36 hours at least — a complete mystery to me. *Jeez, this is a huge move.* I was thankful for the darkened cabin in which I could cry without being seen.

To this day, whenever I hear that song I am transported instantly back across the decades to that moment on the plane when I said *totsiens* to South Africa, and began saying kia ora to New Zealand.

CHAPTER 5:
SCARFIE

I remember the cold most vividly — and that was before I had even made it to the deeper south.

I arrived in Christchurch in the middle of the night, the city glistening through recent rain. Johann and Kruger, both now playing their cricket in Ōtautahi, picked me up. I didn't have much time to reflect, just jumped through a shower and brushed my teeth and tried to fend off the cold by burrowing into the couch under a heap of blankets in the flat they shared. The next morning, they dropped me back to the airport for the final leg of my journey. My forehead remained glued to the window throughout the flight, as the plane followed the snow-white Southern Alps down the mainland. It was the closest I had ever been to snow.

I walked off the plane into Dunedin Airport. The sky was bright blue, the sun dazzling, but there was a wintry edge to the spring air.

I met Andy McLean, who I'd been liaising with over the previous months, and Mark Bracewell, then a selector for Otago. I loaded my luggage — my entire life crammed into a single suitcase — into Andy's car and off we drove through the farmland. First stop: University Oval, my new home ground, where I met Ross Dykes and the backroom staff. Then to the Edgar Centre, the indoor training facility where I would meet the majority of my new teammates.

I was nervous — would these guys treat me as an outsider coming to take their pay cheques? — but I shouldn't have worried. Instead, I was overwhelmed by friendliness as players — I particularly remember Sam Wells and Matt Harvie — lined up to introduce themselves. I chatted with Aaron Redmond, who I had bowled to in England. I met trainer Chris Donaldson, formerly a sprinter who had represented New Zealand at the 1996 and 2000 Olympics, and a man who would become incredibly important as my career progressed. I was surprised to find Mike Hesson shorter than me, which I hadn't pictured while speaking with him over the phone.

Andy took me to the house — owned by Jared and Anna King, Andy's good friends — where I rented a room for the first year of my life in Dunedin. It was a Friday before a long weekend and they were away, so Andy showed me around, then left me to get some rest. I felt very weird and alone in an unfamiliar house that was now my home, where I figured out how to blast the heat pump and eventually got the TV working. Odd, I thought, that none of the doors or windows were latched, and I made sure everything was locked before I crashed out.

Mark picked me up early the next morning in the freezing cold and took me on a tour of club games around the city to give me my bearings and introduce me to the local cricket scene. At the first ground, I noticed they were playing on an artificial wicket —

something I hadn't done since I was maybe 10 — and thought that was interesting. At the second, the same. At the third, artificial again — with the added peculiarity of overlapping cricket fields, where the player fielding at fine leg in one game would be standing at mid-on in the other. This was one of the strangest things I had ever seen. I met Neil Broom for the first time, the sarcasm of his Kiwi banter completely unintelligible to me. I just thought he was a bit cocky.

The next day dawned cold and gloomy, with threatening clouds hovering in the sky throughout the morning. I had to get groceries, eking out the limited funds I had before my first Otago pay cheque arrived. I set out on foot, covering what felt like half the city before I arrived at a supermarket in the heart of South Dunedin. I got a few things — bread, some steak, a box of microwave risotto, a bottle of Coke and a bottle of mineral water because the Dunedin tap water at the time tasted undrinkably strange to me — and started back home with my supplies in a couple of plastic bags. At the bottom of the hill, the sky broke open, freezing needles of rain coming almost horizontally at my face. I lifted my jacket to protect myself and continued, but halfway up one of the bags broke and the Coke bottle rolled, fizzing, down the hill.

I suddenly felt very far from home, and started to cry. *What the hell am I doing here? It's the middle of the night back home, with no doubt another beautiful hot day later to edge over the horizon. I am freezing cold, soaked through, on some street I don't know the name of at the end of the bloody world.*

I wanted to leave the Coke bottle to bleed out at the bottom of the hill, but in the end I trudged down to pick it up, making a basket out of my arms to carry my meagre supplies home, where only the longest shower I have ever had could warm my bones. I jumped into bed and put on a movie, trying to clear my mind until South Africa woke up and I could talk to someone familiar. Jared and Anna came back later, surprised by how secure I had made the house in their absence — they had to wait for me to unlock the front door — explaining that they never felt the need to lock even their car, that the back door to the house would always be open so don't worry about having a key with you. They were so open and welcoming — lovely, warming people who helped me quickly put my shopping excursion in the rear-view mirror. Cricket training with Otago started as soon as the weekend was over.

Once the cricket started, I felt more at home. Although there were some teething issues. Playing warm-up stuff on artificial pitches meant I couldn't charge in from a full run-up — I couldn't wear spikes and the surface was too slippery for my full delivery stride. I also kept running myself out when shots, which felt off the bat like a certain single, would stop dead in the long grass. The joke was that my English was so bad that I didn't even understand 'Yes', 'Wait' and 'No'.

I made my debut for Otago against a Northern Districts team featuring Trent Boult and Kane Williamson, who was playing his second first-class game. We bowled first on University Oval, and I didn't have to wait long for my first wicket when I nicked off opener Cameron Merchant with my fifth ball. Later I returned to have Michael Parlane caught behind by wicketkeeper Derek de Boorder. I bowled 21 tidy overs for those two wickets, as ND got through to 275 on the back of a Kane 80-odd. I got plenty of time to take a look at the batter I was told was the boy-wonder of New Zealand cricket.

And they had a good look at the way I went about things, too. I approached it with the usual energy I would bring to any match back home, where the cricket was tough and the mind games could be brutal. I ran in hard, puffed out my chest and followed through until I was under the batter's nose, eyes locked onto his, sometimes offering a little advice on his batting technique. I remember a momentary uneasiness seeping through my team as players exchanged quizzical looks, as if to say: 'What's going on? No one plays like that here.' But then they started to embrace it, particularly Ian Butler, who had just moved to Dunedin after seven seasons with Northern Districts and had an axe to grind with his former employers. He loved the presence I brought to the crease, getting right behind me and pumping me up. Hess remembers the umpires stepping in to have a quiet word with me, letting me know this wasn't quite the way things were done down here, although I don't recall it. It was, regardless, a fiery game, with Trent seeming to take special offence to this blond-haired South African bringing the energy of a fired-up Allan Donald to the placid atmosphere of early-season New Zealand cricket.

When I came out to bat, he returned my gestures with a distinctive and comedic Trent Boult twist, getting right up in my grill. *Man, I'm gonna whack this guy to the moon*, I thought, and tried to absolutely lash the next ball through the covers. Predictably enough, I nicked it and was out caught behind, walking to the pavilion with a nice little send-off making sure I knew the way. I took a further three wickets in the second innings — BJ Watling, James Marshall, Peter McGlashan — to finish off a tidy debut. We drew the game.

I was thankful for my experiences in Bangladesh and Lancashire — and I kept adding lessons as the season progressed. The University Oval pitch was slow, low and abrasive, very quickly robbing the ball of its ability to swing, which was still my primary weapon. When that happened, my natural left-arm angle seemed to merely create width for right-handed batters to hit through the covers, with not enough pace on offer to help me seek an edge. I remember the off-side boundary being peppered until I installed a cover-sweeper, something I would never have done in South Africa where, even without swing, the zip of the wickets gave me enough to work with. Later, it became a bit of a joke within the team that as soon as it stopped swinging — typically, in Dunedin, after four or five overs — I would switch to around the wicket, something I'd never done much of before, and try to bowl a tight line. I often purposefully undercut the ball — the same thing I had once been criticised for — to try and find some movement off the pitch, throwing in a few yorkers and a couple of bouncers to rough up the ball in the hope that it would reverse later. That's when I learned to be at my most destructive in these conditions.

In South Africa, I had never played much with a white ball. Most of the limited-overs stuff I was involved with over there was dressed in whites with a red ball, so it was a thrill to get onto the park in the electric blue of the Otago Volts kit, a white Kookaburra clenched in my fist. Short-form cricket was always something that I loved, a chance to further test, and expand, my range of skills. I remember bowling at the Basin Reserve in what was then called the State Shield, the 50-over competition. I have always tried to put my hand up for the hard overs, taking pride in toughing out the worst of conditions when I feel the best should challenge themselves, and I remember running into a brutal northerly, nailing my yorkers and taking five wickets from my 10 overs, which cost only 34 runs.

I have always put the ODI World Cup on a pedestal almost as high as test cricket, and I was determined to grow my skill set to give me the best chance of playing in one in the future. I remember

New Zealand taking on South Africa in the 2003 World Cup in Johannesburg, watching live as Stephen Fleming scored a classic century — using that elegant manner of his to flay Donald, Ntini and Pollock to all parts of the ground — to defeat the home side. It was an honour, when the State Twenty20 rolled around, to bowl at the man himself, then with Wellington — although the pleasure didn't last long. I bowled him second ball. That was a highlight during a successful white-ball season for Otago: we were beaten finalists in the State Shield and won the T20 competition, which meant we qualified for the Champions League.

The night before the T20 final — ultimately it was abandoned due to rain without a ball being bowled — my Domino's pizza came with a note inside the box, wishing me well for the game, perhaps a sad reflection on how well my local outlet had gotten to know me. I called my parents from the middle of a sodden University Oval, more than a few beers deep after the match was called off and we were crowned champions, to tell them I was off to the Champions League in India. I felt so proud to share that something good had already happened, that this move seemed to be already paying off. We would lose both our games at the tournament and didn't progress past the group stages, though I did snare the wicket of Virat Kohli. The noise of the crowd in Bengaluru was so intense that I couldn't hear the instructions that the captain, Craig Cumming, was giving me from mid-off. It gave me a taste of what international cricket might be like. I wanted more.

We didn't manage to win a single first-class game that season, either, as I finished with 21 wickets from the seven games I played. In the 50-over competition, I was the leading wicket-taker, with 24 scalps. Although I remember feeling like the real accomplishment was a post-match conversation with Brendon McCullum, who had a break in his international schedule that allowed him to play a few games for the Volts.

'Don't worry,' Baz said, 'you'll be playing for New Zealand one day.'

For him I'm sure it was just an offhand comment. For me it meant the world.

I went back to South Africa for the New Zealand winter, sorting out my driver licence and doing a bit of coaching. I returned to Dunedin via Brisbane, where I'd been selected for a New Zealand Emerging Players team, in which I would share new-ball duties with Tim Southee — by this stage he had already played test cricket — and represent New Zealand against a South African side for the first time in my career. It was surreal to take the field against Heino Kuhn, in particular, a fellow Affies old boy and the man who had held the catch that gave me my first wicket for Northerns.

Then it was back to Dunedin. I moved out of Jared and Anna's and in with Andy McLean — I still didn't have a car and I figured it would be easier and less disruptive if I lived with someone I could get a ride to work with. It wasn't a particularly good season, however. I topped the Otago wicket charts in the Plunket Shield, with 28, but they came at an average of 37. The highlight was taking part in my first four-day win with the province, when I took seven wickets across the game against Wellington in Queenstown. They were an opponent that would become a firm favourite. My white-ball form hadn't held up to the previous season's standard either, and I only took a dozen wickets in both the 20- and 50-over competitions — in the latter I conceded nearly 6.5 runs per over, as opposed to 4.7 the season before. Part of it, I think, had to do with the different roles I was being asked to play in the team — long spells into the wind in the four-day games, four or five overs on the trot at the death of a one-day innings — but I'd also obviously been an unknown quantity the year before. Now the whole country knew what I brought to the bowling crease.

If I was to press for higher honours — and the clock was counting down on when I'd be able to represent New Zealand — the challenge would be how to succeed even as I became a familiar opponent. I again played for New Zealand Emerging Players in Brisbane over the winter, but all it really did was concentrate the young fast-bowling talent around at the time — Trent Boult, Tim Southee, Doug Bracewell, Mitchell McClenaghan, Mark Gillespie, Adam Milne, Lockie Ferguson, Ben Wheeler and others — and make the New Zealand team seem very far away. If I'd ever thought it was going to be easier to make the Black Caps than it was to break through in South Africa, I was very quickly corrected.

The prospect of representing New Zealand was also far away because of mundane bureaucratic reasons. In fact, it got further away as I learned that the immigration pathway that could've led to me becoming a New Zealand resident after three years with Otago no longer existed for someone who, like me, only had an employment contract for six months of the year. It was my understanding that under that old system, if I had successfully been granted residency, I could have used that status to leverage the International Cricket Council to allow me to represent Aotearoa, thus shortening the qualification period to three years from four. But, without it, I would need to wait the usual four years. The 2011 Cricket World Cup, which I was hoping I might be an outside possibility for, was suddenly off the table. That meant another year with Otago before I could even begin to dream of international cricket.

Yet I *was* starting to think about the prospect of representing New Zealand less and less in purely cricketing terms and more with a sense of burgeoning patriotism: that is to say, I had fallen in love with the country as the warmth of my greeting never seemed to let up. I'd always felt, growing up in an Afrikaans-dominated community in Pretoria, where people were much more likely to have strong Christian beliefs, that there were sometimes double standards at play. The things people might profess on a Sunday seemed to have slipped the mind by the time mid-week rolled around. There was a definite emphasis on only looking after those in your immediate circles. In New Zealand, where it seemed almost no one was a practising Christian, people would go to the most extraordinary lengths to help me, a newly arrived foreigner who couldn't do much for them in return. It was impossible for me to find a church that felt familiar to the Dutch Reformed faith I was raised in, but it was easy to find examples of Christian values I'd been taught to aspire to.

There was the social side of the Otago team, too. Much like in Ormskirk, I loved the compactness of Dunedin after growing up in a house far from where most of my mates lived. Once a week, a bunch of us would meet in the Octagon, find a bar, sit down and grab a few beers. The next morning, we'd crash into training — a bit dusty, maybe, but nothing a gym session wouldn't thrash out of you pretty quick. We probably drank too much for a bunch of professional athletes, but I was young and Dunedin's student energy easily rubbed off on me. We were a bunch of youngsters, all in the same boat, seeing if we could make cricket work for us, the future lying undiscovered. It's one of the periods of my life about which I have the fondest memories.

The 2010/11 season started with a bang. I took six wickets in the first innings against Northern Districts in a high-scoring draw. The lessons I'd been learning since my arrival were coming to fruition, and under the tuition of my coaches and colleagues at Otago I was becoming the most destructive version of myself as a bowler. Hess, and old hands Nathan McCullum, Craig Cumming and Dimitri Mascarenhas, the former English international then with Otago, were instrumental sounding boards in helping me plot how I would take my wickets. Ian Butler, who we called Butsy, and Warren McSkimming, my fast-bowling comrades, were never short of an idea, Warren introducing me to a delivery we now call the three-quarter ball, designed to go straight off the pitch and enhance the threat of the ball swinging the other way.

In Butsy's case, he had so many ideas that sometimes it almost felt like too many, but he was the ideal foil in training, where we loved setting up match scenarios when we bowled against one another or in tandem against a batter. For the first time in first-class cricket, I had a great group of mates I could lean on and I felt as if I was a treasured part of something bigger than myself. In South Africa, if a coach or colleague had suggested a new role for me in a game — bowling into the wind or a long spell with the old ball — because of my insecurities I would've suspected an ulterior motive, that they wanted me to fail so I could eventually be moved aside, but here, with solid leadership and stability of team selection, I was learning to trust.

I was also adding important technical skills to my repertoire under the instruction of Otago's bowling coach and later Hess's successor at the top, Vaughn Johnson, VJ. I developed a range of slower balls and introduced cutters into my armoury, something I had never really needed to do on the pitches on which I had learned to bowl. I was further unravelling the mysteries of reverse swing, lengthening my bowling stride and lowering my arm when conditions, and the ball, were conducive to the art. In South Africa, I remember Pierre Joubert, my first captain at Northerns, criticising the bowlers for gravitating towards one of the seemingly limitless new balls available at every practice. He wanted to see if bowlers could still pose a threat with something old and worn. At Otago, where finances were more constrained, there would sometimes only be a single new ball to share around at a net session. And the quality of the nets was dodgy enough that sometimes the batters asked not to face a hard zippy new ball anyway. I would grab an old one — Pierre's words ringing in my ears — and work and work and work on shining one side, trying to coax any semblance of reverse swing from it. In hindsight, what at first seemed a liability — a lack of new balls — was the best thing that could've happened to my bowling.

And my wickets column soon agreed. The next game of that season was even better: I took my first-ever first-class match haul of 10 wickets as we beat Auckland, following that with eight wickets in a draw against Wellington. As the Plunket Shield took a break for the limited-overs window, I took 11 wickets from seven games in the 50-over competition, missing several games with a split webbing in my hand, as Otago finished third. I took five wickets in six T20s — but we finished dead last after winning the competition the previous year. As soon as the Plunket Shield got started again, though, I was back in the wickets, taking a five-for against Canterbury. My wicket-taking was only really halted by a rampant Daniel Flynn when we met Northern Districts in the penultimate round: his assault — I was hit for some of the biggest out-of-the-ground sixes I can remember — even led to a heated on-field argument with Craig Cumming about tactics and controlling my aggression, which we later had to sort out in the privacy of Seddon Park's umpires' room. I left that meeting, though, in which Craig explained where he was coming from, feeling that he was definitely on my side — and from that day forward he became something of a Kiwi big brother to me. And, in the end, we escaped Hamilton with a draw.

That led to the last game of the season, against Wellington in Queenstown. The third day of the match was beautiful and sunny, but cold, with a freezing wind blowing off the snow-capped Remarkables in the distance. My first act of the game had been a golden duck in the first innings, in which we made 441 for eight declared. When I began the 70th over in Wellington's reply, the ball old and ready to start talking, they had reached 136 for four. They were going at less than two an over, and it felt that the game was meandering towards a draw as we approached lunch on day three.

All thoughts were about getting inside and warming our freezing hands over a meal until, with the first ball of the over, I got left-handed opener Stewart Rhodes caught for 77 as he inside edged it onto his pad, the ball carrying to Neil Broom at gully. We were almost into the tail, and we suddenly had the opportunity to snare another before the break to put Wellington under real pressure. I immediately came around the wicket to the right-handed Joe Austin-Smellie, looking for a reverse-swinging yorker to target his stumps. It came out perfectly, hooping exaggeratedly with the round-the-wicket angle and smashing into his poles. Next was the hat-trick ball: Jeetan Patel. *Why change?* I thought, and this time an almost identically deadly yorker knocked off stump out of the ground. A hat trick — the third or fourth I had ever taken — and I was instantly buried in the congratulatory hugs of my converging teammates.

When the dust settled, and I'd cleared my head, I came back over the wicket against the left-handed Ili Tugaga, but the method was the same: he couldn't keep out the yorker. Four in four. I was again mobbed by teammates running in from every corner of the field. Now things were getting weird. Mark Gillespie — I was back around the wicket to the right-hander — dug out the fifth, but he could do nothing with the sixth. It left the stumps in absolute disarray, all three pointing in wildly different directions and looking exactly like the pictures of shattered stumps that used to occupy my time in the classrooms of my youth. Five wickets in six balls. And that, said the umpire, was lunch.

It's hard to explain the feeling that came over me during that over — and which has visited me a few other times throughout my career — other than to use a tired cliché: I was 'in the zone'. In those moments, you suddenly know exactly what you need to do and how to do it, and I had an almost supernatural knowledge about how the immediate future was going to work out in my favour — I somehow just *knew* those deliveries had a wicket at the end of them. A kind of tunnel vision descended: I knew what I needed to do and then did it.

Often, in a high-stakes match situation, your head is clouded with a million thoughts and counter-thoughts, and making a rational decision becomes nearly impossible. When you are watching from the couch and you see a bowler attempting what is obviously the wrong option, you, the viewer, are able to see what is obscured to the athlete by the anxiety and stress of the scenario. Later in my career, guys like Brendon and Kane would often talk about trying to think like the 'balcony boy' — that the best players can ignore the white noise going on around them in the middle and make their decisions as if they were calmly observing the scene from the balcony. In Queenstown, I was able to do just that, and for a rare moment I could focus 100 per cent only on what was in front of me.

At the time, I didn't realise the significance of what I had done.

I was stoked, of course: I'd just taken five wickets out of nowhere and blown open a game that looked like it was meandering towards a boring draw. I was sitting in the dressing room and Warren McSkimming looked towards me.

'Do you realise what you've just achieved? This must be some kind of record. I bet there'll be news cameras around the ground soon.'

We sat down to have some food and 15 minutes later I poked my head out and noticed that reporters and their camera operators already seemed to outnumber the few hardy Queenstown spectators.

'I told you so,' Warren said, before our team manager tapped me on the shoulder to let me know I was wanted for an interview. The first journalist asked if I realised that, as far as they knew, no one in the history of first-class cricket had ever taken five wickets in a six-ball over. I kind of shrugged it off — there was still a game to win — but it was starting to dawn on me that this was something special. We got back out and I eventually took the last wicket — Andy McKay, bowled — and we enforced the follow-on. I'd bowled a heap of overs on the trot seeking that final wicket so it was decided I would surrender the new ball — Butsy opened the bowling in my place — and I would rest my legs until the ball was reversing again. I came back later that afternoon to add another three wickets and help Otago to an innings victory, enough for us to finish the season in second place.

It gave me 51 wickets for the season, 19 clear of the next fast bowler, and made me the first Otago bowler to take over 50 in a season since Stephen Boock had done so in 1986/87. There was interview after interview following the game — they all seemed to blend into each other — and it wasn't until after it had aired that I realised one of them had been for the six o'clock news in Australia.

What I'd done had resonated outside the borders of New Zealand. It finally started to sink in that I had achieved something that nobody, in all the thousands and thousands and thousands of first-class overs bowled throughout history, had ever done before.

On the back of that crazy over, public interest in when I was going to be available for international selection skyrocketed. Especially when I followed that breakout four-day season with one nearly as successful. I started the 2011/12 season with eight wickets in the match against Canterbury at Rangiora, before a quiet two games. Things changed when we met Wellington at the Basin, and I took seven for 96, then my best first-class figures, in the first innings of a game we would eventually lose heavily.

Early in the new year I was called into a New Zealand XI to face the touring Zimbabwe side, a game played in Gisborne. Lining up with the likes of Ross Taylor, Daniel Vettori, Kane Williamson and BJ Watling, I bowled well in my one opportunity, with three wickets, the most for the team. Black Caps selector Mark Greatbatch and then Director of Cricket John Buchanan were there and I hoped to receive some clues about whether I was close to the side, but I was simply told 'well bowled, thanks for being here' and I left Gisborne thinking that, given the lack of conversation, I must still be a long way away. I went back to the Plunket Shield determined to press my case.

The last game of the season was, like the year before, against Wellington, this time at University Oval. We won the toss and elected to field, which almost immediately revealed itself to be the right decision. I had taken the first three wickets by the time

Wellington had put 16 on the board, and I returned to rip through the lower order to finish with seven for 46, bettering the figures I had against them earlier in the season. In the second innings, I added a further couple of wickets as Wellington got within 60-odd runs of making us bat again, but in the end surrendered to the innings defeat that seemed inevitable when Hamish Rutherford followed my seven wickets with a double century in our turn at bat. Nine for the match, 46 for the season — again, I was comfortably the Plunket Shield's leading wicket-taker.

I was desperate to qualify for New Zealand. Which is not to say I wasn't incredibly happy playing for Otago — I was — but I just hated the feeling of claustrophobia that this ceiling above me, limiting how far I could climb, gave me. I knew enough, by now, about how cricket form could come and go — the two great seasons I'd just had when I wasn't eligible to be picked for the Black Caps might count for nothing if I couldn't maintain that form when I was. The law of averages dangles above every cricketer: you know it desperately wants to drag you back to the mean. I left for South Africa — another cricket season over, another visa run to perform — hoping against hope that soon my time would come.

CHAPTER 6:
BLACK CAP AND DARK DAYS

The news came in the middle of the night. I'd been back in South Africa for about a week, following the end of the 2011/12 New Zealand season, sleeping in my teenage bedroom, down the hallway from my parents. One night, about 3am, I was awoken by the buzzing of my phone. I saw it was a New Zealand number and rubbed the sleep from my eyes as I stumbled to the lounge and answered. It was Ross Dykes and he told me I was finally eligible for New Zealand. I was almost beyond words when Mum and Dad padded into the room in their nightclothes to find out what the noise was all about. They both gave me a hug and my mum, an emotional character, erupted in a flood of tears.

Relief was perhaps the biggest component of my happiness.

There'd been a few overseas trips early in my career with Otago — the first season I'd returned to Pretoria for a few days to attend my brother's wedding, later we'd gone to India for the Champions League — which meant I hadn't spent the requisite number of consecutive days in New Zealand in that year to fulfil the ICC criteria for qualification. There was some talk about whether I might have to spend another year in New Zealand before I would become eligible, but in the end the family circumstances — after I submitted photographic evidence to prove there had been a wedding, and that I'd been there — were taken into account.

I was ecstatic that the last constraint on how far cricket could take me in my adopted country had now disappeared. I was free to play for New Zealand, though I thought I must be a fair distance from the team as there'd been no indication from Black Caps management that I was on the verge of selection.

A couple of days later, however, I was out with a few mates — one of whom was Heinrich Klaasen, later to play for the Proteas. We'd just eaten some huge steaks and were catching up over a few beers. It was late when my phone rang, another New Zealand number on the screen. The bar was loud, so I walked outside to take the call. It was Kim Littlejohn, the Australian who was then the Black Caps' selection manager. The conversation was short — and very sweet: 'You've been selected for the test team,' Kim said. 'You're going to the West Indies.' I couldn't quite believe it.

Four years earlier, I'd left South Africa in the blind hope I would one day hear this exact news. I could hardly restrain myself — I wanted to scream my joy into the busy Pretoria night — but I managed, when Kim had said goodbye, to give my parents a quick call. They were so happy for me, urging me to head home to celebrate. Inside, my mates wanted to know why I suddenly had a big stupid grin plastered across my face. I told them. Someone immediately ordered a few shots for the table, then a few more beers, then a few more. When I got home, the scene from a couple of nights before basically repeated itself, so similar that now I have difficulty telling them apart. Tears from Mum, a hug from both parents.

The next day my brothers came over for a barbecue. They were excited, too, but most of the talk was about how on earth I was going to pull off the logistical feat of getting the visas I would require in time for the tour. As well as the New Zealand visa that I already knew I needed, I would have to get one that made it possible for me to transit through the United States, plus those that allowed me into the West Indian countries where we were scheduled to play. These were not easy things to accomplish for a South African passport-holder. The American visa in particular necessitated a nightmare of bureaucracy at the US Embassy in Johannesburg: a full-on sit-down interview, submission of my biometric information, medical test after medical test.

Later, Kim called me back to see how I was progressing. There'd been an injury in the ODI squad and he wanted to know if I could make it back to New Zealand in time to leave early enough to play the ODIs preceding the test series. At this stage I had my US and West Indian visas, but was still waiting on my New Zealand one. I was desperate to make the limited-overs segment of the tour — I told him I would do whatever it took, offering to pay for my own flight from South Africa direct to the Caribbean. In the end, Kim called me back the following day to tell me not to worry about it, they would call up someone else, and that I should just focus on getting to New Zealand in time to depart for the tests. I was disappointed, but consoled myself with the thought that a limited-overs opportunity would surely come again in the future.

That Black Caps team was a strange environment to walk into. John Wright had already announced the tour would be his last as coach, citing irreconcilable differences with John Buchanan, the Director of Cricket. Ross Taylor was the captain, but it was almost immediately clear to me that all was not well within his squad. I knew close to nothing about the team and its politics, although even I could tell there was an environment of secrecy, of huddled conversations that would quickly end as soon as you came near. Ross was quite a distant captain who I didn't often see around the team. I didn't really have much of a relationship with many of the senior players — Kruger, Dean Brownlie and Daniel Flynn were the guys I spent most of my time with — and I did my best to keep quiet and focus on the cricket. Not everyone was doing the same.

We stayed in a beautiful resort — The Verandah — on the island of Antigua. I was on the beach on my second day there, relaxing alone after training. I'd never been on a beach like this, with its palm trees, its white sand, clear water only just cool enough to refresh you from the heat of the day. I felt like I had stepped into a postcard. I'd had a swim and was feeling pretty pleased with where life had taken me, when assistant coach Trent Woodhill appeared. We started talking and Trent steered the conversation around to his uncertain future with the Black Caps. He said it was looking like this would be his last tour with the team. Maybe he was simply trying to unload some of his worries, but it felt to me as if he hoped that if the future of the coaching staff came up for discussion within the team I might be able to put in a word for him. I was trying to pull back from the conversation. I didn't want anything to do with the politics of the group, and our chat added to my perception that something was not well in the culture of the team.

I was selected for the three-day warm-up game against the West Indies Cricket Board President's XI, held at the same ground the first test was to be played on, the Sir Vivian Richards Stadium in North Sound. It didn't start well. We batted first and were bowled out for 149 late on the first day. Only Kane passed 50. I opened the bowling along with Chris Martin. It was a good pitch to bowl on, with plenty of grass and nice carry, and I made fairly good use of it, though my three wickets couldn't stop our hosts from taking a huge lead. When I joined Kruger at the crease late on the third afternoon, an innings defeat looked very possible. We still needed about 20 runs to make them bat again, with only Chris to come in after me and 15 or so overs to get through. Kruger greeted me in the middle by telling me just to stick with him. Which I did, the two of us batting out the remainder of the day — I ended on 5 from 57 balls — to save at least a few blushes. Naturally, though, Ross was seething about the way we had played and was fired up when he shook my hand after the game.

He said, 'Well played. You'll be playing the first test, congratulations.'

It was a strange, slightly joyless, way to receive the news. I didn't even know whether I should believe it — or whether Ross's emotions had gotten away from him and that rewarding me for the fight I had shown was a roundabout way of criticising the rest of the team for not doing the same. It wasn't until later, when Wrighty approached me in the sheds and reiterated what Ross had said, that I was sure I was going to make my debut.

I am going to be a test cricketer. The news made for a nervous, excited few days. I was on the cusp of achieving something I'd wanted since as far back as I could remember. At the capping ceremony on the evening before the test, West Indian legend Jeff Dujon addressed the team and then we were presented with our caps for the game. I couldn't even begin to say what he spoke about. No matter how hard I tried, my mind couldn't stay with his words, instead drifting back in time, through all the similar ceremonies I'd been through in my career, across games I'd played on the sun-baked highveld of my youth, in damp England, in frigid Dunedin, the whole of my circuitous journey sharpened to this exact point. When it was over, I needed to clear my head. The words of two men instrumental on that journey, Affies coaches Deon Botes and Colin Dettmer, came back to me: *Control the controllables. Try to put emotion aside. Forget about the schoolboy who covered his books with his cricketing idols. Focus on what's in front of you.*

    I had dinner with Kruger that night, and afterwards the two of us walked back through the grounds of the resort to the chalets in which we were staying. Kruger and I were usually pretty disciplined about only speaking English around the team, but as we padded along the path and he offered his advice — about enjoying the next day as a symbol of how far I had come, about how the way I'd played had been good enough to get me here so don't change now — we slipped into the familiarity of our mother tongue. Two cricketers from the same high school on the other side of the world, speaking Afrikaans about representing New Zealand against the West Indies in the balmy breeze of a tropical Antigua evening.

The alarm finally went off. I'd spent the night in broken sleep, excitement punching holes in my unconsciousness, periodically waking in the darkness to silently plead with the morning to hurry up and arrive. The minutes crawled by, until the squad split in half in front of the hotel and filed into the two minibuses that were to take us to the stadium. It was a bit of a drive, and for the last five minutes of it you could see the ground growing ever bigger as our convoy inched towards it. The closer we got, the more I felt it: *this is it, it's coming*. My headphones were on. I was locked in my own little world, but I couldn't wait to break out of it to show what I could do on the biggest stage I had ever played.

It had been clear, since a day or two before, that this would be an entirely different surface to the one we played on in the warm-up game. We'd watched as the ground staff diligently removed every blade of grass from the pitch, working among the cloud of dust their weed-whackers raised from the earth. We knew it would be dry and abrasive, that the new ball wouldn't swing for long. A bat-first pitch, which is what Ross decided to do when he called correctly at the toss.

For me, it meant more waiting, but it also calmed my nerves as I cast my eyes around the ground, at the big stands rising out of the terraced banks, sprinkled with a small crowd. I thought about my family in Pretoria, where it was the evening, Mark, David, Mum and Dad gathered around the TV, watching. I hoped I'd be able to make them proud. I allowed myself that moment of emotion before Colin and Deon came back to me. *Control the controllables. Focus on what's in front of you.*

We started well, Flynny and Martin Guptill putting on almost a hundred for the first wicket, before the West Indies, led by Sunil Narine, began to make regular breakthroughs — Flynny gone with the score on 97, Baz when we'd made 133. Rossco and Gup steadied things, getting us towards the back end of the day. I was told to pad up — if needed, I would be the nightwatchman. And with our score on 223, Rossco was out, bowled by Narine. There were five or six overs left for me to negotiate. I walked out, a TV camera pointed at my face. I was desperate to get us through to stumps, but it was hard work. Narine and his carrom ball were unpickable to me. We'd been told to watch how he lifted his little finger as he bowled the variation, but I couldn't imagine how anyone could see that level of detail from the other end of the pitch. I just tried to react to the ball off the surface, playing the line, happy to let the big-spinning off-breaks harmlessly beat my outside edge. At the other end, Gup top-edged a sweep to fall for 97. Kane joined me, and we got through with no more damage done, ending the day on 232 for four. The next morning I lasted six balls against Narine before edging him to second slip, and we lost wickets steadily throughout the day's first two sessions to be all out for 351.

Chris Martin bowled the first over of the West Indian reply, with Chris Gayle on strike. He took two balls to get his eye in, and then resoundingly crashed the next four against the concrete ringing the playing surface. I still remember the rifle-shot sound of the big man's bat meeting the ball. He didn't let up, and was racing along when Ross threw me the ball to bowl the seventh over of the innings, desperate to regain some control.

At the top of my mark, all those emotion-laden thoughts I'd had leading into the game disappeared. All that existed, suddenly, was 156 grams of cork and leather in my left hand, and Kieran Powell, Gayle's opening partner, in my sights. I ran in, speared the ball at the pitch and hit the bat hard, Powell going back to defend it to the off side. I was under way, the next five balls treated with similar respect to give me a maiden. But that was as good as things would get for a long while. On the last ball of my second over, Powell slashed at one outside off: the edge flew hard and fast, towards Gup at second slip, but he couldn't get a hand to it in time and the ball skidded to the rope. I was gutted, and things quickly started going worse from there. Gayle, on his way to a quick 150, was in brutal form — cutting, flicking off his legs, slapping through and over cover in an onslaught that soon made our first-innings total look completely insufficient. Powell, heading towards a more sedate 134, was an immovable blockade in support.

It was a tough introduction to test cricket. It was windy and hot and the pitch gave us nothing. I would've loved some guidance or wise words from seniors in the team, some help to formulate a plan, but nothing much came my way. We simply weren't a unified and supportive group at that time, and I was left to struggle through the bruising encounter in isolation. The frustrations were visibly telling on Rossco, too. Gayle, when he wasn't punishing me through the off side, was content to clip me repeatedly through midwicket, taking the ball from outside off stump. When it happened a few times in quick succession, Rossco at first slip angrily kicked the ground in exasperation. It didn't bother me too much — far worse had come my way from South African skippers — but I remember Tim Southee, who happened to be running drinks onto the ground not long after, telling Ross to help me out, it was my first test, to try and support me instead of getting angry. Tim wasn't in the team — arguably, I had taken his place in the XI — and it made me start to reconsider a teammate who had until then given me the impression he didn't like me much at all. It felt good to have someone stick up for me, but in hindsight it maybe said more about the simmering divisions in the team than anything else.

I came back on with the second new ball five or six overs old. Powell, after Gayle had finally perished trying one shot too many against Kane's off spin, had picked up the pace, and he welcomed me back with three fours pummelled, almost arrogantly, to the off-side boundary — over mid-off, cut through point, smoked off the back foot through extra cover. I was starting to get angry, which seemed to focus my mind. I bowled the next ball on a length outside off, asking him to try again. A hint of shape took it away from his attempted drive, catching a faint edge as it carried through to Kruger behind the stumps.

Pure relief: finally, finally, I had a test wicket. West Indies, 304 for two. I'll never forget two New Zealand legends, Daniel Vettori and Baz, rushing in to shake my hand, telling me that it was hopefully the first of many. None of which would come in that game, however. We sank to a nine-wicket defeat that even my best efforts with the bat, stonewalling for 103 balls as nightwatchman in the second innings, could not prevent. My phone, once I was able to check it after the game, was full of messages of congratulations from my parents and brothers. I could count on the same thing happening throughout my Black Caps career, during which my parents battled against the time differences to watch almost every game I played. They became such committed Black Caps fans that they watched even when I wasn't in the team.

The bowling attack was overhauled for the next test in Kingston, Jamaica. It was the first time Trent, Tim and I lined up together for the Black Caps, with Dougie Bracewell completing a pace quartet. We bowled beautifully — Tim and Trent hooping the ball around corners — when the West Indies replied to our middling first-innings effort, and I had the pleasure of Gayle's wicket, caught at gully, before he could do any damage. It felt, after taking all that tap in the first game, that this configuration had clicked, and that we were able to exert real pressure. We quicks shared the 10 wickets.

Only a brilliant Marlon Samuels hundred dragged the West Indies to within 50-odd runs of our first-innings score.

Again, I came in as nightwatchman when the opening stand was broken late on day two. Soon Baz joined me and together we saw out the day. We were more than 100 ahead, still with eight wickets in hand. Rossco and Baz, when I chatted with them the next morning, wanted me to take the game on and be positive. That sounded good to me — I was excited to get out there and play my natural game. But just as the five-minute bell rang, Wrighty came up to me. 'Mate, I want you to bat time. Block it like you did in that first test. I want you to make it through to lunch.' It was another mark of the issues within that team that no one at the top had even bothered to talk through the day's strategy with each other. No one was talking to anyone about anything, it seemed.

In the end, I went with the coach's instructions but soon got a few stern looks from Baz in the middle, as if to say, 'Come on, mate, remember what we talked about.' A Tino Best short ball gave me something to have a swipe at, but it was quick and it rushed me, clipping my glove and carrying through to the keeper. I was out for not many. In the dressing room, Wrighty wasn't happy.

'You're the worst fucking nightwatchman I've ever seen. What was that?'

Out on the field, things weren't going any better. We collapsed, squandering an excellent position. The West Indies won early on day four — the series lost two–nil and my first four test wickets coming at an average north of 50. The Black Caps environment had proven to be less than ideal: it was a sobering introduction to cricket at the highest level. Baz would later write that the team, then, was on the verge of 'imploding' and that he was considering whether he even wanted to be part of it any longer.

My state of mind wasn't improved by a calamitous trip home, in which a mix-up with Trent's guitar, which he had asked me to take as part of my baggage allowance, ultimately caused Kruger, Chris and me to miss a flight and be redirected through San Francisco. That evening, we met in the bar to console ourselves with beer and pizza. The pizza gave me food poisoning. I arrived back in Dunedin bone-tired and shattered by the experience of my first Black Caps tour. My dream had come true, but it certainly hadn't yet matched the picture of it I'd held in my mind for all those years.

During the West Indies tour, it was announced that Hess would replace John Wright as Black Caps coach, and the following tour to India — including two tests — would be his first in charge. I was initially really happy to hear that a man who knew more than perhaps anyone in the world about what I could bring to a team would be at the helm. But there had already been rumblings that not everyone was happy with the appointment. Hess and Baz had worked closely together at Otago, and that left Rossco feeling uneasy. I was duly selected for the Indian test squad, but didn't play either of the tests on that tour, and I started to think that perhaps Hess was wary of picking too many Otago guys to guard against the perception that he favoured players from his home province. I'm not sure, but it added another layer of uncertainty to what became a difficult tour.

A cricket tour can be a brutal place, especially when you aren't playing. We lost both tests and the issues I'd noticed in the West Indies showed every sign of surviving the change of coach. Morale was low, and I could feel it beginning to seep into my own outlook. Most of my teammates only really knew me from playing against me in domestic cricket, and some of them didn't appreciate the energy I brought to those encounters. All the camaraderie and understanding I had spent four years building in Dunedin counted for nothing in the New Zealand dressing room, and I felt again as if I was being misunderstood, viewed as an outsider. Many of my teammates had been playing together since they were kids.

It felt like there was no real place for me among the network of tight relationships built on foundations of a Kiwi humour that was still difficult for me to grasp through my imperfect English. As in the West Indies, I would sometimes approach a knot of teammates talking in the hotel bar, only for the conversation to suddenly end as soon as I came near. As my mental health worsened, it became increasingly hard not to think those conversations were about me.

When I got back to my room each night, the day would replay in my mind as I waited for sleep — mistakes I'd made, things I should have done or said, a joke I mistook for something malicious. Then

I'd wake in the night when the silent hours seemed to stretch even longer, my mind paralysed by self-doubt. The West Indies tour started to prey on my mind. *Am I even good enough to be here? If so, why am I not being picked?* Then older and deeper insecurities would hitch themselves along for the ride. *Do my teammates understand me? Do they even like me?* One night in Bengaluru, locked in a worsening spiral, I remember thinking: *Jeez, what have I done with my life? I've uprooted everything to try and make cricket work, and now I can't even get a game.* I didn't feel like I could talk to Hess or Rossco or Baz about any of this — they all seemed to have enough going on and I also didn't want to do anything to further jeopardise my selection — and I didn't think it was fair to bother anyone back in Dunedin, like Craig Cumming. I was even feeling isolated from my family and, besides, I didn't want them to worry. Later in life I realised that all those people could and would have happily helped me, but my insecurities and selfishness didn't let me see it at the time.

When the tests ended I went back home while some of the boys stuck around in the subcontinent for the T20 World Cup and a few T20s against India to warm up for it. For me, it was about as far from the glamour of an ICC event as possible: to Lincoln, just outside of Christchurch, where I was to play for New Zealand A against a touring India A team. The dorm rooms at the NZC High Performance Centre are hardly the place you want to be when you are heading towards a mental-health crisis, but the loneliness I was feeling — one night, unable to sleep — urged me to take one of my life's most decisive steps. I was mindlessly scrolling through Facebook when I noticed a familiar name online. It was Lana. I said hi and we began to chat. It started really general, but soon I found myself confessing how I'd been feeling — the loneliness, the creeping worry that I'd made a mistake, that I felt misunderstood and without anyone to talk to — and she simply said that she was always there if I needed someone to talk to. We didn't know each other very well, but something told me to take this opportunity. And very soon the focus of my days became not the cricket but the mornings and nights, when our time zones overlapped and Lana would be awake and up for a chat.

When that series ended, there were a couple of rounds of the Plunket Shield to play, beating Canterbury away and then drawing with Northern Districts in Hamilton, before I was called up to the Black Caps squad for two tests in Sri Lanka, which followed the rain-ruined limited-overs series for which I hadn't been required. When I arrived in Galle, the environment seemed to have worsened, if that was even possible, after the guys had failed to get beyond the group stages at the World Cup and the sodden tour of Sri Lanka had further dampened spirits. There was another reason, too, which none of us at the time knew.

Before the first test, Hess had informed Ross that he wanted a change of captain after the tour, and that he would make that recommendation to the board on return to New Zealand. It was almost unanimous within the team at this point that Baz should be given the reins, though we didn't know those wheels had already started turning. The vibes were bad and the thoughts looping through my mind were just as dark, as if implanted there by osmosis.

I was doubting everything: who I was, my faith, my talent, whether I would ever be understood in this environment, whether I belonged, whether I was even liked. My thinking was becoming seriously disordered, and one evening I asked Kruger to shave my head. I thought that when my teammates looked at me all they saw was this vain, fussy South African who only cared about his blond hair looking good and everything around him being neat and tidy.

I thought this might convince them otherwise, or at least send a message that, 'Hey, I'm not in a good space here.' I wanted to reach out properly, but I didn't know how to.

If you look at photos from that tour — my arms around the shoulders of beaming teammates, a big grin below my newly shaved head — you would see a young man happy to be on the cusp of living the life he has worked so hard to build for himself. But I was utterly miserable, filling the empty minutes of the tour with room service eaten in front of the TV, where it was easier to brave long hours of loneliness than it was to try to build connections with teammates I was convinced didn't like me. And, again unwanted for both games of the tour, I wasn't even able to distract myself by trying to win games of cricket. By the time we reached Colombo — the team was thrashed by 10 wickets in the first test — it had all become almost too much for me to bear. In that unthinkably low time, the hotel window momentarily beckoned.

When that immediate crisis had somewhat passed, the only thing I could think of that might give me something to look forward to was buying an expensive sports car, and I spent a lot of money that I didn't really have on an Audi S5, which would be delivered to Dunedin after I had returned home. It gave me a sense that at least I was getting something out of what I was doing. Despite the very dark space I found myself in personally, I remember still being so happy for the team when we won that test, Tim and Trent cementing their positions as the Black Caps' new-ball pair, following on the heels of a monumental and, we'd soon find out, bittersweet Ross Taylor batting performance. I also had the solace that soon enough I would be behind the wheel of my dream car.

When the tour was over, I arrived back in New Zealand and stepped off the plane and almost straight into a game of cricket, the best place for me, substituted into the Otago team then playing Auckland at Eden Park. It gave me an opportunity to at least channel some of the emotion and anger of the past few weeks into my cricket. We won, and that feeling, in the company of familiar teammates, gave me some brief respite, but when I returned to Dunedin, loneliness fell upon me again. The car arrived, and its spell lasted for a week or so as I cruised around the Otago Peninsula. Then its novelty wore off and I realised how stupid I had been. I tried to avoid being alone, finding any excuse I could to invite teammates over for beers or a barbecue.

At least I had something to look forward to: Hess, whose communication with the team was always excellent, later let me know that I would be on the next tour — to South Africa, where family, a contest against my former compatriots and, most importantly, Lana, were waiting. It was amazing just how significant she had already become. With that on the horizon, life seemed immeasurably more worth living than it had a few floors above the Sri Lankan capital.

CHAPTER 7:
CHASING VICTORY

Don't look down, look up — at least that's what local wisdom dictated. And the sky over Cape Town on the morning of 2 January 2013 was bright blue, no hint of the tuft of cloud that so often sits above Table Mountain. The pitch looked a little green, but Baz — on Hess's recommendation, he'd replaced Ross as captain in a swarm of bad press, Ross later opting out of the South African tour — was keen on the local knowledge the two South Africans in his squad, me and Kruger, could offer. Kruger, in particular, had played a lot of cricket at Newlands. Plus, Baz was keen to put his stamp on the team, and batting first would be the bold, positive option. He was always likely to take the advice that adhered to this mindset. So when Baz won the toss to give him the choice, he decided to bat. I'd been in the mix to make the XI, but eventually the experience of Chris Martin was favoured for what would be his 71st and final test match. The configuration of the bowling attack would hardly matter: after our first turn at bat, no bowling attack in the world could've dragged us back into the game.

I was disappointed I wouldn't get to play in front of those I loved. A few days before the game — in fact, on a wild and stormy New Year's Eve in Cape Town — Lana and I had reunited in the restaurant of the team hotel. As soon as I saw her across the room, just as I'd seen her in that Pretoria bar all those years before, I knew I had fallen in love with her. We'd drawn unbelievably close over the past few months as I'd shared the scale of my depression — all of my frustrations, regrets and insecurities — one Facebook message at a time. But in her presence, that night, that unhappiness suddenly seemed to belong to the distant past, almost to a different person. And, unlike all those years ago in Pretoria when she was entirely unimpressed by my efforts, there was an obvious two-way chemistry between us. She'd driven a couple of hours through the storm to be there with me — from a town called Hermanus in the Western Cape — so I thought I must've done something right. We had dinner together the next night, too, after the team capping ceremony at which former New Zealand captain Ken Rutherford spoke, retreating to the Italian restaurant across the road from the hotel, where her company melted away the worry about whether I'd be playing the next day or not.

Mum, Dad, David and Mark were there as well, having driven down from Pretoria in the hope they would get to see me in the test arena, having already watched me play in a warm-up game in Paarl, a town 45 minutes northeast of Cape Town. So when I was told on the morning of the game that I wasn't playing, I was naturally gutted. But already I had the sense that, with Lana, there was something important building in my life outside of cricket, and the excitement of it blunted the disappointment. I couldn't communicate with her, though, as by the time I found out I wasn't playing we'd already handed in our phones, an anti-corruption protocol, for the day.

Instead, as the game got under way, and my old friends Morne Morkel and Dale Steyn — along with Vernon Philander — began scything through our batting lineup, I had a pair of binoculars to my face, scouring the approximate section of the crowd where I knew Lana would be. I finally spotted a familiar-looking white watch waving in the crowd and followed the arm it was strapped to. There she was. I needed to talk to her. By the time we got our phones back after the day's play, it would be too late to make a plan to see her that night. And not seeing her wasn't an option. I walked around the boundary rope, beckoning her down from 10 or so rows up in the stands — despite her embarrassment — so I could quickly arrange to see her again that night at the same Italian restaurant.

There was the small matter of *that* day of cricket to witness first. I remember watching the first ball, bowled by Dale, which absolutely flew off the surface, audibly slapping into AB's gloves despite the distance at which he'd placed himself and his slip cordon from the stumps. We'd just come off two tours to the subcontinent where you never saw guys this fast bowling on wickets as lightning quick as this one. And we were duly routed, lasting 19.2 overs and scoring just 45, as the three South African seamers put on a masterclass and every edge flew to hand. I felt pretty sheepish, given it had been my advice to bat first, but no one could have foreseen carnage this unrelenting. The Baz era began with the embarrassment of the third-lowest innings score New Zealand had managed in its history.

We were at rock bottom.

The tour, I had hoped at its outset, was a chance to make a statement against a cricket system that I felt hadn't wanted me, an opportunity to prove those doubters wrong. I wanted to express my hard-won belief that you didn't need to possess those fast-bowling characteristics so prized in South Africa — to be the fastest, the tallest, the strongest — to succeed as a quick bowler. You didn't even need to be the most talented. You just needed to have the tenacity to work the hardest, fight the longest, to believe and to try and to keep coming back — through the pain and into the wind — to throw yourself once more into battle. My old desire to scrap as hard as possible was always with me, even at my lowest.

Before departing New Zealand, I had been given a central contract with NZC, after Jacob Oram's retirement left a spot free, so I was now officially recognised as one of the 20 best cricketers in my adopted country. I had played with or against almost every player in that South African team: I wanted to show them I belonged at their level, even if I'd taken a scenic route to get there.

It was also an opportune place to tour for a reason I hadn't considered. I obviously knew South Africa — how the country worked and how it sometimes didn't, where to find a few interesting places, a cool nightspot or two. I became something of a guide for my teammates, which helped make me feel like I was part of things. The intense loneliness I had felt in Sri Lanka was easing. And from the outset in South Africa, I had family close. My parents watched every day of the warm-up game in Paarl, as well as being there for the Cape Town test, and my brother Mark and his wife Heloïse were in Port Elizabeth for Christmas, where our T20 side played a Boxing

Day game against the Proteas. It was the first time in four years I'd been around a member of my family on Christmas. Mark would later arrange for us to visit a wildlife park outside of the city — along with Kane and Flynny and their partners Sarah and Rachel — where the truck got stuck and Mark, who spends a lot of his time in the African wilderness, had to lend his expertise in helping to get us going again. Worlds were colliding and friendships were growing.

Mark also came along for a drink with the team following the first test, at Café Caprice, a well-known bar looking out over the lovely beach at Camps Bay, an upmarket Cape Town suburb. He tried and failed to teach Trent a few Afrikaans words as we relaxed and attempted to get some perspective about what had just happened against a very strong South African outfit. We'd shown some fight in the second innings — Baz scored a half century, Dean Brownlie a brave hundred — but we still lost by an innings. We were ordered to the nets as soon as the test was finished, bowlers instructed to bowl fast and short.

None of us knew about the impromptu discussion that took place after the first day, when Baz, Hess, assistant coach Bob Carter and manager Mike Sandle started to diagnose what was wrong with the team and plot a way forward, but already something felt different. There was a new sense of purpose emanating from our skipper. Without knowing exactly where it was taking us, I think we'd started buying into the vision Baz was still forming. At the bar, Baz asked Mark if he was coming back to Port Elizabeth to watch the second test. Mark said he had to get home for work, soon to begin after the summer break.

'That's a shame,' Baz said, 'because your brother will be playing.'

It was perhaps for the best that there was no family there to witness that second test. South Africa batted first and I bowled 33 bruising overs across the first two days, taking the solitary wicket of Graeme Smith, and going at a touch over four runs an over as three South Africans brought up centuries. My enduring memory is Dale Steyn walking out to bat and Baz asking me to greet him with some short stuff. I rapped him on the gloves first ball and, after the second bouncer, he walked down the pitch to say, 'Wags, just remember I still get to bowl at you, and I bowl twenty kilometres quicker.'

I just laughed. 'Dale, mate, I know you'll be bouncing me whatever I do.'

And not just me. South Africa declared north of 500. And, almost immediately, a procession of deflated New Zealand batters were trudging back to the sheds after brief stints in the middle. I remember the bruises adorning Kane's body — an archipelago of huge still-deepening purple welts, one on his back, one on his ribs, another on his inner thigh. Baz soon rejoined us also, shedding his shirt to compare his wounds with Kane. It wasn't what I needed to see before I had my turn.

During the 2011 World Cup, New Zealand beat South Africa in a very heated clash in the quarterfinal. I posted on Facebook about how happy I was with the result. So AB greeted my arrival at the batting crease by telling Dale to really give me something to post about. I only lasted seven balls against him, out leg before when a surprise fuller ball, too quick for me to manage, trapped me in front. We followed on, doing marginally better in the second innings where my dismissal — edging a Dale short ball behind to AB — was the last act of a game we had again lost by an innings. I went to shake Dale's hand and he pulled me into a hug.

'Wags,' he said, 'it's been an absolute pleasure.'

Hess informed me that I would be in the one-day squad for the three matches that followed, which meant, if nothing else, another chance to see Lana. Left-arm quick Mitchell McClenaghan made his debut in the first game, taking four wickets in a win. I could see that after Mitchell's excellent debut I'd be lucky to play, especially following my average performance in the test. We also won the second game, in Kimberley, in the process becoming the first Black Caps team to beat South Africa in a one-day series at home. The squad sat in a big circle after the game and Baz told us to remember we had done something special here, and we each, in turn, spoke to the group about what it meant to us. I said that although I hadn't played, the environment that was starting to build made me feel as if I had made a real contribution. That this felt like my victory also.

The last ODI was in Potchefstroom, and the team flew north to Jo'burg the next day. Lana picked me up and drove us to my parents' house for a barbecue. Things were starting to feel very real between us, even if the end of the tour loomed. We'd both had previous unsuccessful experiences with long-distance relationships and Lana was adamant she didn't want to try that again — this time with a much longer distance across oceans and time zones. But I couldn't face saying goodbye, and it began to brutally dawn on me that this beautiful thing that had bloomed between us over the past few weeks could end almost before it had begun. It even crossed my mind — after the uninspiring start I'd made to my international career — that perhaps I'd be better off staying in South Africa and abandoning my New Zealand ambitions. My head was wrapped in such a mist of emotion that I didn't speak to Lana until I was almost on the plane, and when we did talk she was absolutely, and rightfully, furious with me for failing to arrange a final in-person goodbye. Everything remained in the air as the plane took off, and once again I found myself flying out of Johannesburg with tears in my eyes.

The tail end of the Plunket Shield awaited. We were in a fantastic position to become the first Otago team to win the competition in more than 20 years, until a batting collapse in the last round against Wellington — we were out for 145 in pursuit of 200, Mark Gillespie gutting our middle order — handed the title to Central Districts. I ended the year sixth on the wicket chart with 30 scalps, having played three fewer games than the leader. The season ended in disappointment for the team, but I felt in good shape for the English tourists, especially after my six wickets and some important lower-order runs helped a NZ XI defeat a full-strength English team in Queenstown as they warmed up for the tests.

The first one was at University Oval. I felt relaxed going into the game, thankful to wake up in my own bed and drive to the ground just as I would for an Otago fixture. The entire first day was lost to rain. But we began well the next day when we won the toss and chose to field. England were already one down when Baz threw the ball my way, and I started with a nothing ball, outside off, which Alastair Cook ignored. The next ball was even worse — short and wide — but Cook, in unfurling a trademark cut shot, somehow slapped it straight to point. For the next ball — to Kevin Pietersen — Baz walked over to me and asked if I thought I had an inswinging yorker in me, suggesting we target his pads. It came out perfectly, full and fast and swinging in late enough to sneak past the bat and hit him dead in front. It was as much Baz's wicket as mine, and those two early scalps meant I could settle into the game, taking two more as England made just 167. We replied with 460-9 declared, made in quick time on the back of an exquisite 171 by Hamish Rutherford on debut. I bowled 43 overs in the second innings as we toiled and toiled against a stonewalling Steven Finn, who as nightwatchman helped his team bat out the final day for a draw that only one team — us — ever looked like a chance of winning.

We knew our standing with the New Zealand public and media wasn't great — though Baz was amazing at taking that heat on his own shoulders and shielding the team — and that game felt like an important step in regaining some of that lost affection. Things were beginning to turn around behind the scenes, too, built on Baz's knack of clearly communicating your role to you, and his seemingly absolute belief in your ability to do it. Mine — look to swing it when conditions suited and build pressure in a third-seamer containing role when they didn't — was a familiar one, but the way he spoke made me feel as if I was the only person in the world capable of doing it to the level he needed. I felt entirely backed by him and, for that, I would follow him anywhere. Whenever he spoke, I listened. I'd never before played under a captain so obviously born to lead.

In Wellington, it was our turn to follow on — and then our turn for rain to save us. The series was still on the line for the final test at Eden Park. Again, we had the better of the game from the outset, going big in the first innings thanks to a Peter Fulton century, bowling them out cheaply thanks to six wickets from Trent, before another Fults century helped set them a target of 481 to win and gave us over four sessions to bowl them out. It would be agonisingly close and fate seemed to be with the English when, midway through the second session on day five, on a slowing wicket on which fast bowlers needed every ounce of luck the universe could spare, I bowled a beauty of a short ball at Matt Prior. He got into a tangle, the ball deflecting off his bat handle and onto his helmet, from there falling onto the bails, somehow leaving them in their cradle, before landing on the pitch and spinning back against the stumps, again — somehow — failing to remove the bails from their perch.

Prior would score a match-saving century, surviving the final few overs in the company of last-man-in Monty Panesar, as the noise of the Auckland crowd — big for a test match in New Zealand, but still dwarfed by the empty seats — reverberated in strange ways off the acres of exposed concrete. We were bruised, everything hurt, and we were distraught not to get over the line for what would've been a famous victory.

It wasn't to be, but we were told in the dressing room after the game that more Kiwis had watched that final session than had ever tuned in for a New Zealand test match. We would've done anything for the win, but to hear that our fight was helping New Zealand fall back in love with test cricket, and with their men's cricket team following such a tumultuous period of poor performance, was some consolation as, after a long season and a lot of overs, I was wringing blood from my socks and trying to gently encourage one of my big toenails not to slide off completely. Later that night while yarning with Trent and Timmy, I had the lovely feeling that these guys were starting to get to know me as a person — that I was seen as more than some South African coming to try and steal their jobs. We were all growing in confidence, in belief, and starting to draw together as a team. Something beautiful was beginning to happen.

From there, it was back to South Africa and Lana, who — after some seriously long discussions during that England series — had agreed to make a go of things. And the months that followed only confirmed the feeling that had been growing in me since I first laid eyes on her that stormy evening in Cape Town. I wanted to show her what she meant to me and prove that this wasn't a long-distance relationship I was prepared to let flounder on the oceans separating New Zealand from South Africa. By the time I left Pretoria a few months later, Lana had agreed to be my wife.

Much had changed since the last time I was in the English capital as a wide-eyed kid in constant danger of getting lost in the crowds. This time, as if to illustrate that change, I would be playing a test at Lord's, the home of cricket. It was the sort of thing the Neil Wagner of five years ago could only have dreamed of.

We played a warm-up game against Derbyshire before we moved down to London, where the IPL players joined the squad. A sense of wonder came over me as I entered the ground, then the dressing room, with its blazered stewards motioning you the way to go among all the dark polished wood and palpable history, towards your own monogrammed towel in your seat. It hit me again — bowling spikes scraping on the steps — as I approached the turf itself for the first time, joking with Hamish Rutherford, my good mate from Otago, about how far this all seemed from Dunners. And even more so when I walked to the middle and realised the extent of the famous Lord's slope.

England batted first and, as we had been told it would be, the pitch seemed pretty flat as our hosts made slow but steady progress through a rain-interrupted day. Wickets fell sparsely but regularly, and I got Ian Bell, a batter whose cover drive was perhaps *the* shot I most wished I possessed, when he tried it one too many times against a wide one angled across.

The next day, with a new ball, everything changed for us and Timmy, particularly, was simply too good as he swung the ball around corners and England lost their last six wickets for 40 runs to post 232. We made 207 in reply before England managed 213, Tim taking another six to give him 10 for the game. Lana had to say goodbye from the stands before racing straight from Lord's to Heathrow, and back to Pretoria.

A chase of 239 was going to be tricky — it would've been the highest innings score of the game — but as I had a shower and the batters got under way I thought we were in really good shape to chase a famous victory. My shower was interrupted by a roar from the crowd, and then another. By the time I got out we were two down for not much, and Stuart Broad had embarked on one of *those* spells, seeming to summon an almost supernatural energy from the crowd and channelling it into a succession of unplayable deliveries. Before I knew it, it was basically time for me to pad up. Soon after that, with the score at 41 for seven as Broady kept on slicing through us, I walked out through the Long Room, where the clipped accents told me they would see me again shortly, and into the middle, where my 17 ended in an embarrassing run out that also concluded the game.

We were truly humbled, torn apart by a master of his craft at the top of his game in conditions tailormade for him. We tried to remember, as a team, that many positives had come out of the match, not least Tim's 10 wickets and the fact that deep into the game we were in a position to win it.

The second test, at Headingley, didn't go too much better. Trent went down with a side strain early in our second turn in the field, having taken five wickets in the first, and it meant a big workload for the rest of us. Most of my overs were bowled up the hill that used to be a characteristic of the ground, and into a blustery wind. England were piling on the runs and I was getting more and more exhausted, my speed dropping lower and lower, England scoring faster and faster as they looked to set us a target. Baz joked that this was the first time he'd ever seen me lose my engine.

I was bowling to Joe Root, who'd scored a century in the first innings, when he got down and reverse paddled a full ball for four — not something anyone did back then to fast bowlers in the longest format of the game. He gave me a little nod.

'Don't take it personally, Wags.'

Of course, I took it very, very personally. He was out soon after, caught attempting to hit me over cover. I enjoyed that very much. They declared an over or so later and we were all out chasing a huge total we never looked like getting close to, which resulted in a 247-run loss.

As some of the squad stuck around in England for the ODI series and then the ICC Champions Trophy that followed it, for me it was back to South Africa and back to Lana. We now had an enormous number of logistics to negotiate — a wedding in South Africa the following year and the not-inconsiderable task of getting the paperwork sorted for her immigration to New Zealand so we could really begin our lives together. After all that was organised, she would join me in Dunedin a few months later.

I hadn't played in much of the previous Otago T20 campaign due to international duty, but largely without me the boys had won the competition, qualifying us for the Champions League T20 in India that year. We first had to get through a qualifying tournament, which we did undefeated, and then into the main draw. We won more than we lost and shared the points from another fixture that was lost entirely to rain. It left us in a good position as we settled in over a bottle of nice whisky courtesy of Baz to watch the second-to-last group game, between the Perth Scorchers and the Mumbai Indians, which Mumbai would have to win by an absurd margin to nudge ahead of us on net run rate and end our tournament by going through to the semifinals themselves. The Scorchers batted first and made a middling 149 from their 20 overs. Still, Mumbai needed to reach that score in just 14.2 overs. Then Dwayne Smith and Rohit Sharma went berserk, and they did it with an over to spare. We were out, the whisky turning from celebratory to consolatory even as it still warmed our stomachs. The Mumbai Indians went on to win the tournament.

But it was a good time with a great bunch of mates. We'd enjoyed ourselves — perhaps, as it turned out, a little bit too much. When I got to Bangladesh, where we were playing two test matches, my body-fat percentage was at an all-time high. I felt pretty fit, but the skinfold test couldn't be fooled and trainer Chris Donaldson put me on a strict regime, even taking my minibar away from me. I wasn't picked for the first test — nothing to do with my fitness, just the need for an extra specialist spinner — and I worked incredibly hard with Chris during the week to drop all the naan bread that a month in India had induced me to consume. I felt in top shape when I was called into the team for the second test, in Mirpur, after the first in Chattogram ended in a draw.

We lost the toss and bowled first. My role, in the unhelpful conditions I remembered well from my visit to Bangladesh half a decade earlier, was to keep the pressure on through the middle overs and see if I could get the ball to reverse swing later in the innings. The ball, naturally, stopped moving conventionally in the air almost immediately, and by the time Baz sent it my way for the 11th over, any swing was merely a memory and Bangladesh were motoring along at more than five runs an over. I bowled unchanged until lunch, taking a wicket in my seventh over when I uprooted the off stump of Marshall Ayub with a full, fast one. I would return to get Tamim Iqbal for 95 in the second session with my one short-ball wicket of the innings, before rain closed the curtain on day one.

In the morning, wickets started to fall regularly as soon as I was given the ball — Mushfiqur Rahim, Sohag Gazi, then Rubel Hossain — to give me my first five-wicket bag for the Black Caps. It was a testament as much to Chris as it was to me, that the extra work I had put in to get in the best possible shape and the confidence I took from being in absolute peak condition helped in the role — to bowl a lot of overs when conditions were unhelpful — I was already making my own. Five wickets was a tangible achievement to leave Bangladesh with, and combined with the two wickets I took in the second innings, my bowling average fell below 40 for the first time in my career. Although, it would've been nicer if we'd won. Rain robbed us of that chance by washing out the entire final day.

I was nine games into my career and yet to know how it felt to win an international match. Test cricket, I was learning, was relentlessly unforgiving and gruelling. It was also difficult to get into a rhythm, with two-test series often months apart, and the team was still young and figuring out the game at the hardest level. But we had a big home summer — first the West Indies, then India — in which to attempt to nab that victory. We knew it had to be close.

The first test was in Dunedin, which now, since Lana had joined me in my little townhouse, felt more like home than ever. The intense doubts I'd had about myself and my decisions had quietened — the team environment was much improved from those early days, and that coupled with Lana's arrival had me feeling connected to a strong unit both on and off the field.

We lost the toss and were put in to bat — but we started the summer almost perfectly. A big opening stand segued into an even bigger one, for the fourth wicket, between Rossco and Baz. Ross made his first double century, and Baz his first hundred as captain, the partnership feeling like a symbol of the healing the team had done since the latter had replaced the former as skipper. The partnership was the backbone of a huge score — 609 for nine declared — that put us in absolute control of the game, made more absolute when Timmy and Trent carved up the West Indian top order to have them all out for 213.

We enforced the follow-on, by which stage the pitch had flattened out and the West Indies made 507 — I bowled 30 hard overs for my three wickets, eventual double-centurion Darren Bravo given not out on review for a caught behind I thought clearly brushed the sweatband touching his glove — to set us a target of 112 to win. We made 79 of them before rain washed out the back end of the final day. Ten tests, still no victory. Things were starting to get a little frustrating, though Brendon over a few beers that night greeted the result with his usual calmness — he knew, I suppose, that we were starting to come together nicely as a group, instinctively learning each other's roles, and that something really good was brewing among us.

The tour moved on to the Basin Reserve. Another Ross Taylor century set the game up for us before Boulty took over. I've never seen Trent bowl as fast or as unplayably as he did on that cold, overcast Wellington day, the third of the test. A succession of full, inch-perfect, big-swinging deliveries, into the right-handers and away from the left, very soon had the West Indies in disarray. When their first innings was through and we enforced the follow-on, Trent merely got stuck into them in their second. He took the final wicket of the game — another inswinger shattering the stumps — which gave him nine for the day and 10 for the match.

I was on the winning side in a test match for the first time in my life — also the first time Baz had captained the side to victory. I remember looking around at my teammates in the changing room and seeing the hard-won happiness animating their faces. This was the feeling you played for, of a goal achieved by shared labour. For the first time, I was able to sing the team pledge, which we only did after a win.

There was another Wellington tradition we had to honour: the limo ride up Mount Victoria for the bowlers and the wicketkeeper, which had been instituted by Simon Doull, Dion Nash, Adam Parore and co. in the late 1990s. Everyone who bowled in the test match, the tradition dictates, has a right to a place in the limo. Kane, who had bowled five overs across the game, didn't think he was worthy of a space alongside me, Trent, Tim, Corey Anderson and Ish Sodhi, but we insisted. He did, however, flat-out refuse to take full part in the photo of the bowling squad at the top of the hill — instead, you see his then boyish and unbearded face peeking out from behind an open door. The photo made it to the media and a rumour started that it was actually a woman's face, that the limo tradition was something else entirely than a bunch of mates with champagne and cigars.

I got back to the hotel at midnight, where Lana was watching a movie in bed. She took one look at me — slurring the odd word, giggling like a schoolgirl — and laughed.

'I can see you enjoyed your night.'

'I definitely did,' I told her. I squeezed every bit of enjoyment from my first test victory as possible.

We'd follow that victory immediately with my second in Hamilton, thrashing a dispirited West Indies team by eight wickets within four days. Rossco scored another century and Timmy took his hundredth wicket — which Trent, for some reason, decided not to celebrate with the team afterwards, instead driving back home to Tauranga, something we never let him forget. I'd had an average series, eight wickets at 45.50, but this moment was about the team, which was growing ever more cohesive. Now I just had to make sure that I did enough in the next series to prove I deserved to be part of it.

CHAPTER 8:
THE SHORT STUFF

If a question remained about the composition of the bowling attack, it was me. Tim and Trent had established themselves as one of the best new-ball combinations in the world, but my record was still fairly ordinary. Going into the India series in early 2014, I had taken 39 test wickets at an average of nearly 38. It was coming down, but it was still a long way short of where I wanted it — and where I thought it could be.

As Australian cricket writer and broadcaster Jarrod Kimber would later point out in reference to my career, the Black Caps have never really had a shortage of workhorse-style fast-medium third seamers — someone able to bowl long spells into the Wellington wind in the Ewen Chatfield/Iain O'Brien mould. You'll find them in every provincial team around the country. So if I was to keep my nose ahead of the chasing pack, led then primarily by Doug Bracewell and Matt Henry, I would have to be the best of that bunch, and keep getting better at doing what I did. Or — not that I had really thought about it at the time — start doing it in a different way.

First there was Christmas, which would usually be at Craig Cumming's house with the rest of the Otago orphans, but this year I wasn't alone. Lana was with me in Dunedin and we decided instead to celebrate by ourselves with a traditional South African feast — mainly meat — of which we cooked enough to feed multitudes, rather than merely the two of us. The Dunedin climate didn't quite conform to South African tradition that year: it was overcast and cold, but at least it wasn't raining as I stood beside the barbecue. Not that weather or almost anything else could have punctured our bliss: we were both bursting with happiness, looking forward to our wedding the next year and our lives together after that.

I warmed up for the visit of MS Dhoni and co. with a couple of Plunket Shield games — a win against Canterbury, draw against Auckland — but I was far from convinced that I would get the tap on the shoulder for the first test at Eden Park. Especially after we looked at the pitch, which, at one end on a good length for a spinner, seemed to be suffering from some kind of disease: the grass was dying and there was every chance that it could dry out later and offer a good amount of turn. Baz often spoke about selection as a horses-for-courses situation, so I was almost resigned to being replaced by a second spinner as I warmed up. The nets at Eden Park, where you run up over used pitches, have always unsettled my rhythm, and this felt like the worst I had bowled in a while, which made me even more sure I wasn't going to play. But maybe Baz hadn't noticed: eventually he gave me the nod.

I love playing at Eden Park, the site of so much history — cricket and rugby — with the chance to weave your own name into its tapestry. Some cricketers hate it, the huge near-empty stands and its strange rugby-ground proportions, but not me. I hoped this time to come out on the winning side after being so close against the English during my last outing there. Initially, though, the signs weren't good.

We lost the toss and were put in to bat, finding ourselves in early trouble at 30 for three. But when Baz joined Kane at the crease our fortunes changed, the two of them batting together for most of the day — Kane made a century and Baz, the next day, was the last batter out for a belligerent 224 in a team score of 503. Trent and Tim then made significant inroads into the much-vaunted Indian top order.

When I was thrown the ball, everything in my action seemed to click. It might be the quickest I have ever bowled. The spell was crowned by a beauty: coming round the wicket to Murali Vijay, I pitched it full and angled it into middle before a hint of movement off the seam took it past the outside edge of his forward defensive shot and removed the off bail with the subtlety of a pickpocket slipping a watch from a wrist. Another beauty had Dhoni edging behind, before some short stuff netted me two more tail-end wickets. They were all out for 202.

Probably the less said about our second innings the better: we crumbled for just over 100, and I got hit in the head by a Mohammed Shami bouncer. The impact was so hard, I remember, ringing through the Masuri helmet, that a weird taste flooded my tongue. I was out soon after, trying to murder the ball out of the park, which left India a big but achievable target of 407.

The Indian fans in the crowd sensed a famous come-from-behind win, especially when their hero, Virat Kohli, joined Shikhar Dhawan at the crease and a big third-wicket partnership began to build. The crowd was getting louder and louder, and I could hear people shouting things like 'You're not a New Zealander, you shouldn't even be allowed to play for the Black Caps' in Indian accents. But what sticks with me is how vociferously a nearby group of Kiwi supporters had my back. Whenever my nationality was questioned, this group would call out something like: 'Ignore that, Wags, you're one of us now, we're right behind ya.' Whenever I finished an over — good or bad — they'd be on their feet, cheering me down to the fine-leg boundary.

Initially, the plan was as it had been in the first innings: bowl full, nick them off. Baz, as usual, had set me an ultra-aggressive field. Something like four slips and no one in the covers. Virat crunched me for a couple of drives through the vacant area, and Baz's response was to put in a catching cover with little run-saving utility. Another crunching Virat drive had me worried about all the runs I was leaking, but when I looked over at Baz he was just smirking as if everything was going to plan. Those moments are so important for a bowler. I knew he, like that group in the crowd, was right behind me. Later, when India got past 200 with Virat and Shikhar still at the crease and looking in control, Baz suggested a new plan of attack.

'Let's go short,' he said.

There was some talk about playing on Virat's ego. We dropped square leg back, to join fine leg on the boundary, and put in a widish leg gully, keeping the short cover to give me options. First ball, full, and Virat creamed it through the off side for four. The next ball, a bouncer, he ducked under. The next — another attempted bouncer but badly bowled, wide outside off — he tried to pull through the leg side. All he could do was get a bottom edge, which BJ Watling fell forward to collect. Had Virat cut instead of pulled, he surely would've thrashed it past point. But I was learning that it is not always the technical excellence of a particular ball that matters: sometimes it's about intent, energy and belief in a plan — and that when you've got a batter's mind working to come to grips with what you are trying to do, concentration can lapse and mistakes can happen. With the team behind me, confidence was no problem. We converged to celebrate.

'Mate,' I said to Baz, 'that's 100 per cent your wicket.'

There was still a lot of work to do, with Shikhar looking good to guide his team home. The plan remained the same, bowling short and over-the-wicket to the left-hander. Then it was suggested I come around the wicket, with a short leg under the helmet. 'Try to make him uncomfortable with a different angle.' The first ball of the eighth over of my spell was as perfect a bouncer as I have ever managed, climbing perilously at Shikhar's throat, his body buckling into the shape of an 'S' as he tried desperately to avoid it, but giving him neither enough room nor time to do so. The ball brushed his gloves and again carried through to BJ. I roared as belief returned to the team, beating my chest in the direction of those doubters in the crowd. The spell — one of the most important in my career — ended after 10 overs, with those two big wickets to show for my effort.

Later, another short ball — this time a slower-ball bouncer, very close to being a back-foot no-ball because I had gone so wide on the crease — accounted for MS Dhoni, who along with Ravindra Jadeja had almost dragged India back into the game. That wicket ended India's hope. They were bowled out 40 runs short of the target, and I took eight wickets in the game, my best test-match figures to date.

I wasn't really thinking too deeply about the bouncer-heavy spells of the second innings or considering them as a template to move forward with until after the game when we were sitting in the sheds, revelling in the happiness of a hard-fought victory. Then Baz, player of the match for his double century, approached.

'I think you've found your niche. We've found how you should bowl in test cricket. I think this is going to be you,' he said.

His words hit me straight away, and the more I thought about them, the more they made sense. If we had two of the best swing bowlers in the world opening the bowling, why should I come in after them, with an older ball, and try to do more of the same? I could lean into this new method, which played into a natural strength of mine, using my accuracy with the bouncer and the round-the-wicket angle I'd found so effective for Otago, and see how far that could take me. In those moments and the coming months, I felt myself clicking into my true role within the team, and within our attack. But for now, we had a series to win.

The second test, at the Basin, will forever be remembered for Baz's match- and series-saving triple century, the first by a New Zealander. After a poor start to the game, Baz's innings began with the hope that maybe — if the weather played a huge role — we could cling on for a draw, and it ended two days later with a push for victory, a bursting-at-the-seams Basin Reserve like an outward expression of the belief that was developing within the dressing room. To see Baz slash a ball to the third-man boundary to move past 300, the crowd erupt and stand and clap and keep standing, to see them right behind Baz after everything — as we were behind him in the sheds — was an emotional moment.

Just as good, it earned us our second series victory in a row. When Prime Minister John Key visited the sheds after the game to congratulate Baz on his achievement, he was shown around and introduced to each member of the team. When introducing the PM to me, Baz goes, 'Can you help this guy out, he's still on a South African passport, can we make him a New Zealander please?'

I helped Otago finish off the Plunket Shield — we came second — and stuck around just long enough for the NZC annual awards night before employing that passport to fly back to South Africa, where on 19 April 2014, almost exactly a year after our engagement, Lana and I got married on a beautiful estate in the rolling country west of Pretoria. I could hardly believe my luck as Lana walked down the aisle: this gorgeous woman who had seen me through the lowest moments of my life, and who was the main ingredient in the overwhelming happiness I had now found, was going to be by my side as the rest of life's strange adventure rushed up to meet us.

If I had the method, I still needed a body that would allow me to employ it, and after the Indian series, my body was bruised, battered and sore. I'd always been known for my ability to bowl long spells, but up until that point it had been through almost willpower alone and I would always feel it the day after. Long spells with a higher proportion of short balls — the most energy-sapping ball in a fast-bowler's armoury — would take even more out of me.

I needed to get to work, and Black Caps trainer Chris Donaldson and his Otago counterpart Adam Keane were instrumental in the process. Lana and I got back to Dunedin — we had honeymooned in Santorini — just as winter was closing in on the city. Adam immediately said, 'Look, if you are going to have success with this, you're going to have to be fitter and you're going to have to be stronger.'

The regime would begin early in the morning, after I dropped

Lana off at the school where she worked, with running, running, running — it didn't matter if there was sleet falling from the sky or thick frost blanketing the earth. Then a break, some food, then weights — which I'd never really been big on before, preferring to keep my body lighter and relying on rhythm for my pace. Then I'd pick up Lana from work and either head home to recover on the couch, or, several times a week, back out for skills training. It was a gruelling, hard winter.

But the results were self-evident. Soon I was squatting 200 kilograms, and there was one running session when Adam urged me to put absolutely everything I had into it, which I did, struggling through pain to post a personal best. After two or three weeks of training, we did the same again — and this time I ran it faster but it was so much easier. I was starting to see all my numbers improving, and I was also feeling better about myself and my body, and the confidence flowed into my bowling — I knew I could bowl 10 or even 15 overs on the trot, keeping it at a higher pace for longer, and also wake up in the morning with much less pain than would have previously pulsed through my muscles. I realised this had to become a habit because the dividend it paid was just so high. Strength and fitness became more of a focus — as my bowling developed to suit the team's needs — than swing or seam position or all the other things I had previously put so much store in.

All the talk, though, when the squad assembled to train for the winter tour to the West Indies, was about the role that spin would play, and Otago off spinner Mark Craig was called into the Black Caps for the first time. My senses told me I'd be lucky to get a game, and so it proved as we won the first test in Kingston and lost the second in Port of Spain, both matches going in with two specialist spinners. I was gutted, obviously, especially after the off-season work

I had put in, and it was the first inkling I had that this new role ran the risk of me being perceived as a one-trick pony, that while ensuring I'd be picked for some tests, it would almost certainly exclude me from others. But I felt part of the team regardless, and the contrast with my first tour of the West Indies couldn't have been more stark. And it meant I was raring to go when called into the team for the final test, the decider in Bridgetown.

I took four wickets, utilising the lessons learned in Auckland, including the big scalps of Darren Bravo and Shivnarine Chanderpaul, caught tickling a short one to the keeper down the leg side. Still, the West Indies took a first-innings lead into the game's second half, only erased by a Kane masterclass, his 161 allowing us to declare, giving the West Indies a chase of 308 for victory. I took a solitary wicket as Tim, Trent and Mark did the majority of the work in ensuring a 53-run win. It was just the second time a New Zealand team had beaten the West Indies in a test series in the Caribbean — that same 2002 series win had also been the last time the Black Caps had won an away series against a team other than Zimbabwe or Bangladesh. We were building nicely.

From the tropics to England. I'd performed my new role just as was asked in Bridgetown, but it still felt a little strange to push aside most of the skills — swing and seam — that had helped me get to the top level now that I was there. I wanted to make sure I didn't forget them completely, especially as we had a test tour of England scheduled for the New Zealand winter of 2015, and I wanted to prove I could be called upon, when that series came around, to contribute in the more traditional third-seamer role the conditions would dictate. A spell in the County Championship with Northamptonshire, I thought, would keep me fresh and reacquaint me with the Dukes ball used in England.

It wasn't an easy side to walk into. Early on, I spoke up in our changing sheds about some of the lessons we were learning in the Black Caps, about putting the team first and only worrying about your own performance in so much as it contributed to what the team was trying to achieve — how if you play for your mates it all seems to become a hell of a lot easier. But no one seemed to pay it much mind and I soon found out why when Andrew Hall, who had been in the South African squad when I was around the group years ago, took me aside and informed me of the dynamics within the club. A bunch of the senior players, including Andrew himself, had already been informed by management they would be let go at the end of the season, the club intending to build a squad around its younger members. It had created a real divide within the team, and we didn't play well.

My county debut against Nottinghamshire was memorable mainly for the mess Alex Hales made of my figures on the way to a century and victory, while my second game, against Somerset, included tussles against my old South African mates Johann Myburgh and Alfonso Thomas. It was great to see Alfonso again — even if he took my wicket when I came in as a nightwatchman — and to pick his brains about how to succeed in the county game, as he had done for many years. I took five wickets against Durham, including winning my first battle with Ben Stokes, but that was outshone as soon as we batted by Durham's opening seamer, Christopher Rushworth, who ran through us with nine wickets in the first innings and a further six as we followed on.

My first taste of county cricket wasn't what I had hoped for, but it was hard to find your way in that team environment. And I duly struggled, taking just 10 wickets across five games at an average of over 70. Northants would be relegated to the second division at the close of the season.

The next New Zealand assignment was in the United Arab Emirates, where we were playing Pakistan, in conditions as far from county cricket as it is possible to get. Abu Dhabi, site of the first test, boasted a slow and abrasive pitch, thought to be worthy of only two specialist seamers — Trent and Tim. We lost after none of our bowlers, pace or spin, made much of a dent and Pakistan put on a huge first-innings total that kept us out of the game from the outset. The next test was in Dubai, where the wicket offered much of the same. We went with the same side, and this time held on for a draw.

I was excited when it was announced that Dan Vettori, who I had debuted alongside, would be returning in Sharjah to play his final test. I hoped for one more opportunity to take the field with such a legend of New Zealand cricket, but it wasn't to be — for the same reasons as in Dubai and Abu Dhabi. Not playing had made for a long tour of net bowling and running drinks, though by this time Lana had joined me and we tried to make the most of touring life, exploring the city and all its incredible diversions. Mentally, by the time that third test came around and I found out I again wasn't playing, I clocked off, my mind moving on to the cricket that would follow.

It was the morning before play on the second day when we were called together. It felt serious. There was a strange current running through the team, expressed in the heavy eyes of those who had already been told. I thought maybe there had been a security threat. But then Mike Sandle uttered the awful words: Phillip Hughes, struck on the back of the neck while batting for New South Wales in a Sheffield Shield game, had died. The dressing room went completely quiet.

For a few minutes, everything stood still, each of us locked into a silent, private moment of grief and shock. I didn't know Phil personally, as some of the guys in the team did, but I think we all had the feeling that this could've happened to any one of us. When talk resumed, the main sentiment expressed was that no one wanted to play this game, and we were thankful when play, for that day at least, was called off. We returned to the hotel, to Baz's room, and everyone who wanted to spoke about what they were feeling. Brendon talked about having grown close to Phil when they'd spent some time opening together for New South Wales. Luke Ronchi shared how his friendship with Phil had been forged when the two were at the Australian Cricket Academy together.

Then we dispersed.

Sitting in the hotel, waiting to hear about whether the rest of the game would go ahead, felt dark and heavy, so Lana and me and a few others went to the mall adjoining the hotel. We just needed something else to fill our heads and to keep us away from social media, where video of the incident was circulating. I searched the faces of the people — tourists and locals — inside this amazing mall and found it so surreal to see in them no trace of this thing that had stopped all of our lives in their tracks. Later on, we reconvened in Brendon's room, had a few sombre drinks, then dinner, where we were informed that the test would go ahead.

The next morning was so strange, the boys moving like zombies through pre-game routines, tears rolling down the cheeks of some, everyone just wanting to be on the plane home to their families. We placed our black caps on the handles of our bats and leant them against the boundary hoardings as a mark of respect. We each took to the field with Phil's initials written below the fern on our chests. When play started and wickets fell, everything was so dulled by circumstance that even when I wanted to get excited — this was still a test match, after all — I couldn't.

It was a day in which no one bowled a bouncer, and later on I started to wonder whether this would change the game of cricket. *Would short balls still be allowed? What would that mean for me and my new-found approach? Did I still have an appetite to bowl the short stuff now knowing what, in the absolute unluckiest circumstances imaginable, could happen?*

In the end, as support flooded in around Sean Abbott, the bowler, and as we learned more about the freak nature of Phillip's death, not much, other than the addition of some extra safety protocols, would change. For me, I had to try and put it out of my mind — I knew I could never be effective if I was even slightly scared that a ball from my hand could kill someone.

We won the game thanks to the mountain of runs scored by Baz and Kane and the wickets of Mark Craig, but everything was very muted as we assembled that night in Dan's room to try — despite everything — to celebrate his legendary test-match career, which had ended in the strangest and saddest of circumstances.

It was back home to the opening of the Plunket Shield season with Otago, before a break for Christmas and then the test series, beginning on Boxing Day at Hagley Oval, against the touring Sri

Lankans. It was the first test ever to be played at the ground and the first in Christchurch since the earthquakes had wreaked havoc across the city.

I was in the squad, but anxious about whether I was going to get picked. Walking with Lana around Clearwater Resort, where the team was staying, on the eve of the series, I began unloading those insecurities onto her: I hadn't played a test in six months, since the West Indies, and despite everything I'd been told and been feeling about having found my place in the team after the India series, self-doubt kicked in and I was starting to wonder whether there was actually a place at all. Thankfully, I found out just before the toss that I'd be playing — though I would have to wait until the second day for a bowl after the first was dominated by a blistering 195 by Baz.

When I got the ball, the pitch still had a bit of moisture in it, greasy enough on top that I found my front foot slipping as I went through my delivery stride. The harder I tried, the more I slipped — and the worse my rhythm got. Desperation kicked in. *You simply have to make the most of this opportunity*, I told myself. But that only seemed to make things worse and worse. Typically, Baz gave me a very aggressive field, but I was unable to execute what he was asking me to do, going for runs through the vacant cover region. I could see even Brendon, not one to show any outward anger at his bowlers, getting frustrated, which only made me put more pressure on myself. I ended up taking three wickets, but I knew I had bowled badly. Then I went wicketless in the second innings, before we cruised home to an eight-wicket victory.

I tried to contextualise the test as the bad game that everyone has from time to time, that things would come right for the next one in Wellington. But I didn't get the chance, Doug Bracewell replacing me in the team. I watched as the boys wrapped up a two–nil series victory, thanks in large part to a huge partnership between Kane and BJ. After the game, despite me saying no, it was insisted that I join the bowlers and keeper on the Mount Vic pilgrimage, a small measure of the unity building in the team, where everyone was made to feel like they were playing an important role, even if it wasn't an on-field one. But jeez I was hungry to be on the park.

It was something I'd have to get used to. I wouldn't play another test match for a year.

It was back to the domestic ranks, where the cricket was played in the huge shadow of the 2015 Cricket World Cup, co-hosted by New Zealand and Australia. I hadn't even been named in the preliminary 30-man training squad late the year before, so I knew early on that I had no chance of making the team. It was already starting to feel that my limited-overs aspirations were slipping further and further away from me, even if I had an excellent Ford Trophy that year, taking 15 wickets in seven games at an economy rate of under five an over.

Instead, I enjoyed the World Cup as a fan, if one with some inside knowledge and a lot of friendships in the group, recognising in Hess and Baz's preparation some of the things that were happening in the test team, too: everybody seemed to know their role and what was expected of them, and loved playing for their mates, aligned towards a common goal.

Helped by some of the belief the test team was starting to instil, it was inspiring to see the depth of public support for the group. The whole nation, it seemed, was pulled into the slipstream of the grand-final-bound squad. I remember the magic of the semifinal, screaming at the TV as Grant Elliott pulled my old mate Dale Steyn into the stands to win. And then, also, sparing a thought for Dale and Faf and Morne and AB and all these guys I knew so well and who were as distraught as my Black Caps mates were ecstatic. But I was a New Zealander now and I was so happy for my teammates.

Things didn't go as planned in the final against Australia at the MCG, but — like the public at large — I was inspired by what the boys had achieved. It made me want to get out there, train harder, to see how much I could contribute to cricket in New Zealand. And, away from the intensity of that competition, I had a fairly good time of things in the much more low-key Plunket Shield, reverting to my role as a new-ball bowler for Otago and taking 36 wickets from nine games to help us finish in third place.

That inspiration, however, would be tested on the next two New Zealand tours: England and Australia.

I played my hundredth first-class game on the England tour — taking three wickets against Somerset in a warm-up before the two tests — but that was the highlight as Matt Henry emerged as the preferred third seamer in English conditions, taking six wickets across his debut game at Lord's, where we lost, to ensure he played the second, in Leeds, where we squared the series. The spell I'd had with Northamptonshire to prepare for this tour, in the end, had been in vain. And there wasn't much cricket — just an A series against Sri Lanka — with which to press my case for the next tour, the much-anticipated series in Australia. I wasn't even selected for the touring squad, initially, only called across the ditch as injury cover for Tim. And, in the end, he was good to go for the second test in Perth, so I didn't get to play in that drawn match. I took a five-wicket bag in the pink-ball fixture against Western Australia, scheduled to prepare the team for the inaugural day–night test in Adelaide, but it wasn't enough to force my way into the team for our loss in that historic game.

I shared my frustrations with my brother Mark and he advised me to always bring my best: 'If you're twelfth man, be the best twelfth man possible. If you have to run drinks, run them better than anyone has run them before.' I tried to keep that sentiment at the front of my mind.

It was hard, though, with old insecurities about my place in the team and my ability starting to resurface. There were other pressures, too. Lana and I had upgraded from the little flat I had owned for several years, and into a house in Mosgiel. When we signed the mortgage agreement, we assumed that I'd be playing at least some of the test matches that year — and without the match fees I would've earned by doing so, our finances were seriously stretched. The SOS that I answered by jumping over to Australia to cover for injuries interrupted that year's Super Smash campaign for Otago, and when I got back it was decided to let the incumbents remain in place when I returned. We then lost the final.

All of that was somewhere in my mind when, as part of a four-pronged pace attack, I was picked to play Sri Lanka in Dunedin to begin the 2015/16 home summer of cricket. It was almost exactly a year since I had bowled poorly against the same opposition in a performance that had banished me to the fringes of the team for 12 months, so once again I felt like I had to make it count. And this time I managed not to let the occasion overawe me.

I took three wickets as Sri Lanka replied to our first-innings score of 431 with 294, and then returned as Sri Lanka chased the unlikely victory our day-four declaration had dangled before them. I got number three Udara Jayasundera late on the fourth day and made the decisive strike the next, just as Dinesh Chandimal and skipper

Angelo Mathews were starting to make our total look reachable. I'd troubled Angelo almost immediately, getting a fast short one in my second over to rear up at him and clip the shoulder of the bat he'd raised in self-defence. I gave him two more short balls to begin my third over, before a full one — he was camped back, expecting another bouncer — bowled him between his legs. Chandimal was out to Mitchell Santner a few overs later and the rest was a formality, completed later that day.

That performance was enough to keep my spot for the next game in Hamilton. The Seddon Park pitch was nice and green with a good amount of grass on it, but after we won the toss and bowled first, the ball was moving surprisingly little off the surface. It was fast, however, perhaps the fastest surface many of us had ever played on in New Zealand, and the short ball quickly became the go-to weapon — for both sides. Eighteen wickets fell to bouncers — I took four across the match — as another Kane century saw us to a five-wicket victory on the morning of the fourth day. Then, after the series, Baz revealed to the team that this would be his final season of international cricket, and that the second test against the inbound Australian side would be his 101st and final test match. I was desperate to play. I wanted to show my appreciation for a cricketer, leader and man who had done so much for me.

I wasn't required for the first test at the Basin Reserve — the spin of Mark Craig was preferred — and we sank to a huge innings loss before the tour moved to Christchurch. On a green, fast-looking surface, I was in. When Brendon lost his final toss, we were unsurprisingly put in to bat and were in immediate trouble on a pitch that was perfect for Australia's battery of hit-the-deck seamers, 32 for three when Brendon walked to the crease through an Australian guard of honour. Kane was struggling with the pitch at the other end — at the time he had three runs from 44 balls — which only made Baz's innings all the more remarkable. We suspected what was coming when he edged his second ball for four attempting a heave down the ground, and it was confirmed when the fifth ball was smoked over the bowler's head to give him the outright record for career sixes. The rest of the innings was barely believable, a hailstorm of boundaries that ended on 145 off 79 balls, with a host of other records broken along the way, including for the fastest test-match century of all time. It was the innings he was born to play, and more importantly than the records, it put us right back into a game we had started badly.

Unfortunately, though, the pitch had lost much of its juice by the time we came to bowl that afternoon. And Australia made us toil. Joe Burns and Steve Smith, then near the height of his powers, batted throughout almost the entire second day to put on a mammoth partnership that would only end after evening shadows had stretched far across the ground. Baz gave me the ball for one more crack and, after a few overs, we set the field for some short stuff.

My first bouncer to Joe barely got above waist high, but the second was much better, aimed flush at the badge on his helmet. He couldn't keep his hook shot down and Martin Guptill at square leg took an incredible catch. Almost the exact same thing happened when I bounced Steve the first ball of my next over — couldn't keep it down, caught by Gup in the same position. It gave me the licence to continue the attack the next day, though I would have to wait until after lunch before it started to pay off, when, in a single spell of sustained short-pitched bowling, a flurry of four wickets fell in very similar circumstances.

The Aussie batters, we knew, wanted to dominate — and they hated the idea of letting the short stuff go when they thought they could score from it. I wanted to rub up against those egos, and I could feel, during that spell, that more than anything else I was starting to really annoy them. It was a reminder, just when I needed to give one, of how effective I could be bowling at the body — and against some of the best batters to have ever lived. Six wickets against Australia was the kind of thing I had dreamed about as a boy. It also gave us an outside chance in the game — which we still clung to after having set Australia a fourth-innings target of 201. I wanted more than anything to send Baz into retirement with a famous victory.

Australia began their chase late on day four. I was fielding at forward square leg, looking into the low sun sinking towards the distant alps through the big trees on the western edge of Hagley Park. Baz asked me to warm up; I'd be bowling the next over. Matt Henry finished his second over with a bouncer at Joe Burns. He pulled it hard — and straight at me. I felt the ball strike my left hand near the base of my ring finger and I couldn't quite grasp it. Dropped, ironically, in the exact fielding position where most of my wickets were caught in that game.

I was gutted, and I had other problems, too. Blood was pouring from where the webbing had split between my fourth and fifth fingers. Our physio, Tommy Simsek, ran onto the ground for a look.

'Think that's gonna need stitches, Wags, you'd better come off.'

But Baz had asked me to bowl the next over and now I had a dropped catch to make amends for, too.

'Na, mate, I can't, I'm bowling next. Let's just tape it up.'

I bowled the very next ball that followed my injury. As I struggled through the over, the hand was throbbing with pain and beginning to swell. I knew something was broken, but I had worked that bloody hard to get back into this team, had carried enough drinks across enough continents, and there was no way I was letting go of that ball. I could deal with the pain. I couldn't deal with losing my place. And in my third over, David Warner, hopping across the crease to a short one, could only glove it to BJ behind the stumps. We still had a chance.

The x-ray that evening confirmed a fracture, and I spent an uncomfortable night in a lot of pain. In the morning, Lana and I examined the swollen blob where my left hand would usually be and she asked how on earth I was going to bowl with it. 'I'll get it done,' I said. I wanted to give the team a reminder of the kind of character I was and how much this meant to me.

I had it strapped and tried to ignore the pain as I was called upon to bowl more overs than any other New Zealander that day — 18 in a losing cause. From that perspective, it was in vain — but as a tribute to Baz, a legend of the game to whom I'll be forever grateful for helping me become the player and the man I grew into under his leadership, it was the least I could do. Baz always spoke of his ambition to leave the environment in a better space than when he entered it, and as the curtain drew on his captaincy, it was hard to imagine any other leader who could have transformed the fragmented and unwelcoming team I had walked into in the West Indies into the group of mates who that evening celebrated his career at the Rose & Thistle, his local pub.

Sport was such a big part of my childhood, and from an early age I knew I wanted to be a cricketer.

ABOVE All smiles in Sri Lanka with Chaminda Vaas and Shane Bond — but away from the camera I was experiencing some of the darkest days of my life.

LEFT Soaking up my first test victory with the bowling group at the top of Mount Victoria. It's amazing to think about how much the team culture had changed since those early days.
PHOTOSPORT NZ

LEFT From Affies to the biggest stage. I'll always be grateful for Faf's support and kindness as we grew up together in Pretoria.

BELOW Standing proudly alongside Trent Boult and Tim Southee — great mates with whom I've shared so many great memories both on and off the field. PHOTOSPORT NZ

Celebrating success with the Black Caps: a series victory against India in 2014 (top), when I discovered my true role in our bowling attack; and our World Test Championship win in 2021.
PHOTOSPORT NZ (ABOVE) AND GETTY IMAGES (BELOW)

TOP Pure joy after beating England at the Basin Reserve in 2023. PHOTOSPORT NZ

ABOVE Kane has been such a crucial part of New Zealand's success over the years, and it was a special moment to be at the crease with him to secure another epic test victory against Sri Lanka in 2023. PHOTOSPORT NZ

My family have always been there for me — their support in both the good times and the tough times encourages me to grasp at opportunity with everything I have. Above is Zahli, me, Livie, Lana and Josh. At left is Mark, me, Dad, Mum and David.

ABOVE It meant a lot to take a five-wicket bag against England at Seddon Park in 2019 in front of Lana's parents, Theuns and Erika Koekemoer. They've helped me and Lana in so many ways during my career.

RIGHT With Theuns and Dewaldt during a South Africa trip following the England tour in 2022.

My post-wicket celebrations haven't changed much throughout the years — an energy release that encapsulates everything I've put into life's journey.
PHOTOSPORT NZ (ABOVE) AND GETTY IMAGES (BELOW)

CHAPTER 9:
GOLDEN SUMMER

My first wicket, Zimbabwean Brendan Taylor, was lucky, out bowled as he lashed at a full wide ball that deserved to find the boundary, dragging it a significant distance back onto his stumps. The next 10 I took in that match — my debut for Lancashire and the first game of cricket I played after injuring my hand against Australia — were snared through a synthesis of everything I had become as a bowler. In the first innings, I bowled as a traditional seam-up quick behind openers James Anderson and Kyle Jarvis, pitching it up, swinging it, targeting pads, stumps and outside edges. When we bowled again, on the other side of a 90-run first-innings lead, the Old Trafford pitch had lost its zip, and I reverted to the method I'd been perfecting since India at Eden Park: whack it into the pitch, aim at the body. I took five second-innings wickets to give me 11 for the game, my best first-class match figures. Every ball seemed to be coming out of my hand just as I intended. I felt back to the height of my powers.

Yet I still wasn't quite at peak fitness — I had hardly bowled before arriving, once more, in the north of England — and was using a special splint constructed to protect my injured hand. I could field in it, but I had to remove it to bowl. I could basically ignore the discomfort, especially when, as soon as I walked into the Lancashire dressing room, everything suited me to perfection. As opposed to my experience with Northants, the culture in that Lancashire team was excellent, more akin to the Black Caps, where the guys not only wanted to succeed, they wanted to do it for each other. Plus I knew a good number of the squad: I had played against Jimmy plenty and, as a Zimbabwean test cricketer, Kyle had a long association with Pretoria where I had often run into him. Simon Kerrigan had been a teammate at Ormskirk and South African batter Alviro Petersen was in the Northerns team in which I had made my first-class debut. At the top were skipper Steven Croft and coach Ashley Giles, a man whose approach has rubbed some the wrong way, but whose passion, belief and total commitment to the cause meshed perfectly with my own attitude.

Many of my New Zealand colleagues had followed the Aussie test series with the T20 World Cup — bundled out by England in the semis — and then continued on to the IPL, two competitions I would have loved a crack at. Part of the beauty of the IPL is the chance it gives players to learn from the other cricketers in your squad. County cricket was my equivalent. And there were few people whose advice about how to prise out the last few wickets on a flat Old Trafford wicket offering nothing — Hampshire following on and attempting to bat out for a draw — I'd more readily accept than

Jimmy Anderson's. Just watching him at close quarters was a lesson in how to think a batter out.

Even then, with six or seven prodigious years left to run in his international career, he had a claim to being the greatest fast bowler in English history, a pedestal few would deny him now. Like me, he was always an aggressive opponent on the field, never shy of offering a word or two, and over the years some opponents might have taken his on-field attitude as a mark of the man himself. Share a changing room with him, however, and you soon realise he's a lovely bloke, an international superstar but also the first Lancashire player to sit down and have a beer with me in the hotel bar during our first away match. I would come to realise that although he was arguably the best swing bowler in the world, he was human, too, making mistakes and going through tough times on the cricket field and off it. He worked harder at his craft than anyone else in the game, something he inspired me to emulate.

I would need Jimmy's knowledge. The county game can be a relentless parade of cricket at a level that is the closest to test-match intensity I have played. When I came up against Somerset's Marcus Trescothick, many years after he last played for England and now carrying a little weight around his waist and glasses across his nose, I remember thinking he was one of the hardest batters I had ever bowled to, with an easy answer to absolutely everything I sent him on his way to a century. I had a scare when we played Nottinghamshire and a Harry Gurney bouncer, payback for those I had directed Notts' way during my 11-wicket performance in the opening game, caught me on the back of my neck, below the helmet. Thankfully the blow only left me bruised and shaken. Although I took eight wickets across the game, we lost the traditional Roses fixture against Lancashire's rivals Yorkshire, but we would win a T20 game against the same opponents in front of a full house at Old Trafford. By the end of my stint, I'd played nine County Championship games for Lancashire, taking 32 wickets at 29.3. I was in top shape for the return of test cricket.

The next Black Caps assignment was in Zimbabwe and the squad assembled initially in Pretoria, staying at a hotel across the road from my old stomping ground at Tuks. I arrived a few days before to get in some family time, and Lana dropped me off at the hotel just as the bus pulled up from the airport with the majority of the team. We played an inter-squad game on the main ground at Tuks, where I was very familiar with conditions and used them well, and in our downtime I was able to reprise my role as a tour guide, our presence in my old hometown giving me even more inside knowledge to share.

Through Divan Strydom, an old school friend whose dad managed the local Bulls rugby team, I arranged for an afternoon at Loftus Versfeld. On the way we stopped off at an Adidas outlet store and picked up the jerseys of our Super Rugby teams — Mark Craig and me in Highlanders kit, Timmy in a Chiefs jersey, Matt Henry in the red of the Crusaders — and spent a few hours running around and kicking goals on the hallowed turf. I took Tim and Trent for a tour of my old school, across the road from Loftus, blowing their minds with the excellence of its cricket facilities. It felt good to show the guys a bit of my past, some of the history I was bringing into the Black Caps.

We moved north to Harare. Southern Africa can be a tricky place to tour. The threat of crime is high so you often don't have a huge amount of freedom, which means lots of time locked in the confines of the team environment. If it's not a happy squad, that can be a challenge. But we were all enjoying each other's company, punctuating the cricket with plenty of barbecues, good restaurants and general good times. It was the first instance in my international career when I felt truly happy just to be myself in the Black Caps environment without any of the second-guessing I'd subjected myself to on previous tours, able to focus on the cricket and experiences in front of me. I was confident with my game after my time with Lancs, not to mention all the off-field work I'd been doing, and the philosophy implanted in me after that year on the sidelines — of giving to the group whatever is asked of you, even if it's not what you would have chosen to give — was easily transferred onto the pitch. If the team needed long, gruelling spells of short-pitched bowling, I was more than happy to oblige. I didn't go chasing wickets, just stuck to what the team wanted. If personal success came, so be it, but it was only important if it contributed to winning games of cricket. Under Brendon, and now Kane, who had learned a lot about the art of captaincy from Baz, I became comfortable subordinating my ego to the will of the team.

We warmed up against Zimbabwe A in the capital. I didn't get my hands on the ball much as it was shared among the bowlers in contention for the tests, but when I did, I pushed myself hard. Probably too hard for a warm-up game with a lot of tests to follow, but despite my confidence I still felt I was bowling for my place. We moved to Bulawayo for the first test, and I found I had done enough to edge out Matt Henry and Dougie Bracewell for the third-seamer position. It had been a dry Zimbabwean winter, and the resultantly abrasive Queens Sports Club pitch had scoured from the ball any chance of conventional swing by the time I was brought on to bowl the 13th over, Zimbabwe one wicket down and a partnership brewing between Chamu Chibhabha and Hamilton Masakadza. I bowled full for an over to see if there was any movement, found none, and decided to go short.

It was almost immediately effective. I managed to extract some pace and venom from the middle of the wicket that hadn't been there for my colleagues, Chibhabha tentatively pulling a short ball down the throat of a fielder for my first wicket, and a few balls later I rattled Sean Williams with a bouncer that snuck through his defence to strike his grill. The next ball also got through, hitting the replacement helmet, although I thought it must have come off his bat as the ball ballooned over the grass all the way to midwicket. He was given out and I was just getting warmed up.

In my 11th over — I would bowl 13 straight with a break for lunch — I got one to rise sharply at Sikandar Raza and all he could do was fend it to the fielder installed at leg gully. Three balls later, Regis Chakabva, expecting something short, hung back and wafted at a fuller delivery, edging it to BJ. Graeme Cremer hopped awkwardly as he sparred at the next ball, a chest-high bouncer, inside-edging it onto his body, the ball looping to Henry Nicholls diving forward at short leg. Three wickets in the over, and another five-wicket haul.

Then, after a frustrating 85-run, ninth-wicket partnership between Prince Masvaure and Donald Tiripano finally came to an end, I got number 11 Michael Chinouya with one, angled in from around the wicket, that reversed away to take out off stump. I had bettered my best test-bowling figures at the very next attempt, returning for another two scalps in Zimbabwe's second innings as they tried in vain to make us bat again.

A few days later, in the gap between the first and second tests, we were invited on safari at late Zimbabwean cricket legend Heath

Streak's huge farm. At dusk, we lit a big fire at the top of a hill, watching as the big red African sun sank towards the horizon. In true African fashion, we then returned to Heath's farmhouse for an enormous *braai*. All the protein did me well: another three wickets in the second test, also in Bulawayo, gave me 11 for the series, the most of any bowler and almost double the wickets nabbed by the next best pacer. I had also bowled more overs than any other Black Caps bowler. I was named player of the series.

The tour moved back south of the Limpopo River to Durban, where we would meet South Africa at the historic cricket ground of Kingsmead. Lana's brother lived in Durban, and both Lana's family and mine converged at his home a few days before the test for a barbecue in the beautiful weather. After the disappointment in Cape Town in early 2013, I was excited to finally play test cricket with my parents in the crowd for the first time in my life.

We bowled first after losing the toss, chipping away with regular wickets. I got JP Duminy, the same man who had been my first wicket for the Titans, top-edging a pull to fine leg. My old man was sitting next to Faf's dad in the stands, so the next wicket — du Plessis caught by a Kane screamer in the gully — gave him some bragging rights as they reminisced about the old days. I later had Vernon Philander caught at mid-off as South Africa posted 263. We got to 15 for two in reply before rain washed out the remainder of the second day — and then, after a thunderstorm rolled off the Indian Ocean to dump 65mm of rain on the ground overnight, the remainder of the game. The following three days of Durban sun were not enough to undo the damage done to the recently relaid surface. It was bizarre to arrive at a cricket ground bathed in sunshine for three consecutive days to be told there would be no play. We moved over the Drakensberg mountains and onto the highveld: back to Pretoria, where the two-match series would now be decided.

Centurion, the cricket ground that was the focal point of my boyhood dreams. I was desperate to be selected, picturing the scene: *boerewors* spitting on the grills, its scent drifting across the grass; beer flowing on the banks; snatches of Afrikaans breaking out of the general crowd murmur to reach me at my fine-leg station, all of it so familiar yet now belonging to a long-ago world. Things that once would've been commonplace struck me as entirely surreal, like bowling in the Centurion nets with my brother David, who had knocked off early from his job nearby, watching us train in the bright sunlight.

It was great being back in Pretoria, but things were about to take a turn for the worse. In our training run the day before the test, something felt off, my back stiffening throughout the net session into outright pain by the time it was over. I asked the physio for a couple of Panadol, claiming a headache. I didn't want anyone to have any suspicion that I might not be fit to play.

We drove back to the hotel, I got the nod for the game, and my old mate Kruger van Wyk was on hand to speak at the capping function, after which I retired to my room to try every stretch I could think of to relieve the malevolent ball of pain and pressure that showed no sign of abating throughout the evening. I popped a few more Panadol before bed in the hope my back would right itself overnight.

No such luck. I woke up in more pain than when I had fallen asleep, suffering through breakfast in an unnaturally upright position as I still tried to keep it a secret. In the dressing room, I sat with one hand balled into a fist and pressed into this spot in my back, the only thing that seemed to relieve the pain, and I was within a hair's

breadth of getting out of my seat, walking over to Kane and Hess and telling them something wasn't right, that maybe I should sit this one out. But I thought I should at least see if I could get through the warm-up.

It was sore and tight as I struggled through my routine, but when I looked up to see my whole family in the stands, I knew in an instant that I wasn't giving away the chance to play what, in some ways, 23 tests into my career, would be my first at home. I prayed, asking God to help get me through the game, and silently hoped we'd be batting first. Then Kane won the toss and decided to bowl and I just told myself to find a way. *Dig deep. Remember the lessons from the broken hand in Christchurch. Ignore the pain.* If this was to be my last test match, if I was about to completely ruin my back, so be it. At least I would've played a test at Centurion with my family watching on.

I put on my bowling boots and walked out to sing the anthem, test-match nerves fizzing throughout my body. And as soon as I started to jog on the Centurion earth the pain melted away in the white heat of adrenaline. It was like magic, and just as well. We started nicely, creating pressure and chances, but the edges didn't carry and the raised fingers were all overturned on review. When I came on to bowl the 21st over, the Jekyll-and-Hyde pairing of Stephen Cook and Quinton de Kock had put on 73 for no loss.

I was expecting abuse from the Centurion crowd, but instead they were full of support as I worked into my spell. The openers carried on together until my 10th over — again I toiled through 13 on the trot, with a break for lunch — when de Kock crunched an aerial pull shot, but straight to Trent on the boundary. We still had to graft through that excellent top and middle order — a 50 for Hashim Amla, 88 for JP Duminy, a fantastic unbeaten century from Faf who kept me at bay throughout in revenge for Durban — over almost two full days in the field. I was made to work for 39 overs to earn the emotional five-wicket bag I completed by bowling Vernon Philander through the gate. To do it in front of my family meant the world to me. And if my back was sore, at least now I had 39 reasons why. I could have all the massages I wanted as I waited for my turn to bat.

Dale, Vernon and Kagiso Rabada put us to the sword, Kane and Henry Nicholls offering the only real resistance until I came out to throw my bat around, including one over against Dale when I managed to swat him away for three fours and a six. South Africa, however, had a huge lead, and though we bowled well in their second innings, they declared to set us a target of 400. By now the pitch was treacherous — Rossco was out LBW to Dale to one that hit him on the shin after the previous ball from the same length had sailed through nicely — and we had lost our first four wickets with only seven runs on the board. I remember tapping at the pitch with my bat and nearly dislodging a plate-sized section of its crust. I made three and our innings was only given a spine, and some respectability, by Henry's brave 76. The homecoming didn't have the ending I had hoped for and we travelled home from Centurion on the wrong side of a 204-run loss.

It was arranged that we would leave for our next tour, to India, from Tauranga, where the night before our departure most of the team would celebrate the recent engagement of Trent and his fiancée, Gert. Lana and I flew up from Dunedin, Lana planning to stay a few days before heading back to Dunedin and then later joining me in India. Half of the team seemed to live in and around Tauranga and, as we flew out to India, Gert and the rest of the girls encouraged Lana to stick around for a bit longer. By the time I turned my phone on in Singapore, there was a text from Lana telling me how much she loved life in the Bay of Plenty.

When the following flight landed in India, the next text got straight to the point: 'We're moving here.'

India is a tough, tough place to tour and it was made tougher for us when we lost Tim Southee to an ankle injury before the first test. It meant I took the new ball for the first time in test cricket when the game, in Kanpur, got under way. We bowled first against a merciless batting lineup, in equally merciless heat. In the middle of one spell, I had to sprint, very abruptly, from the field to make use of the facilities — I certainly wasn't the first tourist to India to have eaten something that unsettled my stomach — and got back just in time for the next over.

Even the effort of running back onto the field drenched me in sweat, literally as if I had emerged from a swimming pool. Every inch of our dressing room was covered in boots and gear, the fans whirring incessantly, as we attempted to dry our spare shoes to keep up with all the footwear changes required to give us a precious few minutes of freshness. It's hard to explain how difficult it is to play in heat like that until you've done it, but it was just brutal: I lost four kilograms across a test match we did well to stay in for much of the first two days, before the pitch began turning square and we were washed to defeat on a flood of wickets from Ravichandran Ashwin and Ravindra Jadeja.

If anything, the next test in Kolkata was at least as hot — and India again had first use of the pitch after winning the toss. I took three wickets across a game we'd lose by nearly 200 runs, bowling 35 overs in air so thick with heat and humidity that it was hard to breathe. I walked off the field at one point and felt a massive spasm ripple through my back — perhaps the same unsolved issue that had struck in Pretoria — and I asked physio Vijay Vallabh to pop an acupuncture needle into this hard ball of pain. It was like he had punctured a tyre, the lump almost audibly deflating as sweet relief spread across my shoulders.

Despite all the challenges, I was gutted to be dropped for the next test in Indore. Our batting had been consistently a hundred or so runs short every innings and Jimmy Neesham came in to strengthen it. But after Virat Kohli and Ajinkya Rahane put on a 365-run partnership in the first innings — again, we lost the toss and were made to field — there probably wasn't enough strengthening in the world to overcome that. We lost by more than 300 runs, and I went home as the limited-overs segment of the tour began.

I was back to play two rounds of the Plunket Shield — eight wickets against Auckland, six against Central Districts — and felt in great form, able to identify the best plan of attack for the state of the game, pitch and ball, and growing ever more confident in my ability to deliver the more I did it at test level against the best batters in the world. And then returning to the Black Caps environment to play two tests against the touring Pakistanis was like coming home.

The culture of the team had reached the height at which it would remain for the next few years. There was so much fun and laughter, everyone taking the mickey out of each other and having the mickey taken out of them. We'd developed such tight bonds on and off the field. Our families were friends and there were beginning to be a few kids around the setup. A huge effort was made to welcome new players, and their families, into the Black Caps fold. Also, I felt entirely backed by Kane and Hess, and the environment was such that we were genuinely happier for our teammates' achievements than we were for our own. We were absolutely stoked when someone did well, although no one got too high or too low if a game went well personally or if it went badly. The team was tracking in the right direction and that was all that mattered.

In such an environment, it was no surprise when in the first test all-rounder Colin de Grandhomme — he had forced his way into the team on the back of a first-class season for Auckland that included a monumental unbeaten 144 against Otago when I was powerless to stop him — found immediate success on debut. The first day at Hagley was rained off, but the second dawned clear and cold. Kane finally won a toss and we put Pakistan in, though there was very little work for me to do, Colin having a field day, running through the tourists to take six wickets, Tim and Trent sharing the other four between them. We made an even 200 in reply to Pakistan's 133, and then had to work hard to get through an obdurate stand from Azhar Ali and Babar Azam, which I broke in the 41st over, a short-ball barrage finally inducing Babar to hop across a bouncer and glove it down leg to BJ.

It was my hundredth test wicket, and I became the second-fastest New Zealander, after Sir Richard Hadlee, to reach the milestone. It was my 26th test, but I'd been around the team so long that it didn't feel like I'd reached the century particularly quickly. I'm not someone who puts much importance on these statistical landmarks — for me, if I start aiming for a number, it seems to cloud my processes and ultimately my performance — so I was mostly happy to get a distraction out of the way. Much more important was the win, achieved with my contribution of two more short-ball wickets — including an absolute snorter to get rid of the legendary Younis Khan, who could only fend it off his gloves to the keeper.

We were in control of the following game in Hamilton for the first three innings, before a fourth-innings opening partnership between Sami Aslam and Azhar — in which the two batted throughout almost the entirety of the first two sessions of day five — made a draw the most likely outcome, with an outside chance of Pakistan chasing the remaining runs to square the series.

At tea, someone — either Kane or Ross — was talking about how we had to keep believing. We now had a history to draw on of winning from these sorts of positions. We'd routed the West Indies for 103 in their second innings at this ground a few years before. I thought about the perseverance we needed to beat India at Eden Park. Once we started taking wickets, we knew we could get on a roll. Hess fired us up with some strong words, and once we got back out there things just started happening. All five bowlers chipped in with wickets as Pakistan went from 181 for two to 230 all out over the course of 20 overs of sustained pressure. The last three fell to me. That was the series two–nil. Despite our troubles in India — probably the most difficult place in the world to sneak a series win — we were starting to feel incredibly hard to get the better of in our own conditions.

Not all was well with the Otago team I returned to for the Super Smash that season. I had been instrumental in getting Rob Walter — who since I had last worked with him, on that South African Academy tour of Bangladesh, had been with the Titans and the South African national team — to come over. So far, though, his tenure hadn't improved the slump in Otago's fortunes, and we'd finish last in all three competitions, my contribution limited by international duty in all but the shortest format.

I have a lot of respect for Rob, and I pushed hard for him to join the Otago setup, but in that first season I thought he was perhaps trying to graft South African attitudes and mindsets into this new context, and it wasn't working. It was something I'd had to learn in my early days in Dunedin, too. In the Titans setup, for example, a coach could rely on the fact that well-paid members of the squad, for whom cricket was everything, could be at their beck and call every day. In Otago, where guys might've had second jobs or study on the side, or perhaps just needed to pick the kids up from school, it didn't work for the coach to change a practice session from morning to afternoon at the last minute. The success Rob would have with Otago after I moved on was a measure, I think, of how he was able to adapt. I was the leading Otago bowler in that disappointing T20 campaign, snaring nine wickets at an economy rate under eight. The changing of the guard, however, was starting to help build Lana's case for a move north.

If that final Pakistan test entrenched our ability to summon a win from almost anywhere, the next, against Bangladesh in Wellington, absolutely confirmed it. We turned up on the first morning to a Basin Reserve wicket that was eye-wateringly green, but the grass was so thick we thought it might offer easy tennis-ball-like bounce. It was a good toss to lose — you could potentially make yourself look very silly if you chose to bat first on something so vibrant — so naturally Kane won it, and we put them in. Our fears were confirmed when Shakib Al Hasan and Mushfiqur Rahim came together early on day two and batted for nearly the rest of it, combining to produce a 359-run partnership.

I sent down the most overs, 44, I would ever bowl in an innings, many of them consisting mainly of short-pitched effort balls. The outfield was heavy and I often ran into the Wellington wind, but I ended the innings with four wickets. The struggle to get up the morning after was real, rocking out of bed onto blistered feet, my toenails blue-black, a cut on the underside of my foot barely held together by surgical glue, stinging in the shower. Every bit of pain that my mind had refused to acknowledge during my spell came back to haunt my muscles. Thankfully Tom Latham, with 177, led a reply that gave me the best part of two days with my feet up.

It left a lot of cricket to squeeze into the final day. I contributed another 15 overs and another two wickets as we bundled them out for 160, which gave us nearly two sessions in which to chase 217 for the win. No team had ever conceded more than 595 in the first innings and won the test. But thanks to a quick century from Kane, we did it with time to spare. In doing so, we broke a record that had stood since the 19th century. It was a testament to the character and belief we had built, and our experience to understand that sometimes in test cricket you might need to wait four days before conditions allow you to really strike: but then you have to strike as hard as you can.

We moved to Christchurch, where conditions were more to our liking and we condemned our visitors to a nine-wicket loss, only soured for me by a run out whereby I had grounded my bat behind the line but then as I continued past the popping crease the ball hit the stumps at an exact moment when both feet and my bat happened to be in the air. I was feeling good on 26, having spent well over an hour in the middle, but I was out, the umpires even admitting to me later that it was a stupid law. Thankfully, it would soon be changed.

I had time for one Ford Trophy game for Otago — two wickets in a win against Auckland — before three tests against the touring South Africans would complete my home summer of cricket.

Dale Steyn was nursing a shoulder injury and didn't tour, but in Kagiso Rabada, Morne Morkel and Vernon Philander, the Proteas still had one of the most potent seam-bowling attacks going around. Our thinking was, with Jeetan Patel and Mitchell Santner available, to prepare a Dunedin wicket on which spin could play a big role. It meant there was only room for two specialist seamers and, given my familiarity with the University Oval conditions, it was Timmy who missed out — extremely rough given he had taken a five-wicket haul in a player-of-the-game performance in the previous test against Bangladesh. I knew from experience how tough these situations were for the player not selected, and the wicket — as it turned out —

was actually quite damp with enough grass on it that Tim would've been a handy addition.

I bowled pretty well in the opening role, coming back in my second spell to get Hashim Amla with a perfect inswinger that found the gap between bat and pad and knocked over his stumps — up there with the best balls I've ever bowled. A few deliveries later I got JP Duminy with a short one and, much later, another one accounted for Dean Elgar, but not before he had scored 140 out of the South African total of 308. Kane anchored our reply — he made 130 in our score of 341 — and then we had South Africa 224 for six when bad light ended play. We thought we had a chance to push for victory on day five. Until we opened the curtains: it was a dismal Dunedin day on which no play was possible.

We were soundly beaten in Wellington, where we failed to combat the spin of Keshav Maharaj and JP, and moved to Hamilton. There was a bit of a break between tests and as a group we felt we needed to get away from cricket and try to put some distance between us and those two disappointing results. We settled on an evening at Waikato Stud, an institution that racing-mad Baz had a connection with. We caught up with Brendon, shot a few clay pigeons and just had a great time hanging out with each other as mates away from the game.

I felt we were mentally refreshed heading to Seddon Park for the last game of the series, although both Tim and Trent were injured so Matt Henry came back into the team — with immediate success. He took four wickets and I got three as South Africa made 314, which we bettered when Kane — who else? — anchored our 489 with 176. At the end of day four, we had the Proteas five wickets down and still nearly 100 runs short of making us bat again. They were under huge pressure. Until dawn revealed black clouds massed above and thunderstorms rumbling throughout the day. We got to the ground, but it was one of those days when I just knew there was no chance of play. Without rain in that series, there is every chance we could've found ourselves the two–one winners and become the first New Zealand team to take a test series from South Africa. As it was, we lost. Unfortunately, that's how sport goes sometimes.

It was a frustrating way to end what had been an intense period of test cricket, from Bulawayo to Hamilton. I'd played 13 games and taken 56 wickets at 24.25. It was enough for me to be named — to my absolute surprise — as the New Zealand Test Player of the Year at the NZC awards night. I was lost for words, almost embarrassed by the accolade, but it was a hell of a way to conclude what had been a golden summer.

CHAPTER 10:
LEAVING TOWN

The call came from Ireland. The one-day squad, already shorn of its IPL players for this low-key tri-series — featuring New Zealand, the hosts and Bangladesh — had been further weakened by injury. I was on the other side of the Irish Sea playing for Essex, and when Hess got in touch, asking if I was available, I jumped at the chance. I'd never given up my ambitions in the white-ball game, and it felt like this might be my last opportunity.

I wanted a chance to show how well I could perform at the international level in white-ball cricket, a chance I sometimes thought I'd been unfairly denied. It seemed to me that bowlers were being given test-match opportunities on the back of breakout white-ball performances, but that it was a one-way road. We played test cricket so much less frequently — it was almost as if my name was forgotten for half the year. Sometimes, it felt like I was being punished for the success of the test-match method I had become known for — as if no one could see that, beyond it, I had plenty of other weapons.

The short-ball tactics I had been using in test cricket didn't translate that well to the one-day game. The margins for error, especially around leg-side wides and the number of fielders with which you could protect the boundary, were too small. But in domestic cricket, over many seasons with Otago, I had built a good record based on swinging the ball up the top and nailing yorkers and variations at the death.

As my career progressed, I became more and more desperate. I would head into a limited-overs game with the mindset that I needed to do something spectacular for the selectors to take notice, instead of the calmer, process-driven way I approached test cricket, where I knew if I put the team first the wickets column would eventually fill itself. I never thought I was going to take Tim or Trent's spot, but I wanted to be an option for the occasions when they were unavailable, as they were in Ireland. If everything went well, I hoped — though I hardly allowed myself to think about it — the 2019 Cricket World Cup was on the horizon. I jumped on a plane as quickly as possible to get over to Ireland and join the squad.

My initial conversations with Hess made it sound as if there was a decent chance I could get a game. Which made the moment I realised I wasn't going to play, when the injury issues in the squad resolved themselves, pretty tough to take. Hess asked if I wanted to stick around and carry drinks for the Black Caps or head back to Essex. 'It's entirely up to you,' he said, 'but if you want to play cricket, it's probably best you go.'

I returned to Essex feeling as if my dreams of playing World Cup cricket were over, and it hurt. I regret never sitting down with Baz,

Hess or Kane and just getting it out into the open. There was such a culture of openness and good communication that I don't really even know what stopped me, other than not wanting to be seen to be pleading my case when I thought my performances would be good enough to do the talking for me.

Only featuring in one format had other ramifications, too: despite being the reigning New Zealand test player of the year, when the next contract list came out, I actually found I had dropped a position, meaning a little bit less money — but more importantly I couldn't help but feel that my success in the most prestigious format of the game was being undervalued. In the limited-overs era of international cricket, only England's Mark Butcher has played more tests than I have — 71 — without playing a single white-ball international.

My Irish excursion meant I missed two Royal London One-Day Cup games — a competition, ironically, in which I did really well, ending near the top of the wicket-taking charts with 14 at a shade over 25 as we topped our group but were bundled out by the eventual champions, Nottinghamshire, in the semifinals. Originally I was contracted with Essex to play just the first half of the County Championship, the Royal London One-Day Cup and then half of the T20 Blast before Pakistan quick Mohammad Amir would step into my shoes. But we had done so well that they asked me to come back for the end of the County Championship to help secure the title, which we did in the very first game of my return, against Warwickshire at Edgbaston.

My words can't express how much it meant to win the County Championship, a competition that has run since 1890. For someone who is completely besotted with everything about cricket, the history and tradition of the County Championship represented something you find nowhere else in the game. Essex had last won the title 25 years previously, and to see how deeply our victory moved my teammates was immensely special. For me, one of the best things about cricket has always been the people you meet along the way, the camaraderie of the dressing room. Essex, in the shadow of richer and more famous rivals, reminded me of the Black Caps — perhaps short a buck or two, but comprised of a really solid bunch of guys who would do anything for each other and for the team, always finding a way to compete with the bigger kids on the block.

After that, it was back to Dunedin and an Otago side that couldn't have been more of a contrast. Rob Nicol, the former Black Caps all-rounder, had signed up in the off-season to come down and captain the team. He had a keen interest in psychology and tried to import some of those lessons into a dressing room that, I felt, thrived on a simple approach. In the best sides I played in, it was all about working for each other, and trying to have fun together on and off the field. If you went through your processes, the results took care of themselves. I didn't think we needed fancy theories.

Other things about my situation grated, also. Two days after arriving back from England, still intensely jet-lagged, I was asked to get down to Alexandra for a warm-up game when what would've been best for me and my body was a few more days of rest and some time with Lana. Later, when we lost a Plunket Shield game against Wellington within a couple of days, I wasn't allowed to pay for new flights to get back to Dunedin early — as had previously been the protocol, giving guys a bit more time with their families if they needed it — and instead we were told to stay and train as a team in the capital.

In that game against Wellington, we employed one field where there was a deep point and a close-in catcher, but almost no one else was in front of the wicket on the off side. Even the batter, Michael Papps, was laughing as he stole runs with ease. I spoke up to ask why we couldn't just back our skills and go with a conventional field, and Rob and I had a bit of a back-and-forth out in the middle. It became clear that Rob, who I always respected as a cricketer and an opponent, had very different ideas to me about how a team should be run.

In isolation, most of these incidents were small things, but that season when I looked around at the faces in the Otago dressing room, I found myself realising that I'd been there longer than almost all of them. Maybe it was time for a change. For me, and for the province.

It was a relief to get back into the Black Caps squad, where none of those issues existed, for the 2017/18 summer of international cricket. First up, the West Indies at the Basin Reserve, which was the first test I played with new inner soles in my boots.

I hate playing with new gear — once I find a pair of bowling boots that work for me, I try to have as many pairs of them as I possibly can. You never know the effect a slightly higher heel or a harder sole might have on a knee, hip or back once it has been pounded into the hard pitch 250 times throughout two days in the field. But a worsening Morton's neuroma — a thickening of the tissue surrounding a nerve in my foot, causing a pins-and-needles numbness in my toes and a burning pain in the ball of my foot — forced me to try inner soles that offered more for my arches in the hope that it would relieve some of the pressure.

We bowled first. And as soon as I came on to bowl the 18th over, the opening partnership as yet unbroken, my rhythm felt horrible. *These bloody inner soles.* I wanted to rip them out, get the old ones back in and just deal with the pain in my foot. It was becoming a distraction. Kieran Powell hit me for a crisp straight drive.

In the past — for example, that Sri Lanka test in Christchurch that ushered in a long spell on the sideline — my insecurities around my place in the team made things worse, bad rhythm turning awful as panic mounted. But now, thanks to a foundation of security and backing from the team over the past few years, I was able to empty my mind and stop the rot. *Ignore it. Go back to that fundamental hammered into me as a schoolboy. Control the controllables. Forget about the discomfort. Just bowl.* I took a deep breath and came back to the logic on which my success had been built: if Trent was unable to find much movement on a spicy-looking Wellington wicket, why expect to find it myself? Third slip moved to leg gully. Time to go short.

A chest-high bouncer, which Kraigg Brathwaite tried to steer behind leg on the on side, got too big for him. It lobbed from his bat to Henry Nicholls, under the helmet at short leg, for an easy catch. An over or two later, another one — climbing venomously off the pitch straight towards left-handed Shimron Hetmyer's chin — caught his glove as he tried to duck away from the danger. The ball flew to second slip, a wicket that ended the morning session.

After lunch, things got even better. Shai Hope edged a length ball just outside leg stump through to Tom Blundell, on debut for the injured BJ, behind the wickets. The first ball of my next over, Sunil Ambris trod on his stumps. I was on a hat trick, which wouldn't come to be, but it wasn't long before Roston Chase guided another leg-side short ball straight to Jeet Raval at a fine leg gully, where Kane had just positioned him. Five-for, and the West Indies in all sorts of trouble at 97 for six.

Jason Holder, their captain and the last man who could do a lot of damage with the bat, was next, and as I walked back to my mark I thought I'd try something different. *Jason is a tall guy. He'll probably be hanging back for a bouncer. Let's try to get under his bat with a yorker.* The field was set for the short ball and if I missed my length, there was no mid-off to protect the straight boundary. But I had earned the right to have a go.

It was the perfect bluff. The ball came out just as I had hoped — fast, narrowly evading the descending toe of Jason's bat, crashing into the base of off stump. I was on a hat trick for the second time in the innings. Last man in Shannon Gabriel hung around for 35 deliveries, but there was no way anyone was getting the ball out of my hand — and eventually he parried a short one into the slip cordon. I'd bowled 14.4 overs on the trot, conceded 39 runs and taken seven wickets. My best-ever figures. It put us well on the way to an innings victory — and another limo trip up Mount Victoria.

The next game was in Hamilton, and I took five scalps in a comfortable win, where the wickets were shared fairly evenly among our attack. At that time, we talked a lot as a bowling group about being relentless, of there being no easy overs against us. Over the years, we'd been taught some valuable lessons by some excellent attacks that had our batters hoping for respite that never came.

We didn't have the pace of Dale Steyn and Morne Morkel, but we felt we could make things just as difficult for the opposition. While me, Tim and Trent won most of the accolades, I always thought Colin de Grandhomme and Mitch Santner were equally important pieces of the puzzle, both bowling long dry spells that allowed the frontline to rest — and often, crucially, holding up the into-the-wind end just before the new ball became available, allowing me a down-wind spell to try and blast out a wicket so Tim and Trent could return against a fresh batter. The way we operated as a unit, with clear roles that complemented each other, became an important part of our strategy and an enormous aspect of my personal success within it.

After the West Indies series, I returned to Dunedin where the change in format to the Super Smash had done nothing to paper over the issues I felt existed in the Otago environment. Before my first game back, I was told to prepare to bowl the last over of the powerplay and three overs at the death, a difficult T20 role I was happy to perform. But immediately before we took the field against Canterbury, Rob Nicol told me I'd be taking the new ball, a role that I was also happy to do, but that I hadn't spent any of the past few days training towards. I didn't take a wicket and we lost.

Lana's parents had come over from South Africa for Christmas that year, the first time they had visited New Zealand, and early in the new year they were all set to watch me play against Northern Districts at University Oval — until Rob called me on the morning of the game and told me I'd been dropped, telling me I was welcome to stay away from the ground and spend time with family. When I pressed, he couldn't give me a straight answer as to why I wasn't playing — but I insisted on coming to run drinks and help the team where I could.

When I ran into Graeme Aldridge, the former Northern Districts pacer who had moved onto the coaching team, he asked why I wasn't playing. I just had to shrug my shoulders.

'I honestly don't know,' I said.

'Have you ever thought about Northern Districts?' he asked.

'I'd come tomorrow,' I said, my frustration no doubt clear to see.

My disagreements with the direction in which Otago were heading was one aspect, but there were plenty of positive reasons to shift north, too. Lana loved it, and many of our good friends, like the Boults, the Williamsons and the de Grandhommes, lived in the area. There was the warmer weather, which my Pretoria-bred bones appreciated. I also loved bowling at Bay Oval, and if it meant I could train with, and learn from, Trent and Tim, who both played their domestic cricket for Northern Districts, that could only help my own bowling in the long term.

In hindsight, I had perhaps become too comfortable at Otago — in a new team I'd have to push myself to make sure, firstly, that I was even selected. I had no laurels to rest on. So Lana and I started making a few trips up to scope out property, with Trent our permanent eyes on the ground checking out open homes on our behalf. Trent also connected us with a local building company, and through that relationship we were given the opportunity to intercept a beachfront house in Pāpāmoa that had originally been intended as a showhome. It was perfect. We would move north at the end of the summer.

Despite the shift, there was some talk with Otago Cricket of me continuing to represent them. But, in the end, it was mutually decided that we part ways. That meant the next two Plunket Shield games would be my last for a province that meant so much to me, the team that plucked a naive South African boy out of his malaise and put him on the road to achieving his dreams.

No one in the team knew it was my last match, as we narrowly lost to Wellington at University Oval, and I remember the night of the final day — over dinner and a glass of wine with Lana in the Mosgiel house we'd bought together — as a mixture of emotion. Sadness, of course, and gratitude. We were also excited about the new possibilities opening up before us. Dunedin had felt like home — the streets here definitely had names now — but it also felt like the right time to leave.

I played 63 first-class games for Otago, the eighth-most in the history of the province, taking 277 wickets at 26.37. In the 50-over format, I took 103 wickets at 27.26 in my 62 games, the same number of times I represented Otago in T20 cricket, in which I nabbed 67 wickets. I will always be enormously thankful to Otago Cricket, and will always treasure the city in which I grew to feel like a New Zealander. I hope those wickets — and the passion behind every one of them — helped to repay some of the debt I owed.

I felt like I was starting the international summer again when the last test matches, against England, rolled around in March. Many of the other guys in the group — Tim and Trent, for example — had been in and around the squad for the limited-overs segment of the West Indies tour following the tests, eight white-ball matches against Pakistan, a T20 tri-series against Australia and England, and a one-day series against the latter that preceded the two tests.

For me, it was more than three months since I had last played for the Black Caps by the time I laced up my boots against England at Eden Park before the first day–night test match ever played in New Zealand. Because of that wait, I was more nervous than usual as I spent the morning killing time in central Auckland, going out for coffee and chilling in Boulty's hotel room, listening to music. I had my customary horrible Auckland net session, but tried to put it out of my mind as the afternoon approached. We won the toss, bowled first, and I walked onto the park stoked to get back into test cricket.

Twenty overs later, I walked off having not bowled a ball, after Trent and Tim, bowling unchanged, had scythed through the England lineup. In the Auckland humidity, both found a reservoir of swing to draw from and the England batters had no chance. It was some of the most unplayably great swing bowling I have ever had the privilege to witness.

With England at 18 for six at one point, we even looked a chance to replace New Zealand as the team with the lowest test score — 26 against the same opponent in 1955, also at Eden Park — but it wasn't quite to be as some lower-order hitting pushed the score to 58, Trent with six wickets, Tim the other four. When we talked about being relentless, about doing what in the past others had done to us, this was exactly what we meant.

I followed the two wicket-takers off the field as the crowd stood to applaud. I was absolutely stoked for them.

'Jeez,' I said, laughing, 'you could've left something for me to do, I've been waiting for some international cricket for that bloody long!'

Rain had a big say over the next couple of days — during one break in play, singer-songwriter Ed Sheeran visited us in the dressing room to talk cricket — but in between it, thanks to centuries from Kane and Henry, we were able to declare with just over four sessions left in the game in which to bowl England out. At the start of day five — thankfully no rain around — they were 132 for three, needing to bat out the day for the draw.

We chipped away throughout the afternoon, but when Chris Woakes joined Ben Stokes at the crease, the two all-rounders dug in deep for the seventh wicket, and they looked like a good chance to hold on. Especially as the second new pink ball of the innings was old and soft by the time the lights started to take effect. It wasn't going to zip around like Tim and Trent would surely have got a nice new one to do. The outfield was heavy from all the rain, and running in to bowl was hard work. Our attack was tiring. Stokesy, despite nursing a sore back, was starting to look like a permanent fixture at the crease and time was slipping away. I knew it was my job to get rid of him.

There are some players — I am one of them — who it is usually best not to interact with on the field. Offering them a few words of advice is likely to get them more fully engaged in the battle, and then you are in trouble. Stokesy is one of those players. But nothing else had worked and I was getting anxious. *Have a dip at him*, something told me.

Not long before this, Ben had got into trouble after getting into a late-night fight one evening in Bristol. He would later be found not guilty of any offence, but when we met in Auckland the matter was still before the English courts. He pulled me for a boundary and then looked up as I completed my follow through.

'I'm coming for you, Wags,' he said.

I decided this was the moment.

'Is that with your fists or what?' I shot back.

I watched him register the wisecrack with a smirk and then laid down a challenge. 'Come on then, show me what you got,' I added, before stomping back to my mark.

I remember Tim telling me to shut it, and I wasn't sure if I had just made a huge mistake. I loved it, though — charging in against one of the most combative cricketers on the planet under the Eden Park lights, some heat in the battle, the crowd oohing and aahing with every successfully defused bouncer, the noise ricocheting around the stadium.

During the next couple of overs, we exchanged a few words, and a few more, as well as a few good stares at each other. The battle,

I've been told, reminded some of the Allan Donald vs Mike Atherton encounter I'd internalised as a youngster. I wanted to break his concentration, to shift his focus from the ball to me in the hope that he might try a shot or two in anger. And it seemed to work when he backed away to a short one, the 188th ball he faced, and tried to uppercut it over the short off-side boundary. He mistimed it, scooping it in the air to point, where Tim took a seriously difficult catch, the pink ball swirling almost invisibly out of the bright lights overhead. I roared with delight, relieved my instincts had proved correct.

That wicket ended the session, and I came out after dinner refreshed and ready to go, this time Chris Woakes the man in my sights. The pink ball was by now so soft he could've headbutted it away with no harm done, but I hammered away as he ducked and swayed.

With the first ball of the 12th over of my spell I found some energy off the pitch, the ball seeming to hit BJ's gloves just a little bit harder. During those long, hard spells, you need to find a way to keep pushing and sometimes it's as simple as convincing yourself you've found something that wasn't there before. *This is it*, I thought, putting my all into a bouncer that rushed Chris. He'd resisted for almost three hours, but all he could do with this one was almost involuntarily raise his bat in front of his face, the ball looping from his gloves to Henry at short leg. Again I roared, Eden Park roaring back at me.

The next over, Todd Astle had Jimmy Anderson caught to complete the victory. How sweet to beat the English at Eden Park after they escaped by the skin of their teeth when we last met here in 2013.

England were desperate to avenge the loss when we got to

Christchurch. And they looked pretty good to do so when, on the first two balls of day five — on which we were 40-odd runs into a chase of 382 — Stuart Broad dismissed Jeet Raval and then Kane. It looked for all money that Broady would go on another of his famous wicket sprees. But thanks in large part to Tommy Latham's effort — in the middle for nearly five hours for his 83 — when I came to the crease at number nine, ahead of Tim who had gone down with a virus, to join Ish Sodhi, we still had a chance of escaping with a draw.

Before I came out to bat, the fact that we hadn't beaten England in a series in New Zealand since 1984 was being discussed on the TV coverage. It was ridiculous, I thought, that this hadn't happened in my lifetime, and it hardened into resolution: *It doesn't matter how many bouncers I wear on the body, we have to draw this game.*

Ish and I are good mates and as I joined him in the middle he flashed me a huge smile.

'We're going to do something special here today,' I said.

'Yes, we are,' he replied, his face lighting up again to reveal his fang-like canines.

'That's it, bro,' I said. 'I want to keep seeing those.'

My batting had been a source of personal frustration for a long time. I always thought my technique was pretty solid, but I tended to put too much pressure on myself, thinking I needed to do something incredible just to be given a shot one or two places up the order. And, as always when I start to put that kind of expectation on myself rather than focus on the little things in front of me, I'm doomed not to reach what I consider to be my potential. Here was a chance, however, to finally contribute something special with the bat in hand.

I enjoy playing my shots, taking on the short balls I know are coming my way in retribution, but I had to put that away: time, not runs, was the only currency that mattered. I simplified my technique, covering my stumps, trying to leave everything that didn't threaten them, and if need be taking the short stuff on my body. It was the last game of the season, so if I got injured it wasn't the end of the world.

Ish and I kept encouraging each other throughout, even if I had a few choice words with him when he edged an expansive drive over the slips or swept against the spin out of the rough. He was the senior batting partner and had already been at the crease for an age when I joined him, but I just wanted the draw that much. At one point Ish told me he was struggling against the pace of Mark Wood and I was having trouble with spin, so we agreed to take an end each. It worked until England realised our plan and started getting creative with their bowling changes to unsettle our rhythm, but it brought us five or six overs of relative comfort.

The close-in fielders heaped on the pressure. A Broady short ball hit me on the finger and I called for the physio. A chorus of English accents started chirping: 'I thought you were a tough guy, look at you calling for a physio.' I milked it a bit, trying to take valuable seconds out of the game. A few balls later, another short one deflected off my helmet after glancing off my shoulder: another chance to soak up a minute or two as a replacement helmet had to be brought on. *Keep fighting.*

England had their tricks, too. Ish was still putting anything really loose to the boundary, but the English support staff posted themselves around the ground beyond the rope so they could fire it straight back to the bowler and save crucial seconds. The cluster of close-in fielders moved ever closer, Joe Root down on his knees at the edge of the pitch, Alastair Cook, my Essex colleague, trying to get in my head about my upcoming stint with the county team, the sun sinking towards the Southern Alps. 'It's getting pretty dark out here,' I kept saying to the umpires, and eventually Marais Erasmus, consulting his light meter, relented, telling me that the 125th over, to be bowled by Joe, was probably going to be the last. I felt the weight lift from my shoulders. But it was the worst thing he could've said to me.

Sure enough, the fourth ball of the over — the 103rd I had faced — brushed the inside edge of my bat as I stretched forward to defend, ballooning off my pad and into the hands of silly point. England appealed and I was given out LBW. I knew I *was* out, but that it wasn't leg before — and that reviewing the original decision and getting to the bottom of exactly *how* I was out would take up some more time. When I'd last seen Tim, he looked like he was on his deathbed. For all I knew, there was only Trent to come. *Every second counts.*

There were enough deliveries left in the over that we could still lose the game, but at least — as third umpire Paul Reiffel went methodically through the process — I hoped my review would absolutely ensure this over was the last. When I was eventually given out, as I knew I would be, I left the field gutted not to have been there at the end. I walked back to the pavilion expecting to see Trent emerge, but there was Tim, looking as pale as I've ever seen a human, and I wished him luck as I passed. *Oh my word, how are you going to do this?* I thought. But before I reached the changing room, a huge yell erupted. It was BJ, Tommy, Trent and Henry, and they mobbed me. By the time Tim got to the middle, the umpires had called it. We had saved the game and won the series. I walked back down the tunnel to meet Ish on the edge of the field. 'We fricken did it,' I said, as we hugged. He gave me a big smile, a replica of the one he'd welcomed me to the middle with a few hours earlier.

When we got our phones back after the game there were, as

usual, messages of congratulations from my folks, including, as usual, something cheeky from my dad along the lines of: 'Congratulations for saving the game! But next time try and be there at the very end, okay?'

Lana and I planned to drive to Pāpāmoa after that test — Lana had already packed our ute with the essentials we thought we'd need before the rest of our belongings arrived — but I was ruined. The long season, and that last innings, had taken its toll. I couldn't face two days cramped in a car, so we arranged to have the ute shipped up, while Lana, myself and Blake, the golden retriever who had joined our family, would fly.

Unfortunately, on the weekend of the move, a huge storm descended on the country. When our first flight arrived at 9am to transit in Wellington, Lana and I watched Blake being loaded onto the Tauranga flight — and then, very promptly, being unloaded. I looked at the screen. Flight cancelled. Blake eventually trundled off the conveyor belt, going absolutely nuts in the airport, and we were told the next available flight wasn't until the evening.

What the hell am I going to do with a dog in Wellington Airport for a day? The first thing was to take her outside to use the facilities on the nearest patch of grass I could find. It was a humbling moment, as someone shouted 'It's Neil Wagner!' from a passing car. A few days earlier, I was in the middle of Hagley Oval, helping secure a famous result for the Black Caps. Now I was standing in the driving Wellington rain, while my dog did an enormous shit, and I realised, with a sinking sense of dismay, that I had nothing on hand to deal with the situation. I ran into the nearby service station and asked for a disposable coffee cup, which I tried to make suffice as the rain soaked through my clothes — a reminder never to get too high or too low, no matter what life sends your way.

Eventually, Lana and I boarded a flight north via Auckland with Blake on a direct flight to Tauranga — with the promise that Gert, now Trent's wife, would be there to meet the dog. Everything was delayed, but thankfully we arrived in Tauranga at the same time as poor bedraggled Blake. Gert and Sarah, Kane's partner, met the three of us at our new house with a homecooked meal. The ute, packed with the essentials we needed until the moving truck arrived, was also delayed by the storm, so we spent a week camping in our new house, sleeping on a blow-up mattress and tracking the progress of our possessions. In the end, the ute didn't arrive until after the moving truck got there. Not quite the restful time I'd wanted before my next assignment with Essex began, but nothing could diminish the joy of waking up each morning to waves crashing on the beach a stone's throw away, the excitement of another of life's chapters beginning with Lana beside me.

CHAPTER 11:
CHANGING TIMES

It felt like it had been a long season, so I only signed up to play three first-class games for Essex in the County Championship for the 2018 season, to go with eight matches in the Royal London One-Day Cup — we were beaten in the quarterfinals — and a handful of T20 games. In the midst of that cricket, it was news from home that hit hard.

I received a text from Hess. He was stepping down as Black Caps coach with immediate effect. It came out of the blue. Hess had been incredibly important in my career and my life — by seeing enough potential in me to bring me out to New Zealand in the first place, and then by shepherding my career through its fits and starts at Otago and eventually into the Black Caps, where we

reunited. It was under his guidance that I had found success at the international level. It felt strange to think our careers were about to go their separate ways.

Hess wasn't a coach who, for me, offered a huge amount of technical insight, but he was brilliant at instilling belief, at recognising the individual psychological and emotional needs of each of his players, of getting the right people involved and, above all, of clear communication that left you in no doubt about your on-field role. That took the sting out of those times when it was decided the team needed to go in another direction. The biggest testament to what he achieved — alongside first Baz, then Kane — was that he built a culture so strong it would last for years after he left.

And strong enough that his successor, eventually revealed to be Gary Stead, would need to adapt himself to the culture we had already established rather than trying to put too much of his own stamp on it.

When I returned from England — in the meantime, Lana had turned our Pāpāmoa house into a home — one of the first points of business was a meeting with Steady in Tauranga to talk through where I was in my career at the age of 32, and where I still wanted to go.

Gary told me I would be his first-picked bowler in the team, which on one level was nice to hear — a boost to the ego — but on another it came as a surprise. Rankings were not the way this team had learned to speak to each other. There was no hierarchy, merely elements of the whole. Everyone had a role to play. It was an indication that he had a little way to go in his integration into our way of doing things, which to his credit he managed in the coming years as we maintained a high level of performance on the field.

Steady's first tour was of the UAE in November 2018, where the

Pakistan team had just beaten the visiting Australians in a test series. Tim dropped out of the side for the first game in Abu Dhabi and Ajaz Patel made his debut. We won the toss and batted, but made a hash of it, posting just 153. Pakistan replied with 227, an innings to which I contributed a single scalp — of Yasir Shah, my 150th test wicket — from 18 overs of toil. We managed much better the second time around, thanks largely to a crucial 112-run partnership between Henry and BJ that dragged our score to 249, leaving Pakistan a target of 176, which they began late on day three.

By the time play started on the fourth morning, they had already chipped 37 runs from the chase for the loss of no wickets. Ajaz and Ish got things going for us in the morning — three first-session wickets between them — before Asad Shafiq joined the resolute Azhar Ali and put the chase back on track. I didn't bowl until the 34th over, immediately going short, pushing Asad back in his crease, before instinct told me to give him a full wide one, which he nibbled at and nicked. That was lunch. On the other side of it, we needed six wickets, Pakistan just 46 runs.

The current of belief that ran through the team was evident again as we sat down to eat — we'd won from difficult positions before. We thought, *If we just fight hard here, calmly go about our processes and take it as deep as possible, there's no telling what the pressure might do to Pakistan.*

Back on the field, I entered a kind of trance — the zone, again — where I didn't really see or acknowledge that a diminishing number of runs were required. At the top of my mark, it was just me versus the batter, one of whom, Yasir Shah, I got to fend at a wide full one, nicking it to slip. At the other end, Ajaz applied the pressure, and Pakistan began to wilt, even as the runs required got down to 18, 16, 14. I could feel we had them in trouble.

Lower-order batters, their minds scrambled by the relentlessness with which we came at them, decided to try to bring it down in increments of six — Bilal Asif was bowled attempting to hit across the line. Hasan Ali slogged one high to wide mid-on, where Tim, on the field as a substitute, calmly accepted the high-pressure catch. It left 12 for the last-wicket pairing to get, with Azhar shielding number 11 Mohammad Abbas from the strike. But we gave them nothing and eventually — Ajaz and I were operating unchanged in tandem, another 13-over spell for me — Ajaz got one to grip off the deck, beating Azhar's forward press and striking him in front. We had won by four runs, then the fifth-narrowest test win of all time. We celebrated hard that night in the team room, where the table-tennis table was very soon commandeered for beer pong.

We moved to Dubai, where we lost the toss and were asked to bowl on a slow, low pitch that gave us almost nothing. Pakistan ground out 418 for five declared over the first two baking-hot days, as I bowled 37 gruelling wicketless overs. We were all knackered, perfectly positioned to be the victims of some of the best leg-spin bowling I have ever seen, Yasir twice ripping through us — eight wickets in our first-innings effort of just 90, a further six while we fought hard second time around for 312 — as we sunk to an innings loss.

When I found out I wasn't playing the next game, I was confused, thinking back to that initial meeting with Steady in Tauranga. The two messages didn't seem to align, which was a big change to the communication I was used to with Hess. But we were such a tight team that the personal disappointment of being dropped quickly turned to figuring out how best I could give to the team from the sidelines, passing the time with Ish and Matt Henry playing I Spy or in deep conversation about the nature of God or how to solve the world's problems in between running on drinks and providing support. When we won — on the back of Kane's runs and the wickets of Will Somerville, another debutant — we became the first New Zealand team since 1969 to beat Pakistan in an away series. One of the most pleasing aspects of the series was the way those new to the team — Ajaz and Will — had contributed to our success, empowered by the group's belief in them, knowing they could just be themselves and that, in this environment, that was more than enough.

Coming from the Middle East, the deep green of the Basin Reserve pitch was a sight for sore eyes, but we knew how deceptive that could be, having learned the hard way during Bangladesh's monster first innings on a similarly vibrant Wellington deck a few summers earlier. Still, we thought there was enough there to ask Sri Lanka to bat once we had won the toss. This time, we were right, the conditions exploited brilliantly by Tim — he ran through the top order, finishing with six wickets as we restricted them to 282.

The pitch dried out fast, Tommy Latham making the most of conditions to reach an epic 264 not out, setting up a big total of 578. We thought it would be enough for an innings victory, especially when Tim and Trent reduced Sri Lanka to 13 for three. But then, on a fourth-day pitch that had gone to sleep, we ran into an immovable wall, Kusal Mendis and Angelo Mathews both scoring big hundreds, batting throughout the day without offering even the ghost of a chance. We tried everything, but the two Sri Lankans were equal to it all, prepared to take my short stuff on the body — it was proper, tough test-match batting to save a game, and they were too good for us. Most of the fifth day was washed out by rain, and we moved to Christchurch.

I was marking out my run-up at Hagley on day one when Mark Richardson, the former New Zealand opener turned commentator, on the field for the pitch report, looked at me and said, 'Oh, are you playing?'

'Yeah.'

'I thought they were going to leave you out for this one.'

Bloody typical, I thought, *one innings when things don't go my way and already people think I should be dropped*. It could have been just an offhand comment, but either way it fired me up. That voice of self-doubt, the feeling you have as a professional sportsperson that someone is always coming for your spot, never really goes away, but sometimes you can channel it in the right direction.

I stewed on Mark's words as we lost the toss and batted first, Suranga Lakmal bowling beautifully to restrict us to just 178. There wasn't much for me to do as Sri Lanka replied, Trent taking six wickets — Colin and Tim sharing the other four — to skittle them for just over 100. By now the pitch was starting to flatten and two Cantabrians, Tommy and Henry, both scored big hundreds on their home ground, Colin coming in late to hit a rapid momentum-shifting 71. We declared four wickets down, giving Sri Lanka a basically unattainable target of 660.

Right when the Sri Lankans appeared to be digging in, I got Kusal Mendis caught in the covers for 67, celebrating by raising my finger to my lips in the direction of the commentary box, before the big wicket of Dinesh Chandimal — who had stuck to the pitch like a barnacle for nearly five and a half hours — fell when he could only parry a well-directed bouncer to short leg. Two further wickets helped underline my response to Mark and anyone else who had their doubts about my ability to make winning contributions to the team.

After some time with ND, it was back to the Black Caps as Bangladesh arrived in February 2019 to play three tests. It often feels like cricket fans and the media have a tendency to look down on Bangladesh, but we always found them to be — especially out of all the subcontinent teams — one of the most combative in our own conditions, always ready to take the fight to us. So it was no surprise when Tamim Iqbal came out swinging on the first morning of the series in Hamilton, and Bangladesh got off to a flier.

I didn't bowl until the 17th over, by which stage I'd had to pop off the field for a toilet break, where Steady asked what I thought.

'I feel like we're looking a bit too hard for movement and wickets. We need to go back to creating pressure,' I said, suggesting that a short-ball attack might do the trick. He agreed, and I eventually managed to convince Kane of the same once I was back on the field.

In my first spell, I got Mominul Haque tickling a bouncer to the keeper and then Mohammad Mithun pulling to midwicket. I returned later, blasting out the tail, adding three more short-ball wickets to earn a five-for as we restricted the tourists to 234.

I came in as nightwatchman late on day two after centuries from both openers, with Kane on the way to a double hundred, but the following morning fell three runs short of what would have been a maiden test 50 — which delighted Tim and Trent, with whom there had been some money riding on whether I would get there.

The Bangladesh second innings was notable for the huge partnership between Soumya Sarkar and Mahmudullah, who ingeniously counteracted my short-pitched attack — jumping around the crease and taking on the boundary — to score quick runs. But eventually the deficit was just too big, and even though both made 140s, the second new ball proved decisive. We had gone big enough in our turn at bat to condemn them to an innings defeat.

The next game in Wellington followed a similar script. We bowled first, my four wickets ripping the heart out of the middle order as they made 211, before another double century — this time from Ross Taylor — scored in very quick time, anchored our reply as rain threatened to steal our chance of a win.

What I remember most about this game, though, is trying to dial back my post-wicket celebrations. The guys had been mocking me for a while now, and challenged me to see if I was even capable of toning it down. A roar was the way I had celebrated since my early days in Pretoria. Perhaps I had watched a bit too much of Allan Donald.

'I'll try,' I said.

I didn't get an opportunity until the 44th over, when I had Mohammad Mithun out paddling a short one to Tim around the corner, and for my next, Litton Das caught in the deep by Trent. Both times, I tried to limit my reaction to a finger pointed quietly to the sky. But it felt really unnatural. I've always been someone who lets my emotions take over in those moments. Thankfully, we all agreed I should revert to my way of doing things, so the roars and fist-pumps returned as I took another three wickets in another big victory. It gave me five for the innings, and nine for 73 in the match, the best I would manage in my test career. I was feeling in absolute control of my craft — I could pitch it up and swing it, if need be, or go short and at the body with even more devastating effect. My focus quickly shifted towards taking that form south to Christchurch for the last test of the season.

As a group, we decided not to train on the day before the third test. We'd put in a lot of overs over the summer and a high-intensity session the previous day made a rest feel like the thing we most needed. Instead, Bangladesh switched their itinerary around to take our slot to train on Hagley Oval at nine that morning, instead of their original plan to train in the afternoon after having observed Friday prayers at the mosque across the road. Trent and I grabbed a couple of Lime scooters and went into town for a coffee, meeting Christchurch boy Tom at the cafe, and later getting in touch with Tim — captain for the game in place of an injured Kane — to see if he wanted to join us when the skippers' press conferences, delayed by the change in scheduling, were done.

Tim met us at the AS Colour store, and I was at the till paying for my clothes when I first noticed a siren, not thinking much of it. Then Tom got a news notification and pulled out his phone. Reports of gunshots at a Christchurch mosque. *Shit, that sounds bad.*

I could never have imagined just how bad, however. Soon, a message from Mike Sandle appeared on the team's WhatsApp thread, telling everyone who was in town to get back to the hotel. The reports were correct, and the suspect was still at large. Mike's message said that the hotel might go into lockdown, so make sure we were there when it did. By the time we'd processed the gravity of his message, there were sirens everywhere, ambulances streaming past. I felt cold all of a sudden, really cold, and even the rhythm of my heartbeat changed. The world seemed to darken by a few degrees.

Another message from Mike: 'This is not a drill, you need to get to the hotel now.'

Tom rushed off home to be with Nicole, his wife, and the three of us remaining — me, Tim, Trent — hopped on the Lime scooters to race as fast as we possibly could through the city, where dazed residents were emerging from doorways to look around at what on earth was going on. I felt sick.

Trent pulled his hoodie over his head and Tim immediately said, 'Take it off, you idiot, the shooter is still at large, they might think it's you.' Like everyone, we were freaking out, terrified, and just wanted to get around some familiar faces. We met Mike at the entrance of the hotel, the Rydges, and you could see in his eyes the seriousness of what had happened. We were directed to Tim's room to get together as a team. All you could hear outside was the overlapping of ambulance and police sirens.

That's when, with our phones out, we started piecing together the full picture. Terry Minish, our security manager, was in the room, having gone with the Bangladesh team across Hagley Park to the mosque, where they planned to join the Friday prayers. Had it not been for the last-minute changes to the schedule, the entire Bangladesh team could very well have been inside. As it was, Terry managed to escort the Bangladesh boys back to the safety of the Hagley Oval pavilion unharmed, but in the process they'd all witnessed some of the horror spilling out of Masjid Al Noor.

I was talking about what must've happened when Trent started nudging me.

'Shut up, shut up!' He motioned to Terry, who I hadn't noticed. Terry's face was as white as a ghost. 'You can see he was there, and he's cut up by this,' Trent said in a frantic whisper.

Terry, though obviously in shock, was able to give us an inside account of what he had seen, the severity of what had happened — but there were still so many things we didn't know. *How many shooters were out there? Would Christchurch go into lockdown? Would we be able to get back to our families?* I just wanted to see Lana. Fake news began circulating that there was a gunman at the hospital, just across the road from Hagley Oval. We contacted our Bangladeshi colleagues, sharing with them our deep sadness and shock, and letting them know that we were thinking of them. At dinner, served in a private room, we were informed that the game, to nobody's surprise and everyone's gratitude, had been cancelled.

I remember the fear as I lay in bed that night, unable to sleep, listening to the ceaseless sounds of the sirens and helicopters, feeling sick to my stomach. When my parents woke up in South Africa and saw the tragedy plastered across the news, they instantly got in touch to check, first, that I was okay, and then to send their love and support. They were used to awful things happening in South Africa, where Mum had once been caught up in a traumatic armed robbery as she went to pay her bills at the post office, but they were shocked something so terrible had happened in New Zealand.

At the airport the next morning, waves of anger and disgust washed over me — how could someone have done this, and for something so stupid and evil? In every face I passed I could see sadness and shock and grief. I was heading home to Lana. But there were a lot of people out there at that moment whose loved ones weren't coming home, who had been taken from them in the most senseless way imaginable.

These thoughts swirled in my mind until I finally got home, burying my face in Lana's hair as I held her tight.

CHAPTER 12:
TOWARDS THE TOP

Ever since our wedding day, people had asked Lana and me when we were going to start a family. It was definitely something we both wanted, but initially we were in no rush. We wanted to enjoy each other and the early days of our marriage and didn't want to put any pressure on ourselves, especially as Lana suffered from severe endometriosis, an incredibly painful condition affecting the ovaries that can make it more difficult to get pregnant. Since she had moved to Dunedin, Lana had returned to South Africa three times to have the condition surgically treated, and on the last occasion one of her ovaries was damaged during the procedure, making a straightforward pregnancy even more unlikely. When she came back to New Zealand after that surgery, her gynaecologist told her that our best chance of getting pregnant would be via in vitro fertilisation, IVF.

When teammates and friends began one-by-one having their first child, and then in many cases a second, the enquiries about when we would join them came thick and fast. It always came from a place of love and curiosity — but sometimes when we were already feeling down about the situation, it was an unwelcome reminder that it wasn't going to be as easy for us. The specialists we saw agreed there was almost no chance we were going to fall pregnant naturally, and accordingly our first round of IVF treatment would be government funded. We went on the waiting list. A year or so later — the week before our planned move to Pāpāmoa — Lana got a call telling her that we were next in line. Get ready. When Lana replied that we were moving, we were given two options: stay in Dunedin for the treatment or move and start again at the bottom of the list up north. We had invested so much in the move, it felt like we had to go. We told ourselves that it just wasn't our time, and that it would happen when it was meant to.

We were told it could be up to two years before we reached the top of the new list, and initially, we felt really isolated. We didn't know anyone from the other areas of our lives who'd been through the same thing, but soon, in the various waiting rooms in which we found ourselves killing time, we realised how many people were struggling with the same issues we were. By some miracle — we are still not really sure why — Lana got a call after just a few months in Pāpāmoa letting her know it was almost our turn. She immediately got me on the phone. 'We can start,' she said, through an almost audible smile.

We spoke about it for a week, figuring out how Lana's potential pregnancy, and then a young baby, would work in and among my upcoming cricket commitments. We knew it would be a challenge, with overseas tours on the horizon, but in the end we both leaned on our faith, taking the unexpected earliness of that phone call as a sign. It was the back end of 2018 when we began the treatment, but just before the embryo was due to be transferred, Lana developed a pain in one of her breasts. When she went to have that checked out, they found a lump in the other one — and that had to be analysed in the lab, which took three weeks. The IVF treatment had to be paused while the worst-case scenarios were ruled out, which they very thankfully were.

It was winter by the time we could try again, and I didn't have any overseas cricket commitments so I could be around for the most part — although there were a few training camps and that sort of thing I had to attend. Also, that was the New Zealand winter when the 2019 ICC Cricket World Cup was being played in England. I was working with Sky TV, appearing on a cricket show, filmed in Auckland, that would preview each Black Caps game and then return the morning after to analyse it. Because of one of these commitments, I couldn't be there the second time Lana had the embryo implanted, which went smoothly with a close friend by her side in my place. All we could do then was wait nervously to see if it had been successful.

A week or so later, Lana got a call from the clinic. She was pregnant. She called me right away, catching me in the car as I drove home from training. I couldn't believe it. I was so happy, and so proud of Lana for how she had dealt with all the disappointment she'd endured along this journey. She had sacrificed so much for me over the years. If anyone deserved something to go her way, it was Lana. I instantly wanted to tell everyone I knew, but obviously a lot could still have gone wrong, especially with Lana's history. I wanted to wrap her in cotton wool, especially as — soon enough — I had to fly to Sri Lanka, leaving Lana to deal with those difficult early months of pregnancy on her own.

That series was the first of the ICC World Test Championship (WTC), a competition that had long been rumoured. Some of the guys were lukewarm about it, wondering how it would work and whether it would feel as significant as the other ICC events, which had a lot of history. But ever since I had first worn a test shirt with my name and number on the back — an innovation introduced for the WTC — at a promotional event at Bay Oval, I was absolutely pumped for it. I was starting to come to terms with the fact that I might never play white-ball cricket for my country. This was a chance to get my hands on some international silverware — even if the rigorous nature of test cricket, which tested your skills and temperament so much more than short-form stuff, meant the ICC Test Championship Mace would be the hardest trophy to take home. To me, that made it the most meaningful.

It was the tournament that had just finished, however, that dominated the early days of that tour. I had watched that almost unbelievable final of the World Cup, and was heartbroken for the guys when the result — decided by the much-derided boundary countback rule — went against them. I could see how much they were hurting. The only consolation I could think of was that they'd been part of one of the most incredible games of cricket ever played, and that the way the team had gracefully accepted the loss was a huge credit to them and the country they were representing. But I knew from experience that it would've been impossible for those guys to take much solace from that at the time.

When I arrived in Sri Lanka a few weeks after the final, the boys who had been at Lord's were still struggling so the first thing they did was get together as a group, as the rest of us chilled by the pool, to try and get to grips with what had happened in London and to find a way to stop the hurt of it from spilling into the wider group. After a good two-hour session, we were told to join them, where they had a couple of ice-cold Heinekens waiting for us and I was finally able to get in there and get my arms around the boys to support them, tell them in person how proud I was, and help get their minds off what had just happened — and into the WTC.

I was left out of the first test in Galle — we went in with three spinners and Tim and Trent — where we lost and the tour moved on to Colombo, where we stayed in the same hotel, the Taj Samudra, as on my last Black Caps tour of the country, in those distant, almost unbearable days when I'd been at my absolute lowest. It was a strange place to find myself, seven years on, and it soon got stranger. Lana somehow found a way to inform someone in the Black Caps management of the gender of our baby without finding out herself and had devised a plot so that, despite the distance, we could still find out together. Terry, our security manager, was in on it. He rang me in my room and told me he needed to see me. There had been reports, he said, of someone dodgy in the hotel approaching players about potentially trying to fix matches. 'Can you come downstairs?' he said. 'We really need to talk to you.'

I walked down to find him, knowing that I hadn't done anything wrong but suddenly nervous. When I got to Terry, he asked if I had seen anything suspicious, whether anyone strange had tried to talk to me, and to keep an eye out for anything out of the ordinary.

'Of course, mate,' I replied. 'This is pretty serious. I'll let you know if I see anything. But you know I'd never ever get involved in something like that.'

I walked back to my room a bit shaken. As I stepped through the doorway, my phone rang. It was Lana: 'Don't look down! Don't look down!'

I'd seen a flash of both pink and blue on a plate on the desk, but hadn't thought anything of it so I was still in the dark as Lana told me to wait while she opened the envelope at home and said to look down at the same time as she made the same discovery on the other side of the world.

'It's a girl,' I read, the message written between two cupcakes, one of each colour. I was going to have a daughter.

Later that day, I stood in the same spot, looking through that same window, where years before I had thought really hard about ending my life. Everything looked the same: car park on one side, swimming pool on the other. But the view from inside my head couldn't have been more different.

After years of not knowing when or if it was going to happen for us, my beautiful wife and I were going to have a little girl. If I had taken a step or two further the last time I stood in this spot, I thought, I might never have experienced the intense happiness that was welling up inside me. I was so grateful that something had stopped me. And so grateful that Lana's message was the first thing I saw after that moment.

I thanked God, then focused my thoughts on the future. I didn't want the pain of that moment to pollute the happiness of this one. I wiped a big tear from my eye, nodded in the direction of the glass and tried to put it out of my mind, averting my eyes from the window every time I walked past it for the remainder of our stay. I wasn't selected for the second test, either — we won by an innings to square the series — but I had bigger things than cricket to occupy my mind. I was going to be a father.

Back home, it was into the Plunket Shield season for Northern Districts, with three games — two draws and a loss — to prepare for the English, who were visiting again. I bowled a truckload of overs across those three games, including 40.2 overs in one innings against Otago in which I took six wickets. I always loved bowling a lot of overs in domestic cricket, but usually at some point in the season I would get a call from someone in the Black Caps management telling me that my bowling loads were too high, so I had to ease off. It didn't happen this time, though, and I thought perhaps it was an indication they were thinking of going a different way. Lockie Ferguson had had an amazing World Cup and there was some talk of his express pace coming in to counteract the speed of Jofra Archer in the tourists' armoury, especially with an important tour of Australia, where pace is always regarded as a crucial factor, coming after that. My experiences so far with Steady suggested that no news was usually not good news.

The opening game was at the Bay Oval, the first time my new home ground had ever hosted a test match. I really wanted to help christen it. Lana's parents, Theuns and Erika Koekemoer, were over for the summer and here was a chance to play in front of them in my own backyard. They had become a very important part of my support network, and Theuns' experience as a former top-level rugby player for the Bulls made him an excellent resource as I was learning how to deal with the pressures of professional sport. I was excited by the prospect of an opportunity to pay him back for all his advice over the years with a big performance.

On the morning preceding the game, warming up before training, I could see Kane and Steady in serious conversation. I had a strong suspicion it was about whether I would play. When that conversation ended, I watched Steady start to make the rounds, letting the guys know who had made the XI. He told me I was in, but I felt — once again — that I was playing for my spot.

My feet were a mess. All those overs for Northern Districts were expressed in the shade of my blue toenails pushed back into the flesh, an open cut under my right foot, blisters everywhere. But I pushed through and bowled well in the first innings — 32 overs for three wickets — before BJ put us in control with a double century. Trent was injured early when we bowled again, which meant more work for the rest of us, but this was the kind of situation where I flourished, bowling hard, hard overs — ignoring the pain of my weeping feet — and chipping away.

Bay Oval is a place I love to bowl — flat, but if you really whack it into the pitch you can often find something unexpected, especially late in the game when a few cracks start to open up. It was the 75th over before I took a wicket — Joe Denly, who had anchored the English resistance, caught behind when a length ball reared up to brush his gloves as he attempted to leave it — but once I had Ollie Pope caught in the covers with a knuckle-ball, a delivery I'd been developing in the shorter formats, I knew it was going to be my afternoon. I took the last four wickets — including that of Jos Buttler, taking the new ball that would normally be Trent's, opening with an inswinging yorker that he left to crash into off stump — to finish with five wickets in the innings and eight for the game in our victory.

We only bowled once, thankfully, on Seddon Park in the second game — the wicket was the slowest and most docile I have ever bowled on in New Zealand, where the mixture of fuller-length cutters and three-quarter balls we'd decided would be the way to go wasn't to the liking of two guys in the crowd who were absolutely pleading with me to bowl a bouncer. I eventually relented — *What's the worst that can happen?* — and Ollie Pope immediately top-edged his pull shot to deep square leg. It was the first wicket we had taken in more than 60 overs, and these two fellas went absolutely berserk, running around, leaping up and down, yelling, 'I told you so, I told you so!' And, fair play to them: momentum shifted, I got my tail up, and promptly ran through the lower order to give me another five wickets. I raised the ball to Lana and her parents, who had driven over from Pāpāmoa for the day, on the bank. It was a special moment, and the eventual draw gave us another series victory over England. My 13 wickets, including two five-wicket hauls, at a shade under 20 saw me named player of the series. I had booked my ticket to Australia.

It was set to be a huge series, especially after I'd missed out on playing in the team's last Australian tour. Three tests, including the Boxing Day Test at the MCG — the first time New Zealand had been granted that honour since 1987. Just playing would fulfil some of the most intense ambitions I had treasured as a boy; winning would be immense. As always, the group, attempting not to get too excited, tried to think of it as just another series — but for me, this time, I wondered if that was the right way to go. To win in Australia, I thought, we might need to harness more emotional energy than we usually did. It wasn't *just another series*. But one huge lesson cricket has taught me is how remarkably different each human is in what motivates us to perform. That's one big challenge the coach and captain of a cricket team have — to recognise this while trying to gather those psychological threads into a cohesive whole.

The tour started horribly. Me, Tim, Trent, Kane, BJ and Ross — players with big workloads who also happened to be the experienced core of the team — were given an extra day at home to recuperate before the opening test, a day–night game in Perth starting just nine days after our last gruelling outing against England finished. I woke up on the day we were supposed to fly out to a message that the flight was cancelled, which meant another day at home. The six of us assembled in Auckland the next day, only to find out there was an issue with the plane. Another cancellation before we flew first to Melbourne, where we then had to wait 10 hours for a connecting flight to Perth. The extra rest day, in effect, meant we were still jet-lagged and had hardly begun to acclimatise to the 40-degree heat by the time we had to play. Cricket Australia, we joked, must've been behind this somehow.

That heat was something else. Being a day–night test — and losing the toss — meant we had to begin our work just as it was at its worst in the mid-afternoon. Even the game of golf we played in the days before the match had been enough to drag huge beads of perspiration through our skin in places you hardly think you are even able to sweat. Bowling was an ordeal, but this was a moment I had held in my mind through all the interminable training sessions in the months beforehand. Debutant Lockie Ferguson — Trent hadn't been able to shake the side strain he sustained in Mount Maunganui — was bowling quick, perhaps egged on by the white noise of the Australian media, which had harped on about how important pace would be. But he tore his calf after only 11 overs. I felt hugely sorry for him after all the work he'd put in to get there. And his absence meant a huge workload for the rest of us, especially with the

Australians obviously eager to worsen our position by going after Mitchell Santner to take our main spin option off the table.

It was a struggle to get hydration right. Too little and you'd be in big trouble. Too much and you had to run in to bowl with a big gurgly stomach full of Powerade. I remember the relief of getting down to fine leg, where the big new stands of Optus Stadium threw a slice of shade over the grass. I needed it: I bowled 37 overs across that innings, my strategy based on what I had learned about the Aussies during Baz's last test. They didn't like the feeling of being dominated by the short ball, especially at a less-than-express pace they felt they should be able to punish. Eventually, they'd either go after it — as Steve Smith did twice in the game, caught once at leg gully and once at square leg — or just take it on the body as Matthew Wade seemed content to do, time after bruising time, during a sustained spell in the second innings. I've never been the quickest bowler in the world, but I know how much that would have hurt. I respected the toughness, but it felt like I had got inside his head. 'Keep coming, big boy,' he said, after ducking another bouncer, having already taken many on the body.

They were certainly in ours, I came to think, trading on the dynamics of the big brother/little brother relationship that New Zealand has never managed to shake in the context of our test cricket rivalry. We were twice bowled out for under 200 — in the first innings, as a nightwatchman, I was bowled first ball, chopping on a wide Mitchell Starc yorker I could have left alone, having then to walk back through the crowd and their brutal torrent of abuse that had followed me out moments earlier — to hand the Aussies an easy win that my seven wickets couldn't get close to preventing.

There was a big gap between the first and second tests. We moved to Melbourne to play an inter-squad game, trying to keep ourselves active in the heat, which had followed us east. As Christmas and the game approached, Lana and her folks came over. Exploring Melbourne with them, I could feel the atmosphere of the city sharpening to a fine point. There were New Zealanders everywhere — shouts of 'Love your work, Wags!' or 'Go well, mate!' whenever I stepped outside — and it reminded me of the Pretoria of my childhood, when everything in the week felt aimed at the weekend's rugby field or cricket pitch, the current of the city carrying its citizens' hopes and dreams forward to eddy around the feet of rugby posts or stumps. We had a small function with the team, then me, Lana and her folks wished each other a merry Christmas over a picnic in a nearby park. My nerves had gone into overdrive. That night, as I tried to relax in front of a movie, I smothered them with a bottle of Penfolds Shiraz — a favourite drop — and slept like a baby.

Standing in the middle of the MCG, though, they all came back. *Control the controllables*, I reminded myself. We'd spent a bit of time on the field getting used to the ground itself in the days leading up to the game, but I wasn't prepared for the feel of it almost fully stocked, with one in four of the 80,000 at the ground cheering for us. The first ball, bowled by Trent, back from injury, heralded the loudest noise I had ever heard on a cricket field. Until his fourth ball, when he bowled Joe Burns through the gate and 20,000 New Zealanders in the ground went ballistic.

We were in this, we were up for it. Tim and Trent were beating the bat, and the Aussies were under a bit of pressure. I got the sign to start warming up, the first strains of a new Christmas carol, 'Wagner Wonderland', raising goosebumps on my skin and adrenaline erasing the memory of Perth from my muscles. A few overs in and David Warner, to whom I had only bowled a couple so far, came on strike. I'd got him out with a full ball in Perth and I decided to try the same again, covering the tracks of my plan with a short-ball field. The delivery swung away from the left-hander's bat, caught the edge as he attempted to bunt it down the ground, and Tim plucked a spectacular one-handed catch from the air at second slip. *C'mon!* A surge of emotion raced through my body as the crowd went wild. Later on, the battle resumed with Matthew Wade.

Steve Smith was good enough to resist. He looked ugly at times, but remained at the crease for an age in scoring his 85. I was a couple of overs into a spell when I had to run off the field, down the long tunnel, to the toilet. Above the urinal there was a screen replaying a bouncer he had played awkwardly an over or two before. There were two varieties of bouncer that I bowled: one seam up, the other at a three-quarter angle. The former seemed to come off the pitch at a consistent but slightly slower speed, the latter — sometimes skidding on the leather or hitting the seam at a strange angle — was more unpredictable but often quicker, rising steeply.

I made it back onto the field, feeling pretty cooked by the sprint both ways, just in time to start my over. Kane had been thinking about a bowling change and I'd had to plead with him for 'one more' — two words that had become something of a catchphrase. That replay had confirmed I was troubling Steve with the three-quarter bouncer, and I gave him a couple of good ones, planning another. But at the last minute I changed my mind, altering my grip to the seam-up position. The ball was perfect, coming straight for his front shoulder. He climbed with it to defend but seemed, maybe because of that change of plan, to do so a fraction too early. The ball struck the handle of his bat and traced a slow-motion arc through the air to gully, where Henry, back-pedalling like mad, flung one hand skyward to intercept it.

Australia were 284 for five and, we thought, if we could get

another couple quickly we might run through the tail. But Australia — and how often had I watched them do this over the years? — just built again, Tim Paine and Travis Head putting on a big partnership that would carry the score to 467. In contrast, we folded for 148, Trent last out after having batted on with a right hand broken by a Starc thunderbolt.

It felt like fate was against us, but all I could do was bowl as Australia looked to set up their declaration. I got Davey, backing away and swatting to cover to give me 199 test wickets, and then a few overs later Steve pulled me around the corner where Tim hardly had to move to pouch a catch at backward square leg. It was my 200th wicket in my 46th test. Of New Zealand bowlers, again only Sir Richard had done it faster. Of left-arm quicks, I was the fastest of all time from any country. Those were dreamlike statistics to ponder when they were mentioned by Steady in front of the boys after the day's play, and I truly appreciated the good cheer I got, especially as we were all disappointed with the situation of the game, on our way to another loss on a tour where everything from flights to injuries seemed to have gone wrong. After the test I was officially ranked by the ICC as the second-best bowler in the world, but I didn't pay much attention — I thought there were many better bowlers than me in the world, some in my own team.

Then sickness hit the squad. This was in the days when we were first starting to hear about Covid, though no cases had yet been reported in Australia — and whatever infected the team, it was pretty brutal, forcing us to make changes for the third test, in Sydney. Kane and Henry out, Jeet and debutant Glenn Phillips in — which made the omission of Tim, as Matt and spinners Todd Astle and Will Somerville came into the side, hard to fathom. It was the one time that I ever saw Tim, who had bowled extremely well throughout the series, visibly angry at missing out. It didn't make sense to me, and I was cross on his behalf. That decision put all of us on edge. But I tried to focus on the job at hand as we bowled first, again starting well and keeping the big guns quiet: Steve Smith took 39 balls to get off the mark, which he did by taking a tight single after turning one of my bouncers around the corner. I patted him on the back in congratulations as I walked back to my mark. Throughout the series, Matthew Wade had been telling me to wait for Sydney. I soon found out why, when he came at me hard on the slower pace of the SCG wicket, pulling me for a couple of fours and a big six. But it was Marnus Labuschagne who took the game away from us with a double century that paved the way to our eventual four-day loss.

There was a lot of frustration in the squad about how the tour had gone. And as I was waiting to bat for the final time in the series, the game all but lost, I was stewing about everything. I saw on the screen that the Aussies had named Marnus and Travis in their one-day squad, in part presumably due to the runs they had scored in the tests. Almost without thinking I threw out a cheeky question in Steady's direction.

'Hey, Steady,' I said, 'see how these Aussies are getting picked for the white-ball team on the back of red-ball form? Have I been forgotten about? Am I ever going to be looked at in the white-ball game?'

Steady had a chuckle and said we'd find time to discuss it later. I knew the second the words started to leave my mouth that it wasn't the right way to go about things, but I couldn't hold them back. Some of the struggles in that series were beyond our control, but it still felt like we'd missed a great opportunity to show that we could hold our own against the best of the best.

When we sat down to review that series, I apologised to Gary for putting him on the spot in front of the team. But then Steady explained that he could see where I was coming from, and that there was a white-ball NZ A series against India coming up. Would I be interested in playing to try and state my case?

'Definitely,' I said. 'One hundred per cent.'

We were gutted as we left Australia. I was happy with my individual performance — a team-high 17 wickets at 22.76 — but that was little consolation. We went there trying to write our names into history, but came home with our tails between our legs.

Not long after arriving back in Aotearoa, Steady called. I hoped it was going to be some good news about the A series to take my mind off Australia.

'We feel we know what you've got to offer,' he said. 'We want to give some young guys a chance.' I was so disappointed. Time, it seemed, to let go of my international white-ball ambitions.

Lana, by now, was very nearly at the end of her pregnancy. Her official due date, in fact, coincided with the first test of our next series, against India, but after a few end-of-pregnancy scans and consultations with the midwife and obstetrician, it was decided that for our daughter's health — her stomach wasn't growing quite as much as it should have been — Lana would need to be induced earlier. It looked like I could be there for Lana and my daughter and also play the next two games, which would be rough for Lana, but the reality for professional sportspeople. We organised for both my mum and Lana's to come over from South Africa to help ease the burden.

Lana was induced, but this baby did not want to budge — even after a second and then third induction. Different doctors and midwives had different ideas about how to proceed — one doctor would come in to say it wouldn't be long now, and when the shift finished their replacement would tell us to go home and come back tomorrow. For three days we were in this limbo where no one seemed to know exactly how to move forward. I called Mike Sandle to let him know I wasn't going to get to Wellington after all. Lana was in horrible pain and beyond exhausted after days of contractions.

When, again, we were told to go home, I pushed back. We were worried about what those scans and this long interlude meant for our daughter, and eventually when I insisted that there must be other options, we were told there was a slot for a caesarean section available that afternoon. Lana was too fatigued to think straight. I made the call. 'We'll take it.' I rang the two mums and told them to get to the hospital straight away.

Everything began smoothly. The midwife was taking photos for us to remember the moment, talking Lana and me through the procedure. Then something changed in the atmosphere of the room. The doctor started calling for things and the theatre, suddenly, was full of people and the urgent beeping of the machinery. Lana started to panic when the midwife told her she could no longer take photos. I watched the doctor who had begun the procedure sit down in a chair and literally bury his head in his hands. Someone called for another doctor. *This is my fault. I made the call for the C-section. What have I done?*

I tried to keep my own mounting panic off my face so as not to worsen Lana's. By good fortune, the doctor who had been with us since the beginning of our IVF journey was the one to take over. Our daughter was stuck in a strange position — our doctor later told us he had never seen anything like it in his 25-year career — and what would normally have been a 10-minute procedure to take her out was at least double that. But it felt like forever. At least I thought it did, until she was removed and whisked away from us to the resuscitation table without having made a noise. She wasn't breathing. *What have I done?* I thought again, praying to God, over and over, to just please let her be okay. That minute truly felt like forever. Until it was ended by a piercing heaven-sent cry that cut through the heavy tension in our hearts. We answered it with our own tears of relief, happiness, gratitude and exhaustion. She was okay. Thank you, God.

And soon I had this little darling, Olivia Faith Wagner, in my arms. My world instantly turned upside down. Everything I thought was important suddenly paled into insignificance compared with how I could be the best father to her. She was perfect. But of course she was: just look at her mum.

In the shadow of Livie's birth, I hardly remember the next test in Christchurch. We had beaten India in Wellington, with Kyle Jamieson making his debut in my place and doing extremely well, but my main memories were of getting back around the guys. I shared birth stories and copped plenty of good-natured ribbing from the other fathers in the dressing room — about how much more difficult parenthood was going to be than I thought, about how I wouldn't be keeping my house so tidy now or washing my car every weekend. There was an awareness, too — with Kyle keeping his place alongside me — that my role in the attack might change, that the spells might be a little bit shorter and that, with four other seam bowlers whose primary weapon was swing and who would want to eke every last bit of it from each new ball, I would probably bowl later in each innings and be expected to go straight to the short-ball plan of attack from ball one. But that was okay, whatever the team needed. Because I could also see, as all five of us — me, Kyle, Colin, Trent and Tim — went relentlessly at an all-star batting lineup to set up a comfortable win, that this was a bowling attack, with Matt Henry waiting in the wings, that could take us to the top.

CHAPTER 13:
CHAMPIONS

Covid-19 — its threat growing throughout the 2019/20 summer — had breached the New Zealand borders by the time the next game of cricket I played, a Plunket Shield fixture against Canterbury in Hamilton, began. The match was punctuated by lots of chat about what the pandemic was going to mean for us and whether this would end up being our last game for some time. And just before I left home for our next match, I got a message to hold fire: it looked like a lockdown might be on its way. Lana and I hurriedly arranged for our mums to fly back home so they didn't get trapped in the country, which we just managed before that lockdown came into effect in late March 2020. And that was obviously cricket done for a while.

Initially, life in the Wagner bubble was a dream. An enforced break from the pressures of cricket and life, in which Lana and I could get to know Livie and acclimatise to parenthood with nothing but family to focus on. For the first few weeks, the weather was glorious and we made the most of it by taking our daily walk along the beach and enjoying barbecue after barbecue in the windless early autumn sunshine. It was also scary, of course, when we saw every day on the news the effect the pandemic was having on life overseas and hearing from friends and family how Covid was running rife through South Africa, where my surviving grandfather, Dad's dad, would sadly be killed by the disease — his funeral just one more in a long line of family events I had missed over the years. Not long after that, my grandmother passed away, too, and Dad's business really suffered. It was a tough time to have so much distance between us, not knowing when we would next see each other.

As the uncertainty continued, it got harder and harder to keep our spirits up. A few months into the pandemic, the New Zealand Cricket Players' Association started getting in touch with players, telling us that no one knew what the future of cricket looked like at this point in time — and whether the situation might soon start to affect contracts and incomes — and that it was a very good time to start thinking about how else you might earn a living, and to investigate taking a few steps in that direction. Lana and I both completed our real estate certificates to give us a potential income if cricket was to change beyond recognition in the foreseeable future — and for when it eventually ended. Covid or no Covid, I knew that moment loomed in the not-too-distant future, but until then it had always felt far enough away not to *have* to think about.

And yet, as it seemed like the rest of the world would take a long time to get back to anything approaching normality, by the time our next cricket season rolled around, it was largely business as usual within New Zealand. We had a couple of Plunket Shield fixtures — against Central Districts and then Otago — to warm up for the touring West Indies who, after completing their two weeks in managed isolation, lined up for two test matches. In the meantime, to account for the havoc Covid had caused to the fixture list, the ICC had changed how teams were awarded WTC points — we were now ranked on the percentage of available points we had claimed rather than the points themselves — to even things out after some teams had to forfeit series at the height of the pandemic. It made our path forward very clear: if we won our next four test matches — Pakistan were touring after the West Indies — there was a strong chance, depending on other results, that we would make the final. There wasn't much emphasis put on it within the team, but it was definitely in the back of a few minds as the cricket got under way. As was the fact that we would also climb to the top of the test rankings — we had reclaimed the number-two position by beating India two–nil — if we could win those games.

The first test was in Hamilton. We were put in on a green pitch and Kane and Tommy did extremely well to weather a testing period early on to put us on the road to a big total. Kane went on to score 251 and we then ripped through them in the first innings, victory only delayed, having enforced the follow-on, by a spirited partnership between century-maker Jermaine Blackwood and Alzarri Joseph. I took four wickets in that second innings, to go with my two in the first. All but three of the overs bowled by our team were delivered by either Tim, Trent, Kyle or me, and it was starting to feel even more that this was a frontline attack with enough variety of wicket-taking options to make us truly formidable. Tim and Trent, right- and left-arm respectively, each primarily moved the ball in a different direction in the air. Kyle swung it both ways and generated steepling bounce from his enormous height and lively pace. And I had my short-ball method for when the ball stopped talking for my colleagues.

The second test, at the Basin Reserve, was also my 50th. It was a treasured milestone. There are not that many guys who play 50 tests for New Zealand, given how few test matches we play in comparison to some other countries, and of all the statistical landmarks I had passed recently, this one meant the most. Walking out to bat — again the West Indies put us in — the standing ovation I received was genuinely moving, and it fired me up for the battle to come. We weren't exactly in trouble, but we were a few runs short of where we wanted to be. Henry Nicholls was batting beautifully and is one of the guys I love batting with the most, so relaxed in the middle that we could've been sitting in front of a PlayStation rather than in the middle of a test match. Throughout the innings he hardly mentioned the game, other than to welcome me by commenting on the size of the ovation and by saying the best way to thank the crowd would be by getting stuck into a good partnership.

'Let's be aggressive and score some runs, eh?' he said.

'Mate, music to my ears.'

I always knew that I would receive my share of retributive short stuff whenever I got to the middle, and I loved to take it on. The West Indies — particularly Jason Holder and Alzarri Joseph who were bowling when I arrived — didn't disappoint. I got a short one away for four off Jason, and then just kept going. There was a top edge for six and a dropped catch and suddenly I had passed 20. I took 18 runs — three fours and a six — off an Alzarri over, then monstered big man Shannon Gabriel over fine leg for another six. A top edge over the slips got me to my highest test score, before lunch interfered. Tim and Trent tried to get inside my head, telling me the hundred was there for the taking, better not mess it up. Bowlers love scoring runs, and as a group there was always healthy competition when it came to milestones and high scores. Eventually

I had to get up and walk away from their constant chatter.

It wasn't until the second over after lunch, bowled by Jason, that I managed to squirt one away past point and come back for a second run. My first and only test 50. I never did justice to my talent with the bat, but at least I had finally reached that particular milestone. I ended up with an unbeaten 66 off 42 balls, sharing an almost hundred-run stand with Henry, behind whose 174 my score was the team's second highest, taking us to 460. It was more than enough, as we got through their batting lineup twice — quickly in their first innings, with more difficulty in their second — to win by an innings. When I got back to my room at the Bolton Hotel, one of my favourite places to stay anywhere in the world, there were four Heinekens on ice waiting for me, with a note congratulating me on 50 tests and my first test 50. It put a big smile on my face.

Now the talk within the team started to get a little louder: win the next two games and we were a real shot of making the final. Kane being Kane, however, meant he was keen to put a damper on that kind of chat, bringing it back to the broken-record talk that had helped get us into this position in the first place: go about our processes, put the team first, enjoy ourselves, don't get too high or low and let the results take care of themselves. The public, I always felt, must've thought we were the most boring people in the world, always harping on about the exact same thing, but there was no denying the outlook had worked for us, relieving some of the pressure of playing cricket at international level. When we put too much emphasis on a singular goal — like becoming number one, say, or winning a tournament — rather than the small steps to help us get there, that's when we tended to come unstuck. The approach gave us a calmness with which to chase our big ambitions, knowing that even if we didn't get there but had stuck to our values, failure would be easier to take. That said, we were desperate to give ourselves the best chance of making that final.

It didn't start well when, put into bat on Boxing Day, both openers were gone before our score had reached 15. But Kane and Ross came together, steadied things with a century partnership, the middle order all contributing handy runs to complement Kane's hundred. I came to the crease with the score a dozen shy of 400, BJ batting nicely. Shaheen Shah Afridi was bowling. His yorker, speared at your toes from his significant height, somehow always seemed to reach you quite a bit faster than what the speed gun reported, and the first ball of his I faced was one such delivery that beat me for pace and clattered into the stumps behind me. I began trudging off. Unfortunately, however, given what would happen a few balls later, Shaheen had overstepped and I was called back. He ended the over with another yorker. I missed this one, too — but instead of clattering into the stumps, it struck me squarely on my right foot. I knew instantly it had done some damage. My first thought was disappointment. This game was huge for us and I hadn't even bowled a ball yet. My next was to acknowledge the throbbing pain.

'Mate, I think it's broken,' I said, once physio Tommy Simsek got to the middle.

But adrenaline is an amazing thing and, after he'd given it a spray, I carried on batting, out an over or two later top-edging a slog-sweep against Yasir Shah, but still able to jog off the park for the change of innings, taking every painkiller available to me in the break and coming back out to bowl three uncomfortable overs that evening. As soon as stumps were called for the day, Tommy and I rushed off to the after-hours surgery to see how bad it was.

Often if a cricketer has to be seen during a match they'll be rushed to the front of the queue, but when I turned up to the clinic, there was a little boy — four or five — absolutely screaming in his mum's arms. Tommy and I looked at each other and I thought of Livie, then almost a year old. I didn't care how long it was going to take, this kid had to go first. In the delay, I put my foot up and removed my jandal, giving us an unimpeded view of the bulb of swelling my foot had become, dark purple bruising swirling outwards from where I'd been struck somewhere near my fourth and fifth toes. The x-ray, I was told, showed there was a fracture. *That's not too bad*, I thought. We could just strap it up, ice it, I could dose myself with painkillers and we'd be good to go. It wasn't, however, a view shared by Lana when, the next morning, I had to hobble to the bathroom.

'How are you going to bowl?' she asked in Afrikaans, the language we speak among ourselves at home. 'You can't even walk.'

'I'll have to find a way,' I said.

'There's no chance. You're dreaming.'

All I could think of was how former Springbok fullback Andre Joubert had once played on with a broken hand, just as Richie McCaw would later play through the 2011 Rugby World Cup with a broken foot. *If those guys can do it, surely I can.* I took every painkiller I was allowed, but the agony — as I was given the ball for a short spell before lunch — was overwhelming, even though I got through four overs before the break in play. I went straight off the field to see the on-ground doctor — by chance the same doctor who had treated McCaw through that historic campaign — who took another look at the x-ray. I could hardly walk. The pain was up there with the worst I've ever experienced.

'No wonder you're sore,' the doctor told me. 'You've got two broken toes.'

The second fracture hadn't originally been spotted. I had a break in both my fourth and fifth toes. In her opinion, this was probably it for me in this game — but, depending on how high my pain threshold was, a painkilling injection might allow me to get through some more overs. We had to win this game to keep our title chances alive. If I could be of any help towards that, I wanted to at least try.

'Let's inject it,' I said.

The worst thing about the injection — initially, at least — was how well it worked. My entire foot was numb. I couldn't feel a single thing from two-thirds of the way down my shin. Bowling with this one phantom foot was a very strange experience, and the danger was that not being able to feel my foot, I could easily add another injury or not realise how much worse I was making the existing one. But I ran through my action a few times and felt confident I could contribute. I obviously wasn't going to play the next game of the series and I was headed for a spell on the sidelines. So I could leave everything out there, deal with the pain, use it as something to focus my mind against. I didn't want to sit there for three days watching the other guys do my work for me. When I spent that year carrying drinks for the team, I would've given anything to be out there: this was my chance to prove it at the most crucial juncture. We had a final to make. *Grit your teeth and get through it. It's not that bad.*

And for the game's third day, that was true. I lost count of how many injections I had throughout the game, but I could go off for treatment whenever I needed it, and bowl more or less pain-free until the numbness started to wear thin and the pain emerged again from under it. I bowled 18 overs over the course of the day, nabbing two wickets, including taking my revenge against Shaheen with a short ball that tangled him up and brushed his gloves on the way to the slips. That night, away from those regular injections, trying to sleep with the brutal discomfort in my foot was agony, but at least the next day I didn't have to bowl until the afternoon. We declared just before tea on day four and I managed six overs across the evening session.

It was a strange feeling to arrive at the ground on day five and be unable to walk to the dressing room, also knowing I had a big role to play on the field to keep a dream alive. When we had them four down for 75, we hoped to get it done relatively quickly. Not to be: Fawad Alam and Mohammad Rizwan put on a stubborn partnership that looked like it might save the game for the visitors. I had to put in my share of the work.

I hate injections at the best of times, although at least at the start they didn't hurt. But as my skin became increasingly irritated throughout the game, the spot where the needle had to go in became very tender. To get the relief offered by the injection, I had to first bite into a towel to bear the pain of it being administered. As the day wore on — and I found I had bowled 10, 15, 20 overs in the innings — the pain was so intense it could no longer be buried by the anaesthetic. I was in pain at all times.

But I was able to put it out of my mind when, after that partnership had kept us wicketless for 60 overs, Kyle got one to nip back and keep low to have Rizwan out leg before. Here was our opportunity to strike. I was in the midst of a spell from the other end, and in the seventh over of it, I switched my attack to the left-handed Fawad to around the wicket, hoping for a mistake against the short ball with two fielders in close to capitalise on it. The last ball of my 24th over was short just outside leg stump. He tried to pull it fine, but instead nicked it to BJ. I have let out a number of throat-tearing roars over my bowling career, but that might have been the loudest.

'Come on!' I screamed. 'Come on!'

I'd had to let my emotions take control of me in order to cope with the pain, and in that instant I couldn't restrain them. I nicked off Faheem Ashraf in my next spell, before Mitchell Santner — so often an important foil for the rest of the attack — starred with the last two wickets to seal a dramatic victory with only a few overs left in the test. I knew I was out for the next game, but the WTC dream was still alive — and not even one of my teammates stepping on my ruined foot as we gathered in a huddle could make a dent in the elation I felt. I limped over to the embankment where Lana and Livie had been watching to share the moment with them.

I was very nervous sitting at home in front of the TV, unable to contribute to a game as consequential as that second test. Win and we would officially be the number-one-ranked test team in the world, something the Black Caps had never achieved. We would also remain in the running for the WTC final. I sat there at home, my foot elevated in a moonboot, my fingernails getting ever shorter. Even if, on the scale determined by the last test, this Hagley Oval victory was a fairly straightforward affair — a heap of wickets for Kyle in the first innings, 600-plus runs on the back of another Kane double century, then a second five-wicket bag for Kyle. When, late on day four, Zafar Gohar swung Trent to fine leg, and my replacement Matt Henry tumbled into a catch, we had won by an innings and were at the top of the world rankings. When I debuted, we were eighth and deserved to be there, so unloved we couldn't even find a sponsor willing to pay to put their name on our jersey. It had been a remarkable rise.

I was feeling a bit strange, in the quiet of my lounge, away from my teammates and with Livie sitting on my lap, alienated from the gravity of the achievement. Until my phone rang. It was Trent on FaceTime. I passed Livie to Lana and answered. It was the entire team in a huddle. They wanted me to join them in the pledge. I hopped downstairs as Trent placed his phone in the middle of the guys, and I sang along. It was an emotional moment. I was so moved that the guys had thought to include me. Alone downstairs, self-consciously singing with my mates at the other end of the phone, was one of the most special moments of my career.

It wasn't yet confirmed that we would make the final. In February of 2021, however, when Australia postponed their test tour of South Africa, citing safety concerns amid the ongoing pandemic, they forfeited their opportunity to raise their percentage of points secured above ours. It wasn't the ideal way to achieve it, but we were in. Now it only remained to be seen who would join us, and India soon confirmed their spot when they beat the English at home. So, it would be us versus India, a country of five million against a country with almost that many registered cricket players.

We had two tests against England to warm up for the WTC final. And that English series, beginning in early June and falling outside the WTC, was incredibly important in its own right, a chance to take a series off the hosts in their own conditions, something we had done only twice in our history and not since 1999. It gave me a nice long stretch to recover, which I did with plenty of time to spare — enough to play the final four rounds of the Plunket Shield before flying to England. The IPL that year — held in a bubble — eventually wasn't able to keep Covid at bay and had to be postponed, New Zealand's players either flying home, like Trent, to get a little time with family, ruling him out of the first test, or to the Maldives, where a bunch of guys, Kane and Kyle included, ended up on their way to England.

Those of us who came from New Zealand only had to do a short stretch in isolation, while the IPL boys were room-bound for much longer, sometimes appearing on their balconies — we stayed at the hotel adjoining the Rose Bowl at Southampton — to stare wistfully at us training below. That was as close as they could get. It made for a very disjointed build-up, but we were just thankful we'd soon be playing cricket. That time got us acclimatised to the facilities at the self-enclosed Rose Bowl — to which, in the interests of keeping the teams free from Covid, the WTC final had been moved, having originally been scheduled for Lord's.

The last time we'd toured England, in 2016, the selectors preferred Matt Henry over me. Pitches there tended to be the least conducive to the short-ball attack out of any around the world, often slow and low, but I had worked hard in all my county cricket stints to keep sharp the skills that quick bowlers have traditionally utilised in that country: swing and seam and unerring accuracy aimed at the top of off stump. I had also been working on a new ball, a better-disguised three-quarter ball held with a grip more closely resembling my inswinger to right-handers, designed to kick off the pitch and across the right-hander, further enhancing the danger of my stock ball coming back into their pads.

We won the toss and chose to bat in the first test at Lord's. Devon Conway, my fellow South African import, had now qualified for New Zealand, and he opened, batting across the first day and a half to score 200 on debut, although he was still 14 runs short of that milestone when I walked out to bat at number 11, deathly scared of leaving him stranded. But I felt in good form, standing tall to punch one off the back foot to the off-side boundary, then cover-driving Stuart Broad over it for a maximum, before Devon hit a six to reach an incredible double century. I gave him a big hug in the middle of the Lord's pitch. I knew only too well some of what he'd been through on his journey to represent New Zealand.

I bowled my first spell from the Pavilion End, but I couldn't find my rhythm despite now being quite familiar with the Lord's slope. I tried to go short, but it didn't look threatening and I immediately went for runs. Because of my experience in English conditions, I just knew the sustained short-ball attack wasn't going to work, that keeping the bouncer as a surprise delivery was going to be far more effective.

But when I swapped to the Nursery End, it seemed to click. I was swinging the ball, the new three-quarter delivery was coming out nicely and seeming to create indecision. It didn't result in many wickets — one in the first innings, two in the second — in what petered out into a tame draw after England declined to chase the total we had set them, but I felt I was making a strong claim for a spot in the top XI.

After the match, the competition switched sports as we managed to arrange a game of golf against the English boys at The Belfry — a course that has staged the Ryder Cup and the British Masters. It was a great experience, although Jimmy Anderson and Stuart Broad and the other guys might not have felt the same way after losing and being forced to open their wallets to shout the pizza and drinks afterwards. We moved to Birmingham for the second test.

That I was not a sure thing for the final seemed to be confirmed, counter-intuitively, by my inclusion in the team. A slew of frontliners — BJ, Colin, Kane, Tim, Kyle — were rested, while Trent came back in having been released from isolation during the Lord's game. I went in with that familiar feeling of playing for my spot, especially as the Rose Bowl pitch has a general reputation for taking spin and I couldn't see how I would make the team if we played a specialist spinner. There was a lot to play for, and an amazing atmosphere to play it in. The British government was starting to lift some of its Covid restrictions, and Edgbaston was allowed to fill up to 70 per cent of its capacity. The energy of the crowd, suppressed after months of lockdowns, was freed by a flood of lager and the noise, emanating in the main from the Hollies Stand, was awesome, almost the equal of the MCG on Boxing Day. It was so loud.

Tommy Latham, captaining in Kane's place, lost the toss and England chose to bat. Because of all the changes — the bowling attack consisted of me, Trent, Matt Henry, Ajaz Patel and Daryl Mitchell — our roles needed to switch around, and I was bowling as more of a traditional third seamer, taking the ball earlier than I had become accustomed to doing so. When I returned for my second spell, Henners had made a breakthrough and I had a new batter, Zak Crawley, to bowl at. I set him up by swinging a few into him and then bowled a full three-quarter ball. He covered the anticipated inswing but the ball carried on going across, catching the edge, which carried to Daryl at third slip. It was a proper left-arm swing bowler's dismissal — something I had watched Trent do dozens of times — and, I thought, a good illustration of the range of skills I had at my disposal.

England made 303, to which we replied with 388. Then Henners, bowling like a genius, had the first three batters back in the shed by the 11th over, setting me up to rip the heart out of the middle order, trapping Ollie Pope leg before, then getting Dan Lawrence tentatively playing at one that nipped away — my three-quarter ball again — and later dismissing Mark Wood with a short ball. Everything was working just as I wanted it to and, as a demonstration of everything I could bring to the bowling attack, my contribution to the eight-wicket win was basically perfect. Although, I wasn't the only one firing. Ajaz had bowled extremely well and Henners was player of the match for his six wickets. Everyone was making a compelling case to be included in the team for the final.

We had beaten the English, comprehensively, and done it with half of our best team sitting out the game. That made it one of the most pleasing series wins I was ever a part of. Now for the WTC final. But first, I needed to be selected.

It was back to Southampton for the build-up, where it was key to try and keep ourselves distracted from the final, which we did with more games of golf at the course within the complex, by eating at the restaurant as close together as allowed — two to a table, tables a metre apart — and hanging out in the team room, playing darts and table tennis, or getting our pitching wedges out and chipping golf balls down the hotel hallways. One evening, I manned the barbecue with a bit of help from BJ and Colin, cooking a mountain of meat for the entire team and support staff, evening sunshine angling through the barbecue smoke as we washed it down with a few quiet beers and Trent took care of the music, some good Kiwi beats adding a familiar touch of home to what was a lovely evening, the team gelling and everyone enjoying each other's company. It truly did feel like we were one big family.

It all helped distract from my nervousness, both about the game itself and about whether I'd even be playing. I made frequent mention, in the media rounds before the match, to how this would be my World Cup final, the closest I would ever get to the feeling plenty of the other guys in our squad had experienced in this country a few years before. Trent and I had adjoining hotel rooms and we asked for the door between them to be unlocked so we could go back and forth, spending the time talking about life, kids and cricket, killing time with each other. Trent is one of my best mates — him and Gert, plus their boys Bowie, Parker and Charlie, had come to feel almost like our family away from our family — and is always an important sounding board, whether we are on the cricket field or fishing. In those rooms, we shared our fears about selection, both of us taking turns to reassure the other that we'd be in the XI for the match.

I think the weather helped my cause. We kept a close eye on the forecast as it worsened during the build-up — but you never really know in England and we stayed optimistic there would be enough time to get a result, especially with the extra sixth day scheduled. India, when they announced their team early, had included two spinners, Ravichandran Ashwin and Ravindra Jadeja. Ajaz had bowled really nicely in Birmingham and I believe — I'll never know for sure, but it's the inkling I got from the vibe around a team I knew like the back of my hand — that the last spot for the final came down to the two of us. With all that rain forecast, I suppose it was felt that the extra seamer was the way to go. But it wasn't until quite late in the piece that Steady approached me.

'You'll get your World Cup final, Wags,' he said. 'You will be playing in this game.'

The relief was immense. I was in. Now we had to win the bloody thing.

I had a decent sleep. I woke up a few times throughout the night with the excitement of the game on my mind, but I always tended to before a test. In the morning, I padded over the carpet to the curtains, pulling them open. Rain. Lots of rain.

We walked across the ground for lunch under a flotilla of

open umbrellas. By the time I had crossed the boundary, dodging puddles as best I could, my socks were drenched. The sky was the colour of lead. Everyone looked around at each other with an acknowledgement there would be no play. It was back to our rooms, trying to fill the dead hours with Netflix. Then to the team room, where the darts and the banter and the little games started up, the guys getting competitive in the search to distract ourselves from the slowness with which time seemed to be slipping by.

The next day wasn't sunny, but at least it was dry enough. It was the first time I'd got a look at the pitch, which I thought looked good, a tinge of green but no real demons — a bit there, however, with the overcast conditions, that meant you certainly wanted to bowl first, which we chose to do after Kane won the toss. It was time to switch on, focus everything towards what I needed to do in the middle. It was cold, so I walked out to sing the anthem with my jumper on, feeling the heat of the pyrotechnics — installed to up the sense of occasion — on my face and on my forearms through the cable knit. The familiar opening chord of the national anthem filled the air. That's when it really hit me. *You're playing in the final. You're playing against India. There's nothing better than this. This is the pinnacle.*

India started well, Rohit Sharma and Shubman Gill dealing nicely with the swing on offer for Trent and Tim, and counter-punching hard. Their partnership passed 50, before Kyle got Rohit with a full outswinger, which he nicked to Tim at third slip, in the 21st over of the innings. The mode of dismissal assured me that, when I was asked to bowl the 25th over — earlier than I had anticipated — there was still plenty of swing on offer. I used it to shape the first two balls back towards off stump, Shubman defending both watchfully. A few overs previously, a short-of-a-length ball from Kyle had reared viciously off the pitch to strike Shubman on the grill, and I had the sense that, given my reputation, he thought I'd been brought on to rough him up some more. I liked to play with the tension that expectation created and so I kept it full, bowling my new three-quarter ball, which he pushed at defensively, attempting to cover the inswing he thought was coming, and nicked to BJ. The plan had come off exactly as I envisioned it. Both openers gone, the game wide open, a wicket in my first over.

We would get one more scalp — Cheteshwar Pujara, LBW to Trent, a few overs after one of my bouncers rapped him on his helmet grill — before bad light and the threat of rain meant a stop-start end to the day. Virat Kohli, India's captain and the batter likely to hurt us the most, was looking good and playing me well, somehow able to pick the three-quarter ball better than anyone I had bowled it to so far. I saw him explaining to Ajinkya Rahane how to read the delivery — even if they were speaking in a language I couldn't understand. Virat was the key, and he ended the day unbeaten on 44.

Which is all he would get — Kyle got him leg before a few overs into day three. It was a huge moment. Ajinkya threatened, too, but after he scored a patient 49, he swatted at one of my short balls and was caught at square leg. It was India's highest individual score of the innings, which Kyle, Tim and Trent brought to an end by swiftly running through the tail. Kyle, just getting better and better with every outing on the international stage, ended with a five-wicket bag.

We also started well. Devon and Tom put on 70 for the first wicket, Devon making 54 before he was caught in what was the last over of the day. The next — what should've been day four — was lost entirely to the weather, nervous energy pervading the squad as we watched rain fall from the viewing area. There was so much to do to achieve a result. And India struck back on the morning of day five to have us five down at lunch — we were six down soon after — before Kyle and Tim chipped in with a vital 21 and 30 respectively to help Kane, out for 49, get us to 249. India ended the day on 64 for two — both openers having fallen LBW to Tim. That evening, there was a lot of resigned talk in the team — disappointingly I thought — about how India would surely block it out from here and look for the draw.

My thoughts, the next morning, were that we needed to be thinking about how to win from here, even if it meant risking a loss. But all the chat in our group focused on patience, dragging it out and waiting for a mistake. I found it very frustrating, but Kyle — bowling seriously well — soon got everyone starting to believe when in consecutive overs he dismissed Virat and then Cheteshwar. When Trent got Ajinkya not long after, Rishabh Pant came at us with a frenetic pace, until he skied one and Henry Nicholls made a great grab to send him back to the pavilion for 41. My solitary wicket of the innings was the dangerous Ravindra Jadeja, who had been content to duck under any short stuff on the line of his body. I wanted to try and get him fending at one, aiming to rap his gloves. Close enough: he nicked a bouncer outside off to BJ. And, with an end open, Tim and Trent cleaned up the tail. We needed 139 runs to win. Maybe our patience had paid off after all.

It was a small chase and we felt really good about our chances as Tom and Devon walked to the crease. But we knew India would make it tough. Ross was the only uber-superstitious batter in our dressing room, but in the tension of that occasion, superstitions were suddenly everywhere: don't move, sit down, don't drink. We were watching the action on the TV in the changing room, which relayed the pictures to us a second or two after the cheers of the Indian supporters — first when Tom was stumped off Ravichandran, and then when Kane was given out leg before to the same bowler a few overs later. Kane, of course, was huge for us. As soon as we saw the replay, all of us were yelling, 'Review it! Review it!' at the TV screen, which thankfully he did — and the ball was missing leg stump. When Devon *was* out leg before in Ravichandran's next over, it brought Ross to the crease, our two best batters out there to try and take us home. The nerves were intense as we edged our way closer and closer to the target. When we got within striking distance, Trent stood up, pointing at the batters to come in turn and saying, 'You've got 10 runs in you, you've got 10 runs in you, you've got 10 runs in you, and I've got five in me — surely we're doing this, right?'

When there were about 10 runs left, we started arranging in huddles, giving each other sly little hugs but then quickly reminding ourselves we weren't there yet. But we were close enough that our new-found superstitions started to wane, all of us creeping closer to the door looking out to the middle, Kane and Ross starting to put the pedal down as the end neared.

There are no words that can do justice to that time — when victory was assured — and I stood there trying to take in the feeling, a million things from the road I had walked to be here going through my mind. The New Zealanders in the crowd were belting out a rendition of 'Zombie' by the Cranberries, the titular word replaced by 'Kohli': 'In your he-ead, in your he-e-e-ead, Kohli! Kohli! Kohli-ee-ee-ee!'

The moment Ross flicked the winning runs to the boundary is both vivid and blurry — I can't remember who I hugged or who hugged me as we jumped with joy, a band of brothers under the black cap. My World Cup final had ended in glory. We had won. We were the champions of the world.

When, finally, Kane was preparing to raise the Mace — a world map overlaid across a cricket ball — Tim pointed out the size of

New Zealand, so tiny it was like a sculptor's afterthought. 'That's us! That's us!' I looked again at the familiar shapes, Māui's waka and the fish pulled from the deep. I had helped win this for my country. *My country. That's us.* Kane raised the Mace over his head and the fireworks exploded as we celebrated deep into the Southampton evening.

CHAPTER 14:
LAST HIGHS

Back in New Zealand we had the usual end-of-tour assessment. Mine was one of the most positive I had ever received, the coaching staff noting the work I had put in to become a more complete bowler. I knew my pace had dropped a fraction as I entered my mid-thirties, but it was noted that I was finding more swing than I ever had for the Black Caps and enhancing its threat with other varieties, like the new three-quarter ball. The benefits of the move north, and the extra training it had meant with Tim and Trent, two of the best swing bowlers in the world, was paying dividends. I still had the short-ball weapon for when conditions and match situations demanded it, but I felt I had the skills to prosper in whatever environment I was asked to take wickets.

A few months later, the team reassembled in Auckland to take care of some commercial commitments. In addition, there was another meeting with the coaching staff to talk through the coming season. And I was entirely taken aback when Shane Jurgensen, our bowling coach, asked me if I had ever considered retiring and what my plans were for after cricket.

'Get screwed, what do you mean retirement? We just had a chat a few months ago and you told me how well I was tracking. I'm not even close to thinking about that.'

I could sense there was an air of embarrassment in the room created by the vehemence with which I had rejected the suggestion, but I was very conscious that my place in the XI wasn't as assured now as it had been. My thoughts were so focused on ways to stay in the team that I may have misread the tone of the question, which I think was meant, mostly, as a genuine question about my future.

There was a lot of change starting to happen in an environment that had been stable for so long. BJ Watling was gone, having signed off with the WTC final, when I had described him to the media as the heart of the team. And he was such an important part of my success, too, the man who would tell me what was and wasn't working, when I was hitting the gloves nicely, or when we needed to target the hip and move leg gully a shade finer. So many of my wickets would not have happened if it hadn't been for the thought he had put into them. He was a great sounding board about life, too — not usually the most talkative person, but get a few beers in him and he hardly shuts up. Luckily, he's full of excellent advice.

But I wasn't ready to follow in BJ's footsteps. And that conversation was my first indication that the end of my international career was being contemplated by the management and support staff. I'm sure coaches are always thinking about succession planning and bringing along the next generation, but as a player the knowledge that other people were openly thinking about a scenario when I wouldn't be there made the occasions from then on when I was left out of the XI harder to take. Those decisions started to feel less like horses-for-courses selections, and more like this horse was being appraised for the quality of glue he might make. I sometimes wish I had been able to spend less time worrying about selection — the stress and anxiety is such a killer on the body — but at other times those same feelings helped motivate me to get over disappointment and try again. It is a delicate balancing act.

Our tour of India, always a tough place to visit as a quick bowler, gave me no opportunity to make a statement. The Kanpur in which we played the first test was a world away from my previous sweat-drenched visit to the city. At this time of the year — the first test began as November 2021 drew to a close — it was cool, and with sunshine hours in such short supply we began at 9.30 in the morning to increase the chances of a full day's play. Despite conditions that looked reasonably helpful, I was left out when we went in with three spinners. Although in the end it was our quicks who had the most success for us, Tim taking eight wickets across the game, as we narrowly hung on for a draw after their slow bowlers fell one wicket short of running through us in the second innings. We moved to Mumbai.

I was told pretty early on that I wouldn't be playing, so I tailored my training towards the Super Smash to which I thought I'd be returning when I got home. In the lead-up to the test, I was out in the middle of Wankhede Stadium bowling with a white ball when Indian coach Rahul Dravid strolled over to me to ask why I had never represented New Zealand in limited-overs cricket. Then he asked if I'd ever considered throwing my name in the ring for the IPL auction. I could be pretty handy in these conditions, he said. *Jeez, you can't ask for a better compliment than that.* Those encouraging words instantly got me very excited about something that I'd never considered much of a possibility. I continued training, attempting a knuckle-ball. In the sticky heat, it slipped from my hand, missing my target by the width of about four pitches, the ball heading at beamer height into the midst of where the Indian guys were training. I can still hear the peals of laughter ringing out from the balcony where some of my teammates were watching. That brought me back to earth pretty quick.

We lost that test — we were bowled out for just 62 in our first innings — but it wouldn't be right not to mention Ajaz's incredible performance, bowling 47.5 overs to take all 10 Indian wickets in their first turn at bat, becoming only the third player in the history of test cricket to take 10 in an innings. Like Mitch and Colin, Ajaz had bowled some important spells for us over the years and had perhaps never been hailed as much as he should have been for the role he played. We were so stoked to see him write his name into the history books, especially in the city of his birth.

After the test, Ravi Ashwin approached and asked for my details, also encouraging me to register for the IPL auction. The other good thing to come out of that tour was the bat that Ravindra Jadeja gave me from his collection, an absolute cannon that I still use to this day.

I was excited to head back to the Super Smash with my T20 ambitions renewed by the conversations with Rahul and Ravi. So I was absolutely gutted when coach Graeme Aldridge told me they weren't going to use me in that year's competition. By now I hadn't played a T20 game since February 2019 and I just wanted a shot to prove my worth. I couldn't help but look around at all the franchise leagues popping up around the world and think how fun it would be to challenge myself in those environments. It was extremely frustrating to believe I had plenty to offer but never getting the opportunity to find out. Scenarios like this were the sorts of things that really messed with my mind — no matter how hard I worked, sometimes the final decision was out of my hands.

Even so, when the IPL auction came around, Ravi messaged me to tell me to keep my fingers crossed for the second half. I might get lucky. In the end, I didn't even make the cut that would have put my name up for consideration. I knew it was a long shot and didn't take it personally — but it had been a frustrating and largely cricketless couple of months by the time our next test, against the touring Bangladeshis, began at Bay Oval on the first day of 2022.

It was the hottest test match I have ever played in New Zealand. Every day the mercury nudged 30 degrees, a hot wind blowing across the ground. We lost the toss and were put in to bat on a green-tinged surface, bowled out for a middling 328. Bangladesh had always challenged us and you could see just how up for it they were — the WTC win put a huge target on our backs. The pitch had dried out by the time they came to bat, and they proved incredibly hard to remove from the crease, almost all of their top order making significant contributions to their score of 458. It would have been less if my delivery that top-scorer Mominul Haque nicked behind had not been adjudged a front-foot no-ball — despite the replay, I think, showing a fraction of my boot behind the line. Baz, who was commentating in the series, came up to me later and merely said, 'Well, just don't get that close and you'll never have that problem.' Thanks, Baz. Unfortunately, he was right.

It left us significantly behind in the game. And when Ebadot Hossain snared three quick wickets late on day four and returned the next morning for another couple — it was a seriously good spell of fast bowling — we were condemned to our first-ever test loss against Bangladesh. We were disappointed, but we tried not to over-analyse it. We knew we hadn't been good enough, and they brought their absolute best in conditions — dry pitch, stinking hot — that were as kind to them as any they were likely to face in this country. In the second test, at Hagley Oval, normal transmission resumed — we scored big in the first innings, then bowled them out twice to win by an innings, Ross, in his final test, taking the last wicket to sign off on a legendary career.

Ross had been part of the team since before I got anywhere near it, and I'd always had a mountain of respect for him — for what he achieved as a batter, of course, but even more for the kind of bloke he was and the friend he became. He watched me closely from his perch at first slip over the years and would often give me a word of encouragement or advice in the midst of long fruitless spells, sharing his wisdom on the field just as he loved to share a joke and a glass of red wine in the shed after. So many things had or were changing in the squad, underlined by the fact that long-term manager Mike Sandle — Roman as we called him — who had done so much to help build the culture of our team, would also step aside following our next test series, against South Africa. 'Manager' has never been such an insufficient term for the size of the role he played in the Black Caps' success and, more importantly, the lives of all the guys. He was a key driver of the unifying idea that family came first, and his mantra — a problem shared is a problem halved — has also become one of my own.

That South Africa series was slightly strange in that, thanks to Covid, both games would be played at the same ground, Hagley Oval. Matt Henry — one of the nicest, kindest people you could imagine, and a hell of a bowler who in any other era would have played 50 tests by then — came into the team for the game on his home ground. Henners had been such a great team man, always finding ways to contribute to the success of the bowling group, even though that was the exact thing keeping him out of the XI. So it was a thrill for all of us to watch him destroy a quality batting lineup — 23 for seven from his 15 overs — and then take his form from the golf course into the middle to smash a quick 50 from number 11. Tim did the majority of the damage the second time around and we beat South Africa by an innings. We looked good to get our first-ever test-series win against the Proteas.

The weather was extremely warm for the week that separated the tests, which we spent playing golf at Pegasus Golf & Sports Club, 45 minutes north of the city, in between our training sessions. A warm nor'wester raked over Christchurch, sucking moisture from Hagley Oval. The wicket, although they had pumped it full of water, was far less vibrant than the shade of green we usually expected of a day-one Hagley pitch. There were a lot of unknowns playing on the same ground so soon after the last test, but we stuck with our usual Hagley formula: lots of seamers, bowl first if given the option. Unfortunately, South Africa proved they had perhaps read the pitch better. They chose to bat, scoring 364 — I took four wickets — then bowled us out for 293. We ran into a rampant Kyle Verreynne in the second innings, which left us a target of over 400, a total we never really looked like chasing against a top-class bowling attack as we sank to an almost 200-run loss. We had let slip a golden opportunity to take the series off them and, even if I had bowled well — nine wickets at under 24 — I was starting to become aware of more and more media chatter about what my slightly reduced pace meant for my future.

We had just wrapped up a Plunket Shield game at Bay Oval — there were plans for the team to come back to mine after for a big feed — when I checked my phone. There were a heap of missed calls and messages crowding the screen. From Lana. When I managed to get through, she told me she'd had a miscarriage. I immediately cancelled the team function and rushed to be with her. We were in deep grief, but also amazed. We had no idea that it was even possible for us to get pregnant naturally — we'd been repeatedly told it would never happen — but this was a brutal way to find out. When Lana recovered, we began to discuss the possibility of having another child. We again put no pressure on ourselves, nor yet really began investigating whether we would have to go the IVF route again.

It was Father's Day 2021, about six months since Lana's miscarriage, and I was outside presiding over a pot of bubbling *potjiekos*, a traditional South African stew cooked over an open fire, when Lana told me that her and Livie were popping out to get a few more ingredients from the supermarket. I had no idea, but Lana later told me she woke up that morning and just knew she was pregnant. She was actually heading out to pick up a test. And then — again I was still in the dark — when that came back positive, she wanted to make sure and headed out for more 'ingredients'. When that was positive, too, Lana and Livie came outside to give me the most incredible Father's Day gift imaginable. I was absolutely blown away.

Throughout that season — against Bangladesh and South Africa — we approached Lana's due date, as well as another English tour, as Covid ran rampant through the country. We could see how difficult things were going to get for Lana — she'd be recovering from a second C-section with a newborn baby and a high-energy two-year-old to care for also — with me away playing cricket in England. We tried to get a special dispensation for Lana's parents to get through the border restrictions then in place, but we were declined.

Lana insisted that I had to go — after all, this was our family income — so I called Steady. Given that I had toured England just a year ago, I said, after which everyone told me how well I was tracking, would it be okay if I stayed at home for the first warm-up game so I could be there to spend more time with my new daughter and help Lana? I could also train with Kane, who would be in a similar situation with his second child. He probably didn't mean it as bluntly as I heard it, but I was gobsmacked by his reply: that was fine as long as I realised I was opening the door for someone else. The Black Caps environment I had come to know and love had been rightly proud to put family first. Here I was trying to do exactly that amidst the scariness of a global pandemic only to feel my place in the team was vaguely threatened for doing so.

But of course family does come first and I took the risk, something I have never for an instant regretted. Zahli Rose Wagner was born on 5 May 2022. This time, the procedure went as planned and I could soon hold this little angel to my chest, falling instantly in love, as did her big sister, beside herself with joy when she first met Zahli. It was one of those amazing pinch-yourself moments, to watch Livie take her sister gently in her arms and see the love that existed between them already, to feel that love connecting the four of us. And again, I can't even begin to express the depth of my pride in Lana for her strength. It was a beautiful but chaotic time — there were Covid restrictions to how long and often we could stay with Lana and Zahli at the birthing centre — and Livie couldn't understand why I'd have to drag her away from the little sister she would've done anything not to leave. I also had to keep up a very busy training schedule to get me ready for England, and we never would've managed had it not been for Livie's amazing home carer and our neighbours — Auntie Sue, in particular, was indispensable — who stepped in to help.

If that was a tricky period for me, it was nothing compared with how hard it was for Lana when I had to fly to the UK. Again, we were so thankful for all the help and food Lana received from neighbours and friends. She put on a brave face, but I know it was a struggle. Zahli suffered horribly from reflux those first months of her life and struggled to sleep at night. Lana was exhausted, which added to my frustrations after I played in the second warm-up game in Chelmsford — we lost — and I wasn't selected for the first test at Lord's, where we came up against an England team coached by Brendon McCullum for the first time. We all knew the effect Baz would have on the English dressing room — he'd had much the same impact on ours years earlier — so it was no surprise to see them come hard at us in a back-and-forth test they won on the fourth day.

I thought I was a real shot for the next test at Trent Bridge, and when I wasn't selected I took it hard. I knew we had bowling depth in our squad, with Matt, Ajaz and me likely to be fighting for one spot, but with everything that was going on at home I started to wonder what the point of me even being there was, when I could have been so much more useful in New Zealand. Lana was struggling. I desperately wanted to get back to help her. I even approached the manager — Simon Insley had taken over Roman's role — and Jurgo and told them I needed to get back home. They encouraged me to stay on the tour and found a way to get a little bit more support to Lana, which helped top up what neighbours and friends were already supplying. Unfortunately the on-field action didn't lift my mood, either. We lost the game after scoring 553 in the first innings when Jonny Bairstow went ballistic on the last day.

I was feeling pretty bitter. The conversation with Steady I'd had before the tour kept running through my mind and it almost felt like I was being punished for not making that first warm-up game. I probably wouldn't even have played the final test, in Leeds, had Kyle not been injured at Trent Bridge. But it was an opportunity all the same.

We made 329 batting first after another century by Daryl Mitchell — his third of the series — and then had them on the ropes when Trent, bowling as well as I've ever seen, blasted out the top three. I bowled the 12th over, pumped up and angry about the tour, desperate to make an impact. I did so with my second delivery, Ben Stokes chipping a full ball to mid-off. I roared in anger and defiance, thinking of Lana, Zahli and Livie back home — but equally hoping they were deep asleep at that moment. Three balls later I curved one in to Ben Foakes to trap him in front. I repeated the display of emotion.

England were six down and I had the chance for a knockout blow a few overs later, but I couldn't hang on to a sharp return catch off Jonny's bat. The batch of Dukes balls used for this series had a tendency to go very soft in the middle overs, and that's exactly what happened to this one, Jonny and debutant Jamie Overton arm-wrestling the English back into, and then ahead of, the game, one boundary at a time. When they eventually won, I glanced up at Baz on the English balcony, a big smile animating those familiar features, looking very strange in the shadow of an England cap.

By the end of that tour, I seriously wondered if this was the end. I was feeling so low and the omens didn't look good for my prospects. Kyle had become a world-class bowler in a short space of time, Matt

Henry's case for inclusion was becoming stronger and stronger, and Tim and Trent remained one of the best new-ball pairings in the world. For a brief moment I thought that maybe I should give it away, forget about test cricket, throw in my lot with an English county, giving me the stability of six months at home with the family each year and some good high-quality cricket — plus more money than a year-long New Zealand contract was worth. But one big lesson the ups and downs of my life have taught me is how to pick myself up from disappointments and find a way to keep going when things get tough. In my heart I knew I wasn't ready to be done with test cricket. I was sure I had more to give and I wanted the chance to give it.

The changes kept coming. Back home, several of us senior players got together for a coffee to discuss how to keep the flame of our winning culture burning amidst all the new faces, the new ideas coming in. Games we would have once backed ourselves to take deep and eventually win now seemed to be slipping away from us. We needed to continue role-modelling everything that had made us strong, we decided, prioritising the team ahead of ourselves and looking after everyone who came into its environment. As seniors we could keep a hand on the tiller of our culture. Kane had already been talking about relinquishing the captaincy, so it was no surprise when he made that call. Tom Latham had taken the reins of late when Kane was unavailable and he was a good captain, but I thought he might need a few more years before he would be truly ready. So I was pushing for Tim to take the armband — knowing, regardless, that those guys were all in the leadership group and all their voices would be heard. It almost didn't matter who was officially the captain. And, in the end, it fell to Tim. His first assignment: our first test tour of Pakistan in 20 years.

And he would have to do it without his great mate and fellow opening bowler, Trent. I had no notion, throughout that tour of England, that Trent was thinking about declining a NZC contract in order to spend more time with his family, as well as be available to take up lucrative short-term T20 contracts in the many leagues that continued to spring up around the world. The first I found out about it was a phone call, when he told me what he had decided. Test cricket and representing New Zealand meant the world to Trent so I knew it must have been an agonising decision. 'You know what's best for you and your family,' I told him. If this was it, I continued, then he had my complete backing; as well, I'm sure, as that of all of the guys in the team.

It's now becoming increasingly common for Black Caps, like Kane Williamson and Devon Conway, to come to similar arrangements with NZC, allowing them to pursue T20 contracts while continuing to play test cricket, and I feel for Trent that he wasn't treated similarly at that time and allowed the chance to keep playing the longest form. That lack of consistency makes me think NZC need to take a close look at the contracting system and ask whether it's still fit for purpose in the increasingly complex world of professional cricket. Regardless, it was strange to think about going forward without him — it almost felt like I'd be taking the field with a missing limb, so much did Tim, Trent and I feed off each other as a bowling group.

Before I could experience that in Pakistan, however, I realised my passport was about to expire. That is, my South African passport. Despite having represented New Zealand for a decade, I still wasn't a citizen. Ironically, it was more or less *because* I had represented

New Zealand that I wasn't a citizen: constantly heading away on tour meant I never had the requisite number of consecutive days in the country that I needed. Accordingly, every tour I went on required the extra stress and labour of visa applications — sometimes cutting things unbelievably close — and always being last through the airport on return home, as my teammates headed for the fast-moving New Zealand-passport lines. This was the opportunity to finally get my New Zealand citizenship sorted. It took an age of tediously moving through the Wellington bureaucracy — a process too boring for these pages — but eventually, a few days before we flew out of the country, thanks especially to help from the New Zealand Cricket Players' Association, my passport arrived, delivered to me by an NZC staff member as we trained under the marquee at Lincoln.

I was dripping with sweat when I took it in my hand, as the squad — all of whom had been in the loop about my bureaucratic struggles — gave me a round of applause. I was officially the New Zealander I had known myself to be for a decade. This country meant the world to me, the way it had taken me in, buried me in kindness and made me one of its own. I was surprised by just how emotional I got as I received the official record to reflect that love built over time, standing there holding this fern-emblazoned document in my sweaty hand. I used it to fly to Pakistan a day or two later.

The Black Caps' white-ball tour to Pakistan had been cancelled the year before on account of security threats, so security for this tour was tight. We couldn't get out much, but it was amazing to be in Pakistan — the land of Wasim Akram and Waqar Younis — and it was clear to see on the faces of our hosts how much it meant to have us playing test cricket in the country after so long. It was a joy to spend some time with local net bowlers and try to pass on some wisdom. Although, really, we needed the wisdom to flow in the opposite direction.

Even Trent — then playing in the Australian Big Bash League — would have struggled with the Karachi pitch used for the first test, beginning on Boxing Day. Pakistan chose to bat and the plan was that I wouldn't bowl until later in the innings. Until it actually did swing for Tim in his first over and he decided I should have a look with the new ball also. So I got a single over before we went to spin. I didn't get the ball back until the 39th over, by which time every last bit of shine had been scoured off it by the pitch. I took a single short-ball wicket from my 21 overs and was only asked to bowl three in the second innings in a game that ended in a draw.

As did the second test, for which I wasn't selected. Which was probably a good thing, for I only had half my mind on the cricket. Lana's brother, Dewaldt, suffered heart failure during the tour and required major surgery. There'd been some discussion with Steady about me flying home to take care of the kids so Lana could fly to South Africa to be with him, but in the end it was decided that Lana's parents would be able to take care of things on the home front. Instead I watched as an epic test match ended in a nerve-racking draw that left every result available right up until the final over. We would have a few more of those before the summer came to a close.

We flew back home to face the English again, but not before I played my first T20 game in four years when injuries hit the Northern Districts squad and I was called up to cover. I bowled really well and got another game. Then again, and I got another. Then I had cemented my place and a few games after that I was taking two crucial wickets in the final, helping the team to the Super Smash title. It was a hugely rewarding experience to prove on the field — both to others and to myself — that this old dog still had his bag of T20 tricks. And gosh how I would need them, even in the test matches immediately to follow.

By now the so-called Bazball approach to test cricket ushered in by Brendon had been well and truly bedded in. We knew only too well what to expect. The first test was at Bay Oval, the venue's first-ever day–night test match. We won the toss and chose to bowl and — taking the second over — I got my first delivery to curl deliciously in the air, avoiding the inside edge of Zak Crawley's bat and clipping his front pad on its way to the top of off stump. It was a dream start, a huge statement. Or so I thought, until I realised I had overstepped. I couldn't help but think about Baz's advice the previous summer. I couldn't bear to look at him, this time, up on the English balcony — especially after that over went for 14 runs. It was an omen for a game that soon took on a nightmarish quality.

We knew they'd be looking to score quickly so they could bowl at us under lights that evening. But when they declared at 325 for nine in under 60 overs — I took four wickets, although I went at nearly five runs an over — we thought things were pretty even. But, as expected, the pink ball was a different beast under lights and we ended the evening three wickets down, with me at the crease as nightwatchman. I put on a 50-run partnership with Devon the next day, but it was Tom Blundell who truly dug us out of a hole with a magnificent century to leave us only 19 runs behind when we were bowled out as the lights took effect on day two.

If we thought England had come hard in the first innings, this was something else. Beginning day three on 79 for two, first Ollie Pope and then Harry Brook took on my short-ball attack like it had never been taken on before, both hitting me for massive sixes and lots of runs. It was brutal, but also incredibly frustrating — I felt like I was in with a chance almost every delivery and even many of the balls that went over the boundary seemed lucky to do so, coming off top edges or hitting high on the bat. Others fell just out of reach of despairing fielders. It seemed like one of those days of test cricket when everything goes against you. And almost the whole time throughout the assault I was talking to Tim.

'Should we drop the short-ball attack, go full and try to build pressure that way?'

But we agreed that wickets had to be just around the corner, and with Tim's backing, I kept going. It was hard, though, looking up at the scoreboard at one point and seeing I was going at a scarcely believable 11 runs an over: moderately expensive for a T20 game, almost unheard of in test cricket. I did get Ollie, edging an attempted pull through to Tom behind the stumps, but it felt like a lot of damage to absorb for that wicket. Too much, as it would turn out. Again we found ourselves batting in the evening, and when we had lost five wickets by close of play the match was gone.

It hurt. Not just the loss, but the severity of it. The brutal punishment I had taken put my six wickets from across the game well and truly in the shade. We had a barbecue at Kane's house to unwind, the boys grabbing surfcasters to try and catch a feed straight from the beach, later sitting around a bonfire and reflecting on the game and its lessons and trying to clear our minds for the next one. I had to stay away from my phone. It seemed every second notification was for a story about how I was too old, too slow, past it. I tried to laugh it off, but it wasn't easy. I never read much media about my own performances, but it was almost getting difficult to avoid. Back came that unwelcome voice seeping into my thoughts as I stared into the flames, surf quietly breaking in the darkness beyond — *Maybe they're right?*

I was as fit as I had ever been and my body felt great — but then, because of the doubt implanted in my head, every bit of soreness was magnified. *Is my body too old for this? Have I put it through too much? Am I actually done? Should I just retire?* But then, the other voice, which, in all but the darkest times of my life, I could count on breaking in to counteract the self-doubt. *Screw that, I'll show you. Age is just a number. What really counts is how hard you can push and how deep you can dig.* And that feeling was the attitude I took into the next test.

When I play golf, if I have a bad round, I almost can't sleep that night because I want so badly to get back out there and put it right. It was the same in the lead-up to Wellington — I was absolutely determined to make amends. We won the toss and bowled first on a green wicket, which, as captain, you'd be very brave not to do, but we all knew how deceiving the Basin Reserve could be. Timmy and Henners started beautifully, reducing them to three down with only 21 on the board. But that was the end of our success for the day, the Basin sticking to its deceptive script, Joe Root and Harry Brook getting the better of everything we threw at them.

I was racking my brain trying to figure out what I'd done to Mother Cricket, but it felt like she was biting me pretty hard on the arse. I'd bowled to some of the greatest batting talents of all time — AB de Villiers, Steve Smith, Kane, Virat Kohli, Joe Root — and during that series Harry Brook was the equal of them all. His partnership with Joe reached 300 before Henners got Harry caught and bowled the next morning and, although Joe also made a big century, we kept everyone else pretty quiet before England declared on 435. Unfortunately, Jimmy Anderson was phenomenal when we replied — Broady and Jack Leach not far behind — and we could only put 209 on the board, thanks in the main to Timmy's quickfire 73. I was batting when our innings ended and began sprinting off the field to get ready to bowl.

Ben Duckett turned to me and said, 'Relax, mate, you're batting.'

I couldn't believe my ears. I was amazed the English bowling attack would want to head back onto a very heavy Basin Reserve outfield — there'd been overnight rain around during the test — rather than let the batters attempt to Bazball us out of the game.

But Zak and Joe, who were nearby, confirmed it.

'Thank you,' I said. 'That's the best thing for us.'

They looked at me quite strangely, but I instantly believed that we could win from here, as distant as that seemed. It meant, of course, we would need a huge two days of batting — but as Tom Latham and Devon, then Kane, then Daryl and Tom Blundell started first chipping away at the deficit, then edging us in front, I remained adamant we could do it.

'Settle down, Wags. There's a long way to go,' Tim said, trying to keep us focused on the present and put a lid on my wild optimism.

'Mate,' I replied. 'This is it, this is how we get back in, we're going to win this game.'

When our innings drew to a close, England needed 258 for victory. They started — no surprise — in positive fashion on the fourth evening, losing one wicket on their way to 48 from 11 overs. On the recent record of English fourth-innings chases, most were probably backing the tourists, but I could sense the feeling that we were about to do something special starting to take hold in our dressing room.

Tim got rid of nightwatchman Ollie Robinson early on day five, then I had Ollie Pope edging a late cut to slip on the last ball of my first over, a measure of revenge for the Mount. When, next ball,

Harry, our tormentor throughout the two games so far, was run out without scoring, the game's scales tipped our way for the first time. But Joe and Ben — first painstakingly, but with increasing assurance — built a partnership that by its end was pretty close to taking the game away from us.

Tim called me back on to bowl the 57th over. There was no hesitation about our plan, despite how I had fared in the series so far. We set the field for some short stuff.

'This is when you're at your best, Wags,' Tim said. 'This is when you come into your own.'

I was pumped up, so keen to prove to my doubters and myself that I could still summon the old Wagnerian magic. Fourth ball, Ben took the bait, giving himself some room and looking to swat a head-bound bouncer to the rope, or over it. He did neither, top-edging to square leg. Now we had an opening. Which I widened a few overs later when Joe, pulling at a short ball that didn't climb much above his waist, also top-edged, this time midwicket finishing the job. They still needed 56 with three wickets in hand, and keeper Ben Foakes was the man who we felt had to score the majority of the runs. Which he did, losing Broady early — I took the catch off Henners' bowling — before rebuilding with the stubborn Jack Leach. But, eventually, he top-edged a bouncer from Timmy. I was there again, stationed at fine leg, to take it.

England nine down, seven runs still required, Jimmy Anderson — my old Lancashire mate — in my sights. When he swung the last ball of my over away for four, timing it so well it raced through Kane's legs at midwicket, I couldn't believe it. Two to win. Tim followed up with a maiden to give me one more chance at Jimmy for the game.

The belief that I could do this for the team was really strong, but there were a million things going through my mind at the top of

my mark. I tried to smother them — to be the balcony boy — but I couldn't quite. My first ball sailed over Jimmy's head and I could barely allow myself to look at the umpire in case it was called wide. It wasn't, but I knew I couldn't risk getting that close again.

Among all the ideas swirling inside my head, one floated to the top as I readied myself to bowl again: get it into his armpit and make him uncomfortable. What came out was a little more leg side than I had hoped but, in attempting to turn it fine, Jimmy tickled an edge and Tom behind the stumps took a sprawling catch. We had beaten the English by a single run. Pure joy, though there really isn't a word that can do justice to the relief and happiness of that moment. Later on, it was almost equally satisfying to line up to shake the hands of the English team and to share a bit of a grin with Baz, knowing we'd got one back against them this time.

My body, when I woke up the next day after a few beers with the English boys, wasn't happy. There was pain in my back, my hamstring, my foot. All the pain I'd buried beneath painkillers and adrenaline over the series was suddenly demanding attention. But pain was nothing new, and I was pretty sure I'd be able to get myself right for the following series against the visiting Sri Lankans. I had a cortisone injection in my foot — the most pressing of my pain issues, where I had some swelling in my joints — but couldn't get through a fitness test a few days later. I flew to Christchurch for the first test anyway, hoping to come right by the time the match began. After seven overs in the nets, I felt good enough — in pain, but only mild pain on the fast-bowler scale — to play.

I bowled 10 expensive and wicketless overs in the first innings, then in Sri Lanka's next turn at bat I felt myself tightening up. I thought I could bowl through it. Big mistake. It was as if a sniper had fired directly at my right hamstring from somewhere on the bank as

I followed through after my fifth delivery. I bowled the next ball in agony, but had to admit to myself that something was badly wrong and went off the field. The scan showed a bulging disc in my back. And a torn hamstring. My season over, the county gig I had lined up with Yorkshire suddenly off the table. I'd been playing professional cricket for 18 years and this was the worst injury — or injuries — I had ever received.

Of course, I still wanted the chance to contribute to this game — and with a lengthy recovery already ahead of me, did it matter if I lengthened it a little more? Tim floated the idea of me coming in as a pinch-hitter earlier in the fourth innings as we chased a target on the final day, but when the field was pushed back as we neared the total, the fact that I wouldn't be able to run twos counted against me. Then wickets started to tumble as we chased the last runs in the dying light, and Henners was run out with three balls left. Here was my chance.

I jogged out to meet Kane in the middle. He was on strike, somehow finding a gap in the field to put a full ball away for four. Scores even, two deliveries remaining. I turned down the opportunity to scramble a bye from the next ball when Kane missed his pull shot. I was sure that Kane, unbeaten on 121 and seeing it like a beach ball, would find a more risk-free run off the final delivery, especially when, as we met in the middle of the pitch, the floodlights finally flashed on.

But when he missed that last ball I started running as fast as my hamstring allowed, ignoring the pain and seeing only the line of white paint I was scampering towards. I dived, keeper Niroshan Dickwella missed his throw at the stumps, only for Asitha Fernando, in his follow through, to pick it up and throw down the other set of stumps, where only a big dive from Kane saved his wicket. We had won. By the barest margin. The injuries had put a damper on another famous win, but being out in the middle to savour that moment was a great way to celebrate my 37th birthday.

CHAPTER 15:
FINAL SUMMER

The summer of 2023/24 had to be big for me. I knew my career would end in the not-too-distant future, but I still felt I had a lot to contribute and playing a decisive role at the sharp end of two of history's closest games the season before had reinvigorated my passion for cricket — and for being part of this team. Looking ahead at the schedule, I mentally earmarked the England tour of New Zealand scheduled for the 24/25 summer, our last fixtures of the WTC cycle, as my swansong. It would give me a chance to contribute to a WTC that would hopefully atone for the disappointment of the last, which had never recovered after our home loss to Bangladesh.

I tried to let go of my worries that the team was preparing for life without me in the squad. As so often before in my career, I attempted to channel the doubt I could feel surrounding me as motivation.

Except in my darkest moments, all I've ever wanted to do when things are against me and my back is against the wall is to dig deep and fight — through the pain and into the wind.

The recovery from the bulging disc and the torn hamstring took four months — two months fewer than the medical team had initially suggested. I put in a huge amount of work — Pilates, running the streets of Pāpāmoa, gym sessions — to get myself ready for the cricket season. I was almost back to full fitness, bowling in the nets to the Black Caps squad about to head off on white-ball duty, and feeling good. I even signed to play the final three games of the county season with Somerset in the New Zealand off-season, hoping to give myself the best chance possible to be at peak performance by the time our summer rolled around. South Africa and Australia, both favourite opponents of mine, were due to tour, and before that we were touring Bangladesh. When the central contracts were released — and my name was one of the last on the list of 20 — it sharpened my recognition that I was playing for my future every time I walked out onto the field.

When I arrived in picturesque Taunton, fate, in the predictable form of the English weather, seemed to be against me. It rained basically every day we were meant to be playing, and it was impossible to find any rhythm. From a purely cricketing perspective, I probably would have been better off staying at home and training under the marquee in the Mount than flying halfway across the world to train indoors there. We had also received the happy news that we had another child on the way and, by the time I left for England, Lana was visibly pregnant with two under-threes to look after. I could've been there to help her out, rather than managing only 70 overs in one loss and two draws as Somerset finished in the lower half of Division One — although the infectious energy of the great group of guys I found in Somerset did help to get me really excited about the home season to come.

My old mate BJ Watling, having spent a year in the Wellington coaching setup, had returned to Northern Districts as the newly appointed head coach. And despite my relative lack of game time with Somerset, my body felt good as we went into the first match of the season, against Otago in Hamilton. It was the Friday before Labour Weekend, and Seddon Park had a wet, heavy, early-season feel to it as I took the new ball. But the ball was coming out as if in a dream — one of the best spells I'd bowled in a long time. My action felt smooth, the ball shaping nicely. No wickets initially, but in the first six overs I bowled I didn't concede a single run. Worry about my future was evaporating in the face of the control I had over my craft. I returned for a second spell, taking my first wicket of the season. And then I ran across a damp, sandy section of turf, and felt my foot puncture the surface. Immediately, I felt my hamstring tighten. *Please no.*

I came off the field. BJ assessed things and almost straight away told me to sit out, to minimise the risk of aggravating an injury before the tests ahead of me that summer. It was the Friday afternoon before Labour Weekend, and arranging an immediate scan that might've allowed me back into that game turned out to be impossible. We couldn't really do anything until after the long weekend, by which time we weren't even able to arrange a scan that would allow me to play the following game, either. When we managed to finally get one done, it showed that a recurrence of the bulging disc was pinching a nerve, and that was sending pain down my leg and making it seem as if there was a problem with the hamstring when in fact all was fine. The disc could easily have been treated with standard anti-inflammatories and I could have been playing for Northern Districts all along.

Again, I wondered what I had done to upset Mother Cricket.

There were now three weeks until the Bangladesh tour. In Somerset, a physio had suggested that a cortisone injection could take care of the disc, something that had never been talked about among the New Zealand support crew. I would need 10 days after the injection before I could train again and this seemed like the time to try it, as it would give me an opportunity to rest before getting my bowling load up in preparation for Bangladesh. Then I got a call from Steady, who broke the news that I hadn't been selected for the tour — they expected spin to play a big role. I knew it might be tough to get into the XI with seam-bowling slots at a premium, but this time I hadn't even made the touring squad, and it hurt more than usual. At this late stage in my career, every time I wasn't selected gave me one less chance to show what I could still do.

The ICC Cricket World Cup was under way in India, the Black Caps on their way to a top-four finish. Unfortunately, Henners tore his hamstring in the team's big loss to South Africa and was ruled out of both the remainder of the tournament and the Bangladesh tour to follow. I would be his replacement in the squad — if I could prove my fitness. I had to very hurriedly get down to Dunedin where Northern Districts were playing Otago, where I bowled really well, ripping through the lower order in the second innings to ensure we secured a 34-run victory. I was off to Bangladesh.

Lana, by now, was very, very pregnant. I don't really know how she managed, and once again it was hard to leave her at such a tricky time — but she was the biggest advocate for me making the most of the opportunity. Much like my brother's advice all those years earlier, Lana's was always to get out there and put my best foot forward, whether I had the ball in my hand or was running drinks. So that's what I tried to do, even though the only bowling I did was in the nets as the pitches turned square and we drew the series after losing the first game and winning the second on the back of phenomenal performances from Glenn Phillips and Ajaz Patel.

Any thoughts about team selection were very soon put into perspective by the arrival of Joshua Caleb Wagner, a cherished little brother for Olivia and Zahli, a third New Zealand-born member of the family to tilt the balance of the household. When we'd found out Lana was pregnant, I was absolutely sure it would be another girl, so when we learned that a little boy would be joining the family, we were just blown away. As soon as he arrived, and I held his little body in my arms, I instantly realised our family was now complete. Lana, as always, was strong and incredible and I was once again so grateful for the fact that I get to share life with her.

Josh's arrival meant a disrupted Super Smash campaign for ND. We'd kept Lana's pregnancy pretty private and I remember there being speculation that I was injured, Grant Elliott wondering on air while commentating whether something else had gone wrong with my body. I sent him a text to let him know that actually we were just in the hospital following the birth of our third child. This was no time to have any unnecessary noise floating around out there about my fitness. Lana's parents, who had travelled from South Africa, were able to care for Livie and Zahli at home while Lana recovered with Josh, allowing me to get quickly back into it. The test series against South Africa was on the horizon and I needed to get in as many competitive overs as possible before those games arrived.

It was a much-weakened South African side, after the scheduling clash that meant the SA20, South Africa's new premier domestic

T20 competition, was running at the same time they had previously agreed to tour New Zealand. It was disappointing. You always want to play against the best, and even late in the piece we hoped that when teams were knocked out of the SA20, it might mean their players could get over to New Zealand, even if only in time for the second test. In the end, it wasn't to be. I knew the South African system, though, and knew that whoever they sent, they were still going to be tough, quality cricketers. But at that time I didn't really have the mental energy to ponder what this meant for the future of test cricket. I had to focus on my own game.

Steady called me to let me know I had been selected in the squad for the series. But in that phone call he made it pretty clear that I almost certainly wasn't going to be in the XI for the first test at Bay Oval — the selectors felt it would be dry and flat. They were going to play a spinner and three seamers, insinuating that I wouldn't be one of them. He also said the plan was to play four seamers in Hamilton, but that with Will O'Rourke coming into the squad for that game there would be five quicks to choose from. I appreciated his honesty, but nothing he said gave me any confidence going into the start of the home summer.

Like always, I was desperate for a chance to prove that I still belonged at the top level. But from the moment the team assembled at the Mount, it felt like I was on the fringes. I was batting really nicely in the nets, feeling really good. I had been around this team for 12 years by now and knew how the culture worked. Usually when you looked good with the bat, someone would come along and pump up your tyres a bit. But I was getting nothing. I may as well have been batting in a void for all the attention I was getting from the coaching staff. We had three training sessions before the test, and hardly a word about the upcoming series was uttered in my direction. I realised pretty quickly that I wouldn't be playing, but it still hurt when the axe fell. It was the first home test I had been dropped for on form since I'd played Baz's final test, against Australia in Christchurch. It especially hurt that this omission had come at Bay Oval, my home ground, where I'd taken more test wickets than any other bowler. As always, I tried to hide those feelings under a smile and did what I could to help the team.

We won the game comfortably, as expected, and thoughts moved on to Hamilton. I knew now that every game I played was essentially a trial for the next one. It seemed I had no store of goodwill left that would see me through a poor test or series. There were no more guarantees. I might not have even played that second match had Kyle not been ruled out with back soreness that later turned out to be a stress fracture requiring a lengthy recovery. It was a horrible way to be given a chance, but that's the nature of professional sport — you have to do everything you can to take your opportunities, no matter how they come.

Going into the game, I felt like I was starting again. I hadn't played a test in a year — just one full Plunket Shield game, plus the rain-affected stuff in England and a handful of T20s for ND. My great mate Matt Wouldes called up to see if I was playing and I said I was, but that it felt like my spot in the team was hanging by a thread. I had to find a way to push myself as hard as I could to prove my value to the squad, but not hard enough to open the possibility of another injury — anything significant at this stage of my international career would probably end it. I'd lost a kilometre or two per hour, but I'd replaced that speed with the smarts I'd accumulated in taking 819 first-class wickets, 258 of them at test level. When I was young, sheer excitement and bloody-minded belief in my bowling overpowered the nerves. Then I became an established member of the side, assured of a place in a team with a steady selection policy. Ahead of this game, I couldn't have felt less assured about my role and my place in the pecking order. I was more nervous going into the game than I had ever been for a test before. For good reason, as it would turn out.

It was a strange South African side, shorn of most of the players my teammates were familiar with, to come up against. Some of the opposition, though, I had known for over two decades. For example, I played in the same Northerns under-19 side as Shaun von Berg, the leg spinner who made his test debut, aged 37, in Hamilton after a 130-odd-game first-class career in which he had bounced between Northerns and the Titans and other South African domestic sides. I knew the game wouldn't be easy — and that these guys would be going as hard as they could to prove they too deserved their spot — but any team from which the likes of Aiden Markram, Temba Bavuma, Keshav Maharaj, Marco Jansen and Kagiso Rabada were missing was likely to present an easier five days at the office for its opposition. I hoped this would give me the chance I needed to make a statement.

We bowled first and Timmy threw the ball my way for the 16th over, the Proteas two wickets down. I started well and the ball was new enough for me to pitch it up and look for some swing. I almost had Zubayr Hamza out leg before in that first over when I got my fifth ball to shape nicely into him, but on review it was revealed to be climbing over the stumps. A few overs later, though, I got number-three batter Raynard van Tonder out for 32 when all he could do with a short one outside off was fend it to the only fielder in the cordon, Tommy Latham at gully. Forget about this being a so-called third-string South African team: this was a test-match wicket, and the emotion poured out of me.

I have taken a lot of stick over the years for the exuberance of my post-wicket celebrations. I remember reading an article in which Trent reflected on the smile with which he often celebrates his own wickets. He said that, for him, a wicket makes him happy — so of course he wasn't going to stand there 'like a psycho' and scream his head off. No prizes for guessing the psycho I imagine he had in mind. But, for me, the celebration has never been about anger or macho posturing. Many ingredients make up that roar. It's an expression of how far I've come in life, as well as gratitude to God for the opportunity I've had to live it. It's an acknowledgement to myself of the sacrifices I've made, all the work I've put in to fulfil my ambitions. So, too, for my family — love for them, gratitude for *their* sacrifices. There are elements of I-told-you-so directed at those who doubted me along the way.

For me, cricket has always been more than a game: it has been my livelihood, of course, but also the thing I dreamed about more than any other. It's been my ticket to a new identity as a New Zealander and a better way of life for my family. I've never had money or even an education to fall back on: cricket is all I've had to put a roof over my family's head. Maybe that explains why it's hard for me to express all that with a simple smile. Throw in my teammates, my new country, and a bit of my old one. Every wicket is further proof you don't need to be the fastest, the tallest, the most talented. If you're a good person who works as hard as you can, you can make it happen.

Lana, the woman behind it all, is there in that celebration also. Every time something got me down, every time I was dropped and couldn't figure out why, every time I went wicketless or was hit for plenty, Lana has been there to pick me back up, her complete belief in me a counterweight to the various disappointments of life as a professional athlete. Just as she was the one to give me hope when I was at my absolute lowest and couldn't see a way forward. Lana always encouraged me to lead with my passion, my heart, and to turn that into my strongest weapon. So I let it all out in that trademark roar.

And yet, there was no celebration for my next wicket, the last test wicket I would ever take.

We had slipped behind in the game and were in danger of sinking to an embarrassing loss. I'd made an important 33 batting at 10, which helped us claw to within 30 or so runs of the 242 South Africa had managed before experienced off spinner Dane Piedt worked his magic against our top order — he took my wicket, too, stumped after I attempted to launch him into the Hamilton suburbs. There had been banter, during the Bangladesh tour, about my fielding: where had I been hiding, the joke went, to have only taken 17 or 18 catches over my test career? And so when Timmy moved me from midwicket down to fine leg when we were in the field, I took it a bit personally, building on the frustration of the runs that were leaking and the fact that I wasn't bowling.

When a catch did come my way — Raynard van Tonder top-edging a pull shot off debutant Will O'Rourke — and I safely pouched it, it was my chance to send a bit of banter back. Especially after Timmy, in the huddle, jokingly said something like, 'Congratulations on your tenth catch.' I gave him the finger. The photos didn't look great, but it's hard to describe how much of my very close friendship with Tim is based on banter and having a go at each other. Sometimes, when we had someone around the team who was new to the environment, it would cross my mind that they must be thinking Tim and I really don't like each other, but it was always just joking around. There was definitely some simmering tension between us on the field in Hamilton, but the raised finger was genuinely a joking response to a Tim Southee wisecrack.

However, my frustrations continued to build as I waited for my chance to steam in. Will, Tim and Henners all had a crack — that was to be expected, I knew my role in this attack — but when both Glenn Phillips and Rachin Ravindra made their way to the bowling crease before me, my emotional temperature started to boil. I was stewing down at fine leg, my mood made worse by South Africans in the crowd asking why I wasn't bowling and telling me it was obvious my captain didn't trust me. It wasn't until the 37th over that Timmy finally gave me the signal to warm up — after a crucial 60-run stand between Hamza and David Bedingham had been allowed to build.

It took me four balls to break the partnership. I bowled a short one, rising off the pitch at Hamza's armpit, which he pulled. The ball flew off the top edge, carrying to Will Young, running in off the boundary at deep square leg. Teammates converged, and someone yelled out, 'Yes, Waggy boy!' But there was nothing from me. Timmy ran to join the huddle and jumped on my back in congratulations. I told him to get off me. *Where was the support earlier? Why did it take nearly 40 overs for me to get the ball?* I raised my finger to my lips in the direction of the crowd — my way of telling the doubters to quiet down.

When I'd finished the over, Timmy came over to talk as I walked back to my fielding position. It was a heated discussion. He asked what was going on. I told him.

'You know I'm fighting for my bloody spot here, fighting for my career, and I don't get the ball until the thirty-seventh over? You're not giving me a shot to show what I can do. I've given everything I've got for this team.'

Tim and I have been through a lot together, and he tried to remind me that I'll always have his support, but in that moment I didn't want to hear it. *Don't talk to me now, just let me have the bloody ball. I'm here to bowl.*

I didn't take any more wickets, but we bowled them out for an achievable target, which we chased down the next day thanks to another Kane century. There was a lot of laughter in the sheds, a photo of my raised middle finger making the rounds. I thought I had done enough in the game, especially with Australia — against whom I was the most successful New Zealand test bowler in a generation — on the horizon. I had no sense these were my last moments in the team.

The next morning, I got a text from Steady asking if we could grab a coffee before I drove back over the Kaimai Ranges to Pāpāmoa. I thought it would be a fairly standard catch-up to talk through our plans for the Australians. We arranged to meet at 8.45 and then, having sat with him at breakfast, he texted me to tell me to come to a room on the first floor. I had no sense of what was coming. I opened the door and walked into a meeting room, where I found Steady, Tim and manager Simon Insley. *Shit, this must be serious.* I sat down.

Steady spoke first. 'There's no easy way of telling you this, mate. I'm really sorry, but we are not picking you for the Australia series.

We think your international career is over and that you should retire.'

I was shocked into silence. Tim spoke, trying to soften the blow. 'You don't have to retire. You could go back and play domestically and, if you go well, there's an outside chance you could work your way back in for that England series.'

But then Steady continued. 'I'll be honest with you, Wags, we're not offering you a contract. And looking at our future tours, a lot of them are to the subcontinent, which we won't require you for, and we feel this is the best thing for the team moving forward.'

I was hurt and bewildered and angry. But I managed to handle it quite well, keeping a lid on my emotions. Also, I didn't know what to say.

Steady then said that the team wanted to take me down to Wellington to celebrate my career — after which I would go home as the boys moved on to the second test in Christchurch. 'It's entirely up to you what to do, if you want to come down to Wellington or stay home,' he said.

I walked out to the carpark in a haze and got into my car. I drove to the BP around the corner and gave myself a few moments to sit with the news. Then I called Lana and told her what had just taken place. We were both in tears and she asked how this had happened. I said I'd felt it coming for a while now, although the actual timing of it had blindsided me.

'Maybe this is just it,' I said. 'Maybe I just hang up my boots.'

Although the actual decision to do so wouldn't come for a week or two — one of the most difficult periods of my life. It was a time of many late-night conversations with Lana, a lot of long phone calls with distant family, hours and hours of reflection and introspection. At the end of it, retiring from the international game seemed to be my best option, a conclusion I finally arrived at one evening as I sat in bed with Lana at my side. Still, it was a decision I reached with a heavy heart.

I also came to realise how hard it must have been for Steady and Tim, a close mate with whom I had been through so much, to have had that conversation with me. Few sportspeople are lucky enough to write the script of their farewell. A lot of people close to me are doing it tough right now — in business and in life — and their input into my decision helped put what I had been through into perspective. I *had* had a fantastic international career. And many people have had to sit through conversations much harder than the one I suffered through in a nondescript Hamilton meeting room.

But the decision was made more complicated by how NZC wanted to manage the news. I had been told that my test-match career was over, but, later — as I still wrestled with what to do — I was named in the squad for the Australia series. The plan, as Steady had outlined, was for me to be around during the first game. Then, in the gap between the two tests, they wanted me to announce that I had retired. But I thought that retiring in the middle of a series would make it look as if I was spitting the dummy because I hadn't been picked for the first game — especially after the media had picked up on the tension between Tim and me in Hamilton — and that was not how I wanted to be remembered after having given my all to the team for so many years. I told them I wanted to announce before the series that I hadn't been picked — the truth, despite having been named in the squad — and say that I *was* available for the series but that I was retiring from international cricket, and international cricket only, at its end.

Initially, the media team didn't want to go along with how I saw things. But I insisted, telling them that if we just told the truth, there would be nothing to hide. I had been dropped. The selectors didn't think I was good enough to play at the highest level anymore. But the only way I could get closure on my test career while also going down to Wellington and helping out around my mates with a smile on my face was if I did it with everything in the open. Eventually, they seemed to see things from my perspective.

Most of my teammates still had no idea about what had been going on behind the scenes. All they knew was that I had been named in the squad. And so, when we first assembled in the capital and Simon got through his manager's messages, he handed the floor to me. I had grown to be extremely comfortable about speaking in front of the group over the years, but as soon as I stood up on this occasion I felt as nervous as I ever have. My tongue instantly went dry and numb. But I managed to get on top of my emotions and tell the team that all good things eventually come to an end, and that, while it had been an amazing ride, in the morning I would be announcing my retirement from international cricket. It was the right thing to do for the team going forward.

We then headed to a reception at Premier House, where I got to send a few down at Prime Minister Christopher Luxon. He later approached me to tell me he was a big fan and to wish me luck for the series. I had to confess that I wasn't playing and would be announcing my retirement the next day.

'Have you thought about a career in politics?' he asked.

I just laughed. 'I've still got a lot to learn.'

The next morning, it was time to tell the rest of the country. The press conference was announced and I walked out to face the press as a Black Cap for the last time. I tried — sometimes through tears — to express exactly how much representing New Zealand had meant to me and to thank some of those who had helped me along the way.

I wasn't supposed to get on the field. I was just there to carry the drinks and be around the squad. But when I looked around, after someone signalled for a bathroom break and others were off getting treatment or nursing niggles, I was the only one in whites. Almost without thinking, I got up and jogged into position at the Scoreboard End of the ground, where the crowd was a bit sparse. I got a nice clap and cheer.

When left-handed Mitchell Starc came on strike, I had to jog all the way to the Embankment. The whole bank, realising it was me, rose to their feet. I wasn't expecting this, and I didn't really know how to react. A lump started to inflate in my throat. I was trying hard to focus — imagine if my last act with a black cap on my head was to drop a catch — but the cheering just didn't stop. I was shy about the attention because this moment, as nice as it was, should have been about the guys who were actually playing the test. Still, the applause continued.

Jeez, maybe I really have meant something to New Zealand, this country that took me in and made me one of their own. But soon I had to jog off the field. *Here I am, my last few seconds representing New Zealand.* It hit me like a truck that the journey was over, and random aspects of it — backyard cricket with my brothers, those strange first days in Dunedin, the last tense moments as we waited for the World Test Championship-winning runs to be hit — floated to the top of my mind. I sat down next to Mitchell Santner and he made a joke, but I have no idea what it was. My head was buzzing with emotion and memory. I never in my wildest dreams thought that my success could mean this much to people I'd never met.

'Mate,' I said to Mitchell, 'I can't believe that just happened.'

It was even more special that my parents were there to see it. I'm not sure how they did it, but NZC managed to get them both over to New Zealand together for the first time in their lives so they could be there for the Wellington test. In Dad's case, at age 75, it was his first time out of South Africa. He didn't even have a passport the last I'd known about it. Somehow they'd managed to get him one and get it stamped with a visa at record speed. They met little Josh for the first time, got to see our house in Pāpāmoa and were able to walk out onto the Basin Reserve, run their hands over turf that meant the world to me and which Dad had only ever seen through a TV screen.

My whole family came back into the changing rooms. The boys were hurting — they'd just lost a test they'd been in a few good positions to win — but we all cracked a beer, and Kane and Steady spoke about my career and what it meant to them. Then I spoke to the group. I tried to express what being part of this team had meant to me, how it had taken an insecure boy, so unsure of himself and his place in the world, and helped turn him into the man I had become. I was lucky to have little Zahli in my arms, interrupting at just the right time to turn tears into laughter.

Normally we only sang the team pledge after a win, but for this occasion, on my behalf, we got into a circle, put our arms around each other, and I got it under way. It was an emotional moment, and this time I couldn't hold back the tears. These guys weren't just teammates. These were men whose weddings I had been to, whose kids were growing up alongside mine, friends who were a huge part of my life away from cricket. I gave everyone a hug when the pledge was over.

We stayed in the shed until 10 that night, reliving some favourite memories, sinking a few beers, watching some footy. Nothing flashy:

just me, the team, family. It was perfect. The little lamb and the feared fast bowler, the South African and the New Zealander, the son and the father, the boy and the man. In that moment, my worlds had come together.

But the warmth of that evening didn't last as reality started to set in. When Will O'Rourke was injured in the first test, there was immediate speculation that I could replace him for the next match in Christchurch. I held on to hope, too, that the fairytale ending would happen. After all, I hadn't quite retired from test cricket, regardless of how the media might have interpreted it. And Steady knew that. Eventually he called me up.

'Sorry, Wags,' he said. 'I know how much you want this, but we think we need the extra pace. We're going to go with Ben Sears. I'm sorry. I know that's not what you wanted to hear.'

In the end it was a familiar refrain — one I'd heard since my earliest days in Pretoria — that closed the door on a test farewell. They were going to go with the faster bowler. I was gutted, but once again I understood it was his call and I respected it. But when the media asked if I might get the call-up, Tim refused to rule it out. Then when Steady fronted the media, he said that the boys had given me a great send-off and I was happy with my decision — and for a while the media merry-go-round continued.

When I got home, all the emotions of the past month caught up with me. It was exhausting to see this plastered all over the news, even after I'd left the group. I was so drained that all I wanted to do was barricade myself in my house and let everything blow over. No such luck. When Rossco appeared on a podcast, saying it looked to him like my retirement had been 'forced', the media attention ratcheted up even further. My phone was constantly ringing with journalists trying to get to the bottom of what had happened. Ross, seeing the furore that his comments had caused, rang me up a day or two later to say sorry for adding fuel to the media fire.

'Mate, you don't need to apologise,' I said. 'You're entitled to your opinion. And, hey, you're not entirely wrong. They didn't force me to retire, but they did ask me to retire.'

Of course, with two young girls and a new baby at home, locking myself away was not an option. On one occasion, picking up take-aways for the family, it felt like all my fellow customers were watching me from the corner of their eyes, some of them approaching me, asking why I hadn't come out of international retirement for this next test. I was suddenly so angry at how this had been handled. It took everything I had not to just put my head down and walk away, but I managed to put an empty smile on my face and mumble a few pleasantries. I tried, a few days later, to find some solace on the golf course — so often a place that allowed me to recharge my batteries with good friends like Con Dickie, Phil Holmes and Jimmy Napier — but again everyone I ran into just wanted to ask why I wasn't playing and if Ross's comments were an accurate representation of what had occurred. I walked away from the course thinking that even golf had been ruined by how the end of my international career had become a public discussion.

I tried not to leave the house for the next week. The test match was on, but whenever I flicked over to it, it was too hard to watch. I couldn't believe it was over, and that these hollow feelings were all that was left in the immediate wake of my career. Instead of looking back with pride on my test-match achievements — 64 matches, 260 wickets, a member of the inaugural WTC-winning team — all I could think about were the hurtful circumstances of how it ended.

For the first time in my life, I found myself hating cricket.

I drank too much as the days turned to weeks and months, trying to process the end of my international career. I had nothing much to do with my days, other than spend as much of it with the kids as possible. At times, I felt almost as depressed as I had, all those distant years ago, in Sri Lanka. I'd retired from international cricket only, but there were moments when I seriously considered throwing it all in — giving up on cricket entirely. My body was as sore as it had ever been and every joint and muscle seemed to realise something had changed and that now was the time to ask for some attention in the language of pain. My knee screamed the loudest and a scan revealed a torn meniscus — there throughout the season, but unnoticed until now — which required surgery to put right.

And as I began my recovery under the care of physio Craig Newland, and started to think about the story I had to tell and the chapters as yet unwritten in my life, I knew I wasn't done with the game I love so much. I could use the disappointment of the end of my test career as I had always used disappointment: as fuel to drive me onwards. I let go of that anger and felt a great relief. One of the biggest lessons I've learned along the way is that the disappointments aren't what define you — it's about how you pick yourself up afterwards that counts. It might be a cliché, but for me it's been so true.

When I was able, things got serious with trainer Matt Henderson. I told him I wanted two more years of cricket out of my body. 'In that case, we'll have to get to work,' he replied, and he wasn't lying.

I almost puked after our first session and the intensity never let up. Soon, he had me as fit as I have ever been. I started to think about county opportunities, and focusing on what I could give back to cricket, in the twilight of my career, at Northern Districts. I remembered my early days at Otago, when legends like Warren McSkimming and Craig Cumming took me under their wings, and now I might have the chance to play alongside young guys coming through — the Kristian Clarkes and Matt Fishers — and play a similar role.

It was like the lesson I first learned at Eden Park against India many years ago: come at the opposition hard, with intent, and things will often unfold in your favour, even if not quite in the way you had envisioned. Life has been like that, too. With my faith, I believe everything happens for a reason. The searing loneliness of my early days in the Black Caps opened the door for Lana to come into my life, and those dark days — once I got through my lowest moments — in retrospect helped give me the tools to cope with everything thrown my way since. I now think a lot about that mantra I learned from Mike Sandle: a problem shared is a problem halved. I hope that, in sharing my story, it'll encourage others to do the same, thus halving a problem for someone else.

The key for me has been to grasp at opportunity with everything I've had, to open the doors I've found in front of me with passion and excitement and hope. As I put the finishing touches on this book, training hard for what was in front of me when I wasn't remembering everything I'd been through, another opportunity, for the county of Durham, arrived. I took it. The familiar feeling of gratitude for being able to put a roof over my family's head by playing the game I'd come to love again flooded in, even if kissing three kids, and Lana, goodbye in order to do it now adds a touch of sadness.

After a few Royal London One-Day Cup games, on day two of my first County Championship match I bowled a delivery that sent Ben Slater's off and middle stumps flying and I was feeling great, a sense of confidence returning to my game. Three wickets later, I dived in the field, landed on the ball and fractured my shoulder. A week after that, I was back home with Lana and the kids, trying to soak up precious family time and put aside the frustrations of another setback.

I don't know what life has in store for me next. But as I set out to begin these unwritten chapters of life, I know that for my loved ones, for myself, for my team, I'll be going all out.

ACKNOWLEDGEMENTS

There are so many people who have played an important role in my life and helped me along the way as I chased my dreams — so many more than I can mention in the words below, and I'm so grateful to all of you.

I'd like to start with a huge thank you to all of my teammates, coaches, management and support staff over my career. I've always done my best to give everything to the team, and I received so much from you in return.

To my best friends in South Africa, Stanley Buckle, Francois le Clus, Douglas Hewitt and Tiaan de Beer. Thank you for friendships that started at school, and for always being there even when I've been on the other side of the world.

To everyone at Ormskirk Cricket Club — for one of the best times of my life, filled with special memories and friendships that I cherish to this day.

I'm thankful for the enthusiasm and kindness shown to me from

Otago Cricket as I made the biggest move of my life. Special mention to the late Ross and Sue Dykes for their support during my time at the province. To Mike Hesson, for always believing in me, and for getting me on the plane to New Zealand. Andy McLean, for opening your house to me, driving me everywhere, our late-night chats and your ongoing friendship. To Jared and Anna King, for welcoming me into your home and for being the kindest people — you showed me the Kiwi way. To Stephen Duff, for helping me out with a car to get around, taking care of our house when we were travelling, and for always being there for a yarn and some advice. Thanks also to Craig Cumming and Warren McSkimming for your guidance, support and being our family away from family.

Thanks to Brendon McCullum. Baz, your kind words and help throughout my career have been so important to me. I've learned a lot from watching the man you are both on and off the field.

Thank you to our close friends, the Flynns, the Williamsons, the de Grandhommes and the Boults. The friendships we have with you (and your parents) is what makes our life in the Mount so special. Here's to many more years of amazing family gatherings and good times.

To Jeff and Sue Basham, our amazing neighbours. Thank you for the kindness, support and love you have both shown me and my family. The love our kids have for you shows how important you have been in our lives. To Dan and Amie Mafi, for offering a helping hand (and amazing food) to the family when I'm away. Matt, Kat, Terry and Fiona — thank you for the wonderful friendships throughout the years. Look forward to life ahead with many more amazing memories. To Kevin Pead, for always lending a hand and an ear to chat to. And to Con, Phil and Jimmy for all the golf, beers and stories, which has not only improved my golf game but also given me a space to take my mind away from cricket and enjoy your company.

Chris Donaldson and Adam Keane, I would not be where I am today without your passion and drive for helping me achieve my goals. You both pushed me further than I ever thought I'd be able to go and have been a huge part not only in my success, but also in that of many others. And you're both great men, too. Also to Matt Henderson — you saw me at my lowest and in a short amount of time you challenged me to push the boundaries and played a big role in getting me back on the park. I can't thank you enough and look forward to enjoying more rounds on the golf course and in the hurt locker.

To Mike Sandle, for being a father figure and a mate for so many years. You were always there to listen and help out, and played such an important part in creating the best team environment I've ever been involved with. Thank you for your banter and for going out of your way for the families and partners. And for halving the problems shared!

Thank you to James Borrowdale, who helped me take my memories and turn them into this book. I know all the hard work you've put in and the care that you've shown for these words and my story, and I really appreciate it.

A special thank you to the people of New Zealand and fans of the Black Caps all around the world, for making me feel so welcome and all your support from the sidelines. My love for this country made me want to give everything for the silver fern, and the cheers from the crowd are such a boost when the energy levels start to dip.

Last but by no means least, I'm fortunate to have such a loving and supportive family network. To my in-laws, Theuns, Erika and Dewaldt, thank you for always being there — for your love and support, and for trusting me to take your amazing daughter out of your home to the other side of the world. You've always gone out of your way for our family and to look after our kids so that I can play this game and continue to follow my dreams.

Mum, Dad, David, Mark and Heloise, words can't express how grateful I am for your endless support, love and encouragement. You've always believed in me and made me believe that my dreams were possible. The sacrifices you've made have taken me from that young kid in the backyard to the man I am today.

To Livie, Zahli and Josh, it's been such a privilege to watch you grow, and I'm so proud to see the love you have for each other and for our family. I love you all so much. To our little angel in heaven, one day we will all be together.

And to my wife, Lana! Thanks for being my number-one supporter. You've given up many of your dreams and ambitions so I could live mine. And you've made a bloody good time of it! You know everything about me and this game, from the highest highs to the ultimate lows. You've seen me at my best and my worst and through it all you dug in with me and made it look easy. You're the best mum for our kids and your support and love means the world to me. I'm so grateful to be sharing life's journey with you.